Theater and Cultural Politics for a New World

Theater and Cultural Politics for a New World presents a radical re-examination of the ways in which demographic shifts will impact theater and performance culture in the twenty-first century.

Editor Chinua Thelwell brings together the revealing insights of artists, scholars, and organizers to produce a unique intersectional conversation about the transformative potential of theater.

Opening with a case study of the New WORLD Theater and moving on to a fascinating range of essays, the book looks at five main themes:

- Changing demographics
- Future aesthetics
- Making institutional space
- Critical multiculturalism
- Polyculturalism.

Chinua Thelwell is an assistant professor of History and Africana Studies at the College of William and Mary. His research focuses on the racial politics of performance in the Atlantic world.

Theater and Cultural Politics for a New World

An anthology

Edited by Chinua Thelwell

LONDON AND NEW YORK

First published 2017
by Routledge
2 Park Square, Milton Park, Abingdon, Oxon OX14 4RN

and by Routledge
711 Third Avenue, New York, NY 10017

Routledge is an imprint of the Taylor & Francis Group, an informa business

British Library Cataloguing-in-Publication Data
A catalogue record for this book is available from the British Library.

Library of Congress Cataloguing-in-Publication Data
Names: Thelwell, Chinua editor.
Title: Theater and cultural politics for a new world : an edited anthology / Chinua Thelwell.
Description: Milton Park, Abingdon, Oxon ; New York, NY : Routledge, 2016.
Identifiers: LCCN 2016014897| ISBN 9781138929760 (hardback) | ISBN 9781138929777 (pbk.) | ISBN 9781315680989 (ebook)
Subjects: LCSH: Theater—History—21st century. | Theater—Political aspects. | Theater and society—History—21st century.
Classification: LCC PN2190 .T54 2016 | DDC 792.09/05—dc23
LC record available at https://lccn.loc.gov/2016014897

ISBN: 978-1-138-92976-0 (hbk)
ISBN: 978-1-138-92977-7 (pbk)
ISBN: 978-1-315-68098-9 (ebk)

Typeset in Times New Roman
by Swales & Willis Ltd, Exeter, Devon, UK

Contents

Contributors

Daniel Banks is a theater director, choreographer, and educator. He holds a PhD in Performance Studies from New York University and is the editor of the anthology of Hip Hop theater plays, *Say Word! Voices from Hip Hop Theater.* He is also co-director of the arts and services organization DNAWORKS and founder of the Hip Hop Theatre Initiative.

Elizabeth Méndez Berry is an award-winning journalist whose work has appeared in the *Washington Post*, *Vibe*, and *The Nation*. She has provided commentaries on music for NPR, NBC, CBC, and CNN en espanol. She serves as an adjunct professor of Music Journalism at NYU's Clive Davis Institute of Recorded Music.

Paul Bonin-Rodriguez is a playwright and performer who has created and toured plays and multi-disciplinary performances since 1992. He is an assistant professor in the Performance as Public Practice Program at the University of Texas at Austin.

Lucy Mae San Pablo Burns is an associate professor in the Asian American Studies Department at the University of California, Los Angeles. She is the author of *Puro Arte: Filipinos on the Stages of Empire.*

Jeff Chang currently serves as Executive Director of the Institute for Diversity in the Arts at Stanford University. He is the author of *Can't Stop Won't Stop: A History of the Hip-Hop Generation* and *Who We Be: A Cultural History of Race in Post-Civil Rights America.*

Michael John Garcés has been the Artistic Director of Cornerstone Theater Company in Los Angeles since 2006. A director and playwright, he has created work for theaters across the country and internationally. He is a company member of Woolly Mammoth Theater Company in Washington DC, and has collaborated extensively with the Living Word Project in San Francisco.

Hanay Geiogamah is a professor of theater in the UCLA School of Theater, Film and Television and is the founding artistic director of the acclaimed American Indian Dance Theater. Since 1997 he has served as principal director of Project HOOP, the national Native American theater advocacy program. His career as a playwright, director and producer in the theater began in 1972 at La Mama Experimental Theater in New York City. He is a member of the Kiowa Tribe of Oklahoma.

James Kass is an award-winning writer, educator, producer and media maker. He is the Founder and Executive Director of Youth Speaks. He's creator and Co-executive Producer of the seven-part HBO series *Brave New Voices*.

Esther Kim Lee is Associate Professor in the school of Theatre, Dance, and Performance Studies at the University of Maryland. She is author of *A History of Asian American Theatre* and *The Theatre of David Henry Hwang* and editor of *Seven Contemporary Plays from the Korean Diaspora in the Americas*.

lê thi diem thúy is a writer and solo performance artist. She is the author of the novel *The Gangster We Are All Looking For*. Her solo performance theater works, *Red Fiery Summer*, *the bodies between us*, and *Carte Postale* have been presented at—among other venues—the Whitney Museum of American Art at Philip Morris, the International Women Playwrights' Festival, the New WORLD Theater, and the Marfa Theater Company.

Jasmine Mahmoud is the Postdoctoral Fellow of Inequality and Identity in the Program in American Culture Studies at Washington University in St. Louis. Her work examines how aesthetic and geographic experiences entangle, attending to how race, neoliberal policy, and urban displacement interact with contemporary performance.

Gary Y. Okihiro is Professor of International and Public Affairs and Director of the Center for the Study of Ethnicity and Race at Columbia University, New York. He has authored eleven books, and is widely considered to be a foundational scholar in the field of Ethnic Studies.

Will Power is an award-winning playwright and performer. He is currently on the faculty at the Meadows School of the Arts/SMU (Southern Methodist University), and serves as the Andrew W. Mellon Foundation Playwright in Residence with the Dallas Theater Center.

Bill Rauch is the founding Artistic Director of Cornerstone Theater. He is the current Artistic Director of the Oregon Shakespeare Festival.

Cathy J. Schlund-Vials is Professor in English and Asian American Studies at the University of Connecticut-Storrs. She is author of two monographs: *Modeling Citizenship: Jewish and Asian American Writing* and *War, Genocide, and Justice: Cambodian American Memory Work*. She is director of the Asian and Asian American Studies Institute at the University of Connecticut.

Joseph Schloss is a major voice in the burgeoning field of Hip-Hop Studies. He is the author of *Making Beats: The Art of Sample-Based Hip-Hop* and *Foundations: B-Boys, B-Girls and Hip-Hop Culture in New York*.

Chinua Thelwell is an assistant professor of History and Africana Studies at the College of William and Mary, in Williamsburg, Virginia. His research focuses on the racial politics of performance in the Atlantic world.

Mark Valdez is an artist and organizer based in Los Angeles. Mark was the Executive Director of the Network of Ensemble Theaters for eight years and is currently organizing in his home community of Highland Park and creating performances across the country.

Roberta Uno is the founding Artistic Director of New WORLD Theater. From 2002 to 2015, she was a Senior Program Officer for Arts and Culture in the United States at the Ford Foundation. She currently heads the *ArtChange US: Arts in a Changing America* initiative out of the California Institute of the Arts.

Acknowledgments

This anthology is truly the result of a group effort. The book would not exist without the contributions of the Hemispheric Institute for Performance and Politics of New York University. Special thanks go to Diana Taylor, Marléne Ramirez-Cancio, Leticia Robles-Moreno, Marcial Godoy-Anativia, and Lisandra Ramos. A generous grant from the Nathan Cummings Foundation was fundamental to the completion of the project. My gratitude goes out to Maurine Knighton for her support. It has been an honor and privilege to work with each of the authors in this anthology. Jeff Chang and Daniel Banks were especially helpful as they contributed essays and valuable advice on navigating the publishing landscape. There are so many additional people to thank: Francis Tanglao-Aguas, Chris Rohmann, Jorge Cortiñas, Cureema Uzzell, Fred Tillis, Evelyn Aquino, Lee Edwards, Marcus Pinn, Eddie Bustamante, Leah King, Miles Grier, Yvonne Mendez, Talia Rodgers, Ben Piggot, Kate Edwards, Kathy Perkins, Kevin Gaines, Vijay Prashad, Mark Bamuthi Joseph, Guillermo Gómez-Peña, Awam Ampka, Ingrid Askew, Sylvia Robinson, Steven Sapp, Mildred Ruiz, Gamal Chasten, William Ruiz, David Sheingold, Michael Gomez, Jennifer Morgan, Tavia Nyong'o, Karen Lederer—and the many staff members and artists that made the New WORLD Theater a visionary theater and extraordinary community. My immediate family offers a constant source of pride, support, love, and inspiration: Michael, Mikiko, Andrew, and Emily. Most of all, I would like to thank my mother, Roberta Uno; her ideas fill this volume and have shaped my thinking in ways too numerous to mention.

Chinua Akimaro Thelwell, July 2016

Introduction

Chinua Thelwell

Social demographers predict 2042 will be the year when people of color become the aggregate racial majority in the United States.[1] This demographic shift will reshape common understandings of what constitutes American culture and national identity. We are already witnessing the ramifications of America's changing demographics in our electoral politics. In 1988, George H.W. Bush got 60 percent of the white vote, and won in an electoral college landslide. By contrast, in 2012 Mitt Romney won 59 percent of the white vote, and lost by five million votes.[2] Suddenly, in the wake of the 2012 election, primetime media pundits awoke to the political ramifications of America's changing demographics; conservative media couched the conversation in nostalgia for the "real America." An anxious Bill O'Reilly lamented

> Because it's a changing country, the demographics are changing. It's not a traditional America anymore . . . Twenty years ago President Obama would have been roundly defeated by an establishment candidate like Mitt Romney. The White establishment is now the minority.[3]

Indeed, in places like the state of California and New York City the shift to "majority minority" has already occurred.

In response to the changing demographics that Obama's presidency represents, a nativist backlash has called for the taking back of the country. The new nativism is best exemplified in Donald Trump's 2016 Republican Party presidential primary campaign. Trump ran with the slogan, "Make America Great Again" and achieved a level of campaign xenophobia unmatched in recent history. Trump talked about Mexican rapists crossing the border, promised to build a wall between the USA and Mexico, mocked Asian accents, advocated the creation of a Muslim database, called for a temporary ban on Muslims entering the country, made the inaccurate claim that thousands of Muslims in New Jersey celebrated the 9/11 attacks, and tweeted invalid statistics claiming that most killings of white people are carried out by black people. Prior to his campaign, Trump was the main voice in the "Birther Movement" claiming that President Obama was not a natural born citizen.[4] At the time of this writing, Trump is the presumptive nominee of the Republican Party. The issue of changing demographics is becoming a major part of American political discourse.

Theater and Cultural Politics for a New World examines the ways that demographic shifts are impacting American theater and performance culture. This collection of essays brings together the voices and insights of scholars, artists, and cultural organizers, producing an intersectional conversation about the transformative potential of theater to imagine new ways of negotiating and understanding the social world. The book is organized in two parts: opening with the case study of New WORLD Theater (NWT), an experimental theater that produced new models of artistic and community participation and engaged the issue of demographic change long before primetime news media. The New WORLD Theater case study is the point of departure for addressing the five related themes of the book: changing demographics, future aesthetics, making institutional space, critical multiculturalism, and polyculturalism.

From 1979 to 2009, New WORLD Theater, was based at the Fine Arts Center of the University of Massachusetts at Amherst, where it produced and presented innovative theater by artists of color. New WORLD Theater focused on plays by artists of color because the theater programming at the University and surrounding area was historically Eurocentric. By 1979, the Department of Theater at the University of Massachusetts Amherst had never hired a full-time faculty of color, produced a play by a playwright of color, or recruited a graduate student of color—a record not unlike many peer departments and arts institutions in the country. New WORLD Theater offered a space where historically marginalized actors and playwrights could nurture, produce, and present their work. New WORLD Theater offered quality programming, created a national network of like-minded theater companies, established outreach programs in local communities, won many prestigious grants, and helped to desegregate the Theater Department at the University of Massachusetts. Seemingly out of the blue, the theater was closed in 2009 by University officials. Its abrupt end was ostensibly precipitated by the 2008 Recession; although it had a half million dollars of new grants, the University suspended its operations as part of austerity measures intended to eliminate a larger institutional shortfall. The vulnerability of New WORLD Theater in a time of severe economic crisis, is more than a story of a single organizational life cycle. Its greater significance is the portal it provides to understanding cultural politics during a moment of profound demographic change, increasing economic inequality, neoliberal austerity measures, and de-facto resegregation.

The three-decade life of the NWT existed between two significant bookends, the Civil Rights Movement, and the so-called "post-racial" Obama era. In its early years, NWT was a beneficiary of the Civil Rights Movement as arts organizations across the country began to diversify their programming, often in response to philanthropic incentives; and newly desegregated college campuses attempted to diversify their student bodies, change curriculum to include the histories and cultures of minority groups and create broader cultural programming. The theater ended in the wake of the 2008 Recession and in the waning optimism following the 2008 Obama election. An unprecedented moment of collective national hope was under new attacks by the Right as social gains of the Civil Rights era entered the policy arena and courtroom. Many initially viewed Obama's election as a symbolic culmination to the Civil Rights Movement, the ultimate national expression of a more inclusive national attitude regarding race relations. Thus in an ironic development, at the very moment when the American electorate was heralded for expressing more progressive attitudes regarding race through their ballots, the achievements of the Civil Rights movement including Affirmative Action, voting rights legislation, Ethnic Studies, and many diversity programs on college campuses were being dismantled, defunded, or marginalized anew in a supposedly "post-racial" America.

What does it means to be a multi-racial democracy? This question was asked in many New WORLD Theater productions. Many plays portrayed Herrenvolk democracies like Jim Crow era America or Apartheid South Africa.[5] In the third chapter of this volume, New WORLD Theater's founder, Roberta Uno, describes much of the thinking that fueled her project as she outlines a series of lessons learned while running the theater. She begins with a description of her 1983 production of James Baldwin's *Blues for Mister Charlie* based on the murder of Emmet Till and the farce of a trial that followed. I was a child when I saw it, and to this day I remember: two men, one white, one black, walking on the street. A white aggressor blocks the path. He moves left, moves right, refusing to let the black man pass. A murder, a courtroom, not guilty, no justice. Years later, in the wake of George Zimmerman's acquittal, activists began taking to the streets championing the slogan "Black Lives Matter" and sparking a sorely needed national dialogue about a pattern of state sanctioned violence that has been going on for generations. Other plays focused on democracy building from the ground up and the activists who dared to demand equality. As a teenager I saw NWT's production of *Miss Ida B Wells*, a play about the fearless anti-lynching crusader, written by Endesha Ida Mae Holland. I remember an enormous backdrop of notebook paper, each line filled with elegant cursive writing. Miss Wells is telling a friend about a recent lynching. As she describes the KKK, I picture a procession of canine teeth. She pledges to realize the Fourteenth and Fifteenth Amendments and I feel my back straighten with her unwavering determination.

New WORLD Theater was spiritually grounded in activism that is often erased or omitted from record. It was directly related to the student activist movements of the late 1960s and early 1970s. During this time, students demanded a more diverse curriculum, and as a result Ethnic Studies was born. Ethnic Studies began on the West Coast and quickly swept across the country. New WORLD Theater can be thought of as an East Coast, experimental, and theatrical manifestation of the larger Ethnic Studies movement. Both New WORLD Theater and Ethnic Studies responded to Eurocentric patterns in the American academy by attempting to carve out institutional space where the narratives and perspectives of people of color can be acknowledged. New WORLD Theater represents an early attempt to theatrically sketch out a Comparative Ethnic Studies project that moves beyond racial formation theory. In Gary Okihiro's contribution to this volume, a framework for Ethnic Studies is outlined where scholars and activists who are interested in issues of social justice cannot focus only on the social construction of race. They are urged to focus on a range of historically marginalizing social categories by acknowledging "gender . . . class, racial, and sexual oppressions."[6] New WORLD Theater can be considered a performance laboratory for this kind of intersectional theorizing. In other words, early New WORLD Theater productions created a kind of theatrical curriculum that brought together Africana Studies, Chicano/ Latino Studies, Native American Studies, Asian and Pacific American Studies, Women's Studies, and LGBT Studies. This exercise in creating institutional space encouraged cross-fertilization between a number of academic fields, and serves as a model for future theater and scholarship.

Because live theater is inherently ephemeral, archives are important sites for the preservation of performances for future generations. However, archives tend to reflect the power relations of a given society as the histories and perspectives of politically marginalized groups are often excluded from archival representation.[7] Lucy Burns' chapter begins the process of destabilizing outdated notions of what is significant enough to be archived by calling attention to an archive of plays by Asian American women playwrights that was created by New WORLD Theater founder, Roberta Uno, and is held at the University of Massachusetts. Indeed, there is a wonderful New WORLD Theater archive that can be accessed at the WEB Du Bois Library at the University of Massachusetts.[8] Furthermore, the Hemispheric Institute of Performance and Politics at New York University has begun the process of digitizing the New WORLD Theater archive so that future generations can have online access to archival materials.[9]

Whereas the first part of the book focuses on historical case studies, the second part addresses how the related themes of changing demographics, future aesthetics, institutional space, critical multiculturalism and polyculturalism might play out in the twenty-first century. Some of the essays grapple with the challenges of producing theater during a paradoxical moment characterized by economic austerity measures and enormous community-based cultural vitality. Some of these chapters speak towards the backlash against the current trends of changing demographics as new forms of nativism have begun to emerge. Rather than advocating nostalgia for the past, these chapters invite readers to join in the creation of a possible future and imagine what future American theater might look like. Furthermore, these chapters demonstrate that many organizations are carrying the vision of New WORLD Theater into the twenty-first century.

Critical multiculturalism is expressed in essays that focus on theater organizations and practitioners who are challenging traditional Eurocentric canons by producing new artistic methodologies and organizing practices. Rather than employing multiculturalism as a marketing technique designed to reach a larger consumer demographic or a top-down management strategy for superficially talking about institutional diversity, the authors present a kind of multiculturalism in which overtly political anti-racist interventions are made in an arts landscape that often does not grant access to "non-traditional" communities. Related chapters complicate critical multiculturalism by calling for a polycultural approach that moves beyond the rigid perspective that aesthetic traditions exist in an unadulterated and impermeable state. The multicultural model often relegates cultures to separate silos, almost completely cut off from one another. A polycultural approach acknowledges the hybridity of cultures and their mutual ability to influence each other while still calling attention to the fact that cultural exchange is greatly impacted by power dynamics—access to wealth, opportunity, prestige, and citizenship status.[10] A polyculturalist approach (1) challenges a theater canon that privileges one identity over all others, (2) embraces the reality of cultural mixing, (3) acknowledges power relations, and various forms of racial, gender, class, and sexual inequality, and (4) strives towards a dismantling of the very concept of cultural hierarchy.

Future Aesthetics is a term that was coined by New WORLD Theater's founding artistic director, Roberta Uno, to describe forward-looking artistic responses to the changing demographics of the United States. While demographers project 2042 for the general population shift, they accelerate projections to 2020 for children under eighteen. Each day, our country grows by around 8,000 people, almost 90 percent of whom are people of color.[11] In an effort to cultivate the next generation of American theater patrons as the American population grows younger and browner, arts policy approaches have stressed audience development, access, and outreach programs. Such strategies ask new audiences to conform to a traditional American theater paradigm. Instead, Future Aesthetics shifts the focus to where those audiences are already engaged, by bringing hip-hop, spoken word poetry, and related forms of artistic expression into the theater. Artists working within a Future Aesthetics framework are honing techniques to relate new narratives that reflect the perspectives of audiences who are increasingly more diverse, younger, culturally fluent, and technologically savvy. The chapters in this volume identify artists and institutions that are bringing Future Aesthetics approaches into American theater.

The cultural remapping of American theater cannot be carried out without institutions that are committed to a project of social inclusion, artistic risk-taking, and community collaboration. This type of work is challenged by austerity measures, canonical and institutional marginalization that have often resulted in chronic under-funding, low organizational capacity, lack of institutional space, and resistance to change by power holders. The chapters in this volume do not paint an unrealistic, idealized view of the present day cultural landscape, but instead engage the roadblocks and hurdles that practitioners who are dedicated to the project of diversifying American theater often face. Despite the enormous challenges of economic inequity in arts funding and among potential theater-going audiences, these chapters offer evidence of organizations that are thriving and advancing artistic risk and innovation. For example, Performance Studies scholar Jasmine Mahmoud describes how a burgeoning and vibrant non-traditional sector of theaters has emerged in the austere economy of Chicago after the 2008 economic downturn. Mark Valdez, former head of the Network of Ensemble Theaters describes new forms of ensemble-based collaboration that tie together apparently disparate locales such as rural Appalachia, New Orleans, indigenous Hawai'i, and

Baltimore. Executive director of Youth Speaks, James Kass, describes the process of building a thriving nonprofit arts organization that enjoys an enormous network of partner organizations spanning across the nation. Hopefully these chapters will inspire future artists, academics, and presenters to take up the mantle and continue engaging the changing demographics of the country by imagining what Future Aesthetics might look, sound, and feel like.

Taken in total, the chapters in this volume seriously engage Jeff Chang's claim that "cultural change [makes] political change possible."[12] A new world must first be imagined before it can be realized. Indeed, it is in that messy, exhilarating, and transformational category called culture, where marginalized histories can be remembered, new forms of citizenship sculpted, and possible futures can be envisioned.

Notes

1 Manning Marable, "Racializing Obama" in *Barack Obama and African American Empowerment: The Rise of Black America's New Leadership*, eds. Manning Marable and Kristen Clarke (London: Palgrave Macmillan, 2009), 7.
2 "How Groups Voted in 1988," *Roper Center*, http://ropercenter.cornell.edu/polls/us-elections/how-groups-voted/how-groups-voted-1988/, accessed May 2016. "How Groups Voted in 2012," *Roper Center*, http://ropercenter.cornell.edu/polls/us-elections/how-groups-voted/how-groups-voted-2012/, accessed May 2016.
3 Bill O'Reilly, "The White Establishment Is Now The Minority," *Foxnation*, November 7, 2012, http://nation.foxnews.com/bill-oreilly/2012/11/07/bill-o-reilly-white-establishment-now-minority, accessed May 2016.
4 Dana Milbank, "Donald Trump Is a Bigot and a Racist," *Washington Post* December 1, 2015, https://www.washingtonpost.com/opinions/donald-trump-is-a-bigot-and-a-racist/2015/12/01/a2a47b96-9872-11e5-8917-653b65c809eb_story.html?tid=sm_fb, accessed March 2016.
5 Herrenvolk Democracy: A purported democratic society where one ethnic group has sole access to natural born rights while subordinate groups are subjected to state violence, terror, and "tyranny." George Fredrickson, *The Black Image in the White Mind* (Connecticut: Wesleyan University Press, 1971), 61.
6 Gary Y. Okihiro, "Third World Studies," p. 54 of this book.
7 Michel-Rolph Trouillot, *Silencing the Past: Power and the Production of History* (Boston: Beacon Press, 1997). Diana Taylor, *The Archive and the Repertoire: Performing Cultural Memory in the Americas* (Durham: Duke University Press, 2003).
8 "New World Theater Records: 1979–2010," *WEB Du Bois Library*, http://scua.library.umass.edu/ead/murg025_f2_n4.html, accessed May 2016.
9 "New World Theater," *Hemispheric Institute*, http://hemisphericinstitute.org/hemi/en/hidvl-profiles/itemlist/category/577-nwt, accessed May 2016.
10 For more on polyculturalism see Vijay Prashad, *Everybody Was Kung Fu Fighting: Afro-Asian Connections and the Myth of Cultural Purity* (Boston: Beacon Press, 2002).
11 Steve Phillips, *Brown Is the New White: How the Demographic Revolution Has Created a New American Majority* (New York: The New Press, 2016), 5. Bill Chappell, "For U.S. Children, Minorities Will Be The Majority By 2020, Census Says," *NPR,* March 4, 2015, http://www.npr.org/sections/thetwo-way/2015/03/04/390672196/for-u-s-children-minorities-will-be-the-majority-by-2020-census-says, accessed May 2016.
12 Jeff Chang, "Not a prophecy, but description": rethinking multiculturalism in the "post-racial" moment," (p. 221 of this book).

Part I

New WORLD Theater

Chapter 1

Fertile ground

How New WORLD Theater began

Elizabeth Méndez Berry

By the year 2000, almost 450,000 residents of the United States had died of AIDS. When it first arrived stateside in the early 1980s, the disease primarily hit white men, but by the late 1990s, African Americans and Latinos accounted for 61 percent of those living with HIV, with an increasing number of women among those infected. In October 1998, President Bill Clinton declared AIDS a "severe and ongoing health crisis" in African American and Latino communities.[1] And yet it was a largely invisible emergency, one mostly ignored by the mainstream media and often suppressed by the affected communities themselves. Shame and stigma prevented people from acknowledging the cause of their loved ones' sickness and even death. Obituaries were intentionally vague.

On the fifteenth anniversary of the disease's discovery, New WORLD Theater (NWT) produced *Quinceañera*, a piece that shattered that silence and sprinkled it with sequins. The play, a collaboration between Alberto Antonio Araiza, Paul Bonin-Rodriguez, Michael Marinez, and Danny Bolero Zaldivar, tweaked the familiar rite-of-passage celebration, which welcomes 15-year-old Latina girls to womanhood in a frilly dress and a stretch limo, to commemorate a more painful generational shift: an age of loss. As the AIDS activist group ACT UP famously proclaimed, Silence Equals Death. *Quinceañera* spoke up and out—with humor, artistry and love—about the latest group of Latino *desaparecidos* (disappeared), stolen not by dictatorship but by disease. First performed in 1998, it was a powerful commentary on the crisis.

New WORLD Theater was a small theater in a small town, and yet, by developing works like *Quinceañera*, it offered a relief valve not just for the Amherst community, but for the country as a whole. It provided a public service at a public institution, the University of Massachusetts (UMass). At NWT, big issues like apartheid, mass incarceration, AIDS, and racial inequality were investigated. Equally important, the theater provided space for people of color to delve into their everyday lives. It pushed new aesthetic ideas and welcomed artists from South Africa to the South Bronx, including the famous, the infamous, and the unknown. It also made demands on everyone, from its staff to its ensemble to its audiences.

Like many NWT productions, *Quinceañera* was not easy to watch. The play provoked laughter, discomfort and pain; some squirmed at its campiness, others loved it. Towards the end, the three men onstage asked everyone present to name anyone they knew who had died of the disease. At some performances there were many voices, at others, few. But this act of collective remembrance, mourning, and celebration forced those gathered to acknowledge the absences inflicted by the virus. *Quinceañera* named names at a time when many refused to.

The piece was inspired by the artist Michael Marinez's exhibit of the same title. He collected the brightly colored pills left over after his friends had died of AIDS, and made them into rosaries and necklaces and lavishly decorated cakes, creating a glorious installation from grim souvenirs. The performers Alberto "Beto" Araiza and Paul Bonin-Rodriguez—both members of the New WORLD Theater community—began working on a performance piece on the same theme, and they asked artistic director Roberta Uno if they could develop it for NWT. Uno agreed, and proposed her graduate student, Joe Salvatore, to be the play's dramaturg and director; *Quinceañera* became Salvatore's thesis project. It was one of many hybrid productions at NWT, a place where professionals, students and community members worked closely together.

"It was an amazing experience to be working with these four men who trusted this pasty white boy to work with them, and Roberta trusted me as well, which was a huge thing for me," Salvatore told me. "Then it becomes the only LGBT piece at Inroads: the Americas, which is this festival in Miami that represents the Western Hemisphere. It was a profound experience. The artmaking that [Roberta] allowed me to witness, and then that [she] supported me in doing, it's now really embedded in me." Salvatore is now an associate professor of educational theater at New York University; he traces many of his teaching practices directly to his experiences at NWT.

Founded in 1979, New WORLD Theater transformed the University of Massachusetts-Amherst into an incubator of visionary theater, not just a venue but a laboratory. "The idea was not to do *Bye Bye, Birdie* and cast it interracially," Uno said in 1991. NWT "provides a place where people of different ethnicities, different colors, can come together, can learn about each other, can make the university environment more like they wish the world to be."[2] The theater's mission was "to nurture and present high-quality works by artists of color; to empower a diverse, broad-based audience; to communicate across geographic, generational, ethnic, and racial divides; and to foster a creative network of professional and community participants."[3]

NWT came into being in the aftermath of the Civil Rights era, when the struggle for representation had migrated to college campuses, and was suspended thirty years later, after the election of the country's first black president, at a time when affirmative action policies were being challenged and many argued that the country had entered a "post-racial" era, one in which culturally diverse programming was no longer necessary or even welcome.

Between 2011 and 2013, I spoke with people who played a role in the theater throughout its three-decade history, from original staffers to members of the ensemble to grant writers and UMass administrators. We held two group conversations that included Uno, one at the Ford Foundation in New York, where she worked as a senior program officer of arts and culture following her tenure at NWT, and the other in Amherst.[4] Drawing on those conversations, individual interviews, additional research and then-UMass student Maya Gillingham's exhaustive 1991 oral history of the theater's first ten years, a picture of this prescient, provocative theater and its impact emerged.

In 1965, the Massachusetts State Legislature passed the Racial Imbalance Act, which called for public schools to desegregate themselves or lose state funds. That law set the stage for the Boston busing crisis of 1974, during which white parents threw stones at buses carrying black children to class.[5] It was not a time of racial harmony. Two hours away from Boston, UMass-Amherst was mostly white when Stanley Kinard arrived there from Brooklyn in 1967. In a student population of about 16,000, he was one of forty black students, many of them Malawians who were part of a tropical agriculture program funded by the United States International Development Agency (USAID).[6] One year later, in 1968, the first sizeable class of 125 African American students arrived[7] with the support of the Committee for the Collegiate Education of Black Students, a network created by black faculty and staff members from the colleges of the area.

The same year, Dr. Martin Luther King Jr. was murdered. "When Dr. King was assassinated, primarily the African American students' association began to organize and began to advocate that there be a cultural presence reflective of who we were on campus," said Kinard during the Ford Foundation meeting. As a result of that mobilization, which included protests and the occupation of a university building, in 1970, the W.E.B. Du Bois Department of Afro American Studies was founded, with Ekwueme Michael Thelwell (who would become Uno's husband for ten years) as its chair. Over the years, the department attracted the likes of James Baldwin and Chinua Achebe to its faculty. The university's Women's Studies program was founded four years later, and is one of the oldest in the country.

Around the same time, UMass-Amherst's music department was also being transformed. Dr. Frederick Tillis, a native of Galveston, Texas, who was forced by segregation to leave his own state in order to pursue his PhD (he completed his doctorate in musical composition at the University of Iowa), joined the university's music department in 1970, when there were few African Americans living in the Amherst area. He started a jazz program in the department, which had long been a bastion of classical European music. Tillis played an instrumental role in attracting noted black jazz musicians to the program, including Max Roach, who arrived in 1972, as well as Billy Taylor and Archie Shepp. "There was a particular era of twenty to thirty years where black people had something going on at the university, and this was it," said Tillis, describing that period during a 2011 interview at his home in Amherst.

Still, racial tensions continued to simmer. The anger over busing in Boston had bubbled onto the UMass campus, where, according to founding NWT staffer Miriam Carter Langa, many white students from South Boston came to study.[8]

In the late 1970s there were several hate crimes at UMass, including a cross burning outside a student of color's social function and vandalizing of the campus's New Africa House. Shortly thereafter, there was another cross burning at nearby Amherst College.[9] In a May 1979 interview with the college newspaper, *The Collegian*, UMass Chancellor Randolph W. Bromery said, "This is the worst year in terms of women's rights incidents and racial incidents I've seen in the past twelve years."[10]

That was the year New WORLD Theater was born. In 1975, in response to student activists, an office of Third World Affairs had been established with Stan Kinard at its helm. Four years later, Kinard and the school's Student Activities Office hired the university's first racially diverse team of students to assist with student activities: Miriam Carter Langa, a Puerto Rican/Jamaican American woman, and Derek Davis, an African American man. Then Kinard brought on Roberta Uno as the school's first non-white professional activities programmer. She was a 23-year-old Japanese American who had been raised in Hawai'i and Los Angeles and had worked as a high school organizer with the United Farm Workers Support Committee in California. Uno was a recent graduate of Hampshire College, where she had majored in pre-med and also studied theater. Initially, the new hires were charged with organizing events for people of color, like Martin Luther King Week. In an interview with Maya Gillingham for her oral history project, Carter Langa said, "We were all repulsed by the climate at UMass socially—our cultures were not represented, and the people, the outlook, the focus was thoroughly white European." Soon after Uno was hired, she and Kinard took photographs of racist graffiti in the stairwells of the university's library, which they then used as part of a campaign to combat racism on campus and to advocate for the building's renaming after W.E.B. Du Bois, who grew up sixty miles away in Great Barrington, Massachusetts. In 1994, the library was finally named after Du Bois.

During our conversation in Amherst, Karen Lederer, who was a white student at UMass in 1979, said that Uno quickly began planning to expand her role beyond just coordinating pre-existing events, to creating original programming, including theatrical productions. She started raising funds to make the programs possible. In 1979, Uno wrote a $20,000 proposal to start a Third World Theater series, which led then-dean of students William Field to offer dollar-for-dollar support using the school's concessions revenue. "Roberta basically finagled this job that didn't have anything to do with this into this whole other thing. Is that fair?" Lederer asked Uno at our meeting. "Yes, that's fair," Uno replied with a smile.

In a 1989 interview with Glenn Siegel for the theater's tenth-anniversary publication, Field recalled her pitch:

> Here was this young woman, just out of Hampshire College, with a broad vision of what a university's mission should be. I was convinced within the first half hour of her presentation. On a pragmatic level, I had been coming to

> the realization that you can't open minds and reach people through lectures like you can through creative interaction in the arts. I was slowly learning this in my fifties. Roberta knew it at twenty-three. As far as I know, there is no enterprise like New WORLD Theater on other campuses, and it is interesting to note that the program didn't come up, and in fact probably couldn't have come up through normal academic channels.

Uno's first production at Amherst was *In the Rock Garden*, written by Uno herself. It starred a young Hawai'ian exchange student named Mariko Miho, who is now the senior director of development for the University of Hawai'i. At UMass, Miho took a class in multicultural education with Professor Bob Suzuki that, she said, changed her life. "Through Dr. Suzuki, it was brought to my awareness that there was a movement afoot. There were other Asian Americans who were finding their voices," said Miho, whose grandfathers had been held in internment camps during the Second World War. "They too had not known about the plight of their parents because they did not talk about the internment camp experience; it was a source of shame."

Suzuki suggested that Miho contact Uno about her play. "Roberta says, 'Do you have any acting experience?' and I said, 'No, but I'm very interested in your story,'" said Miho. "She encouraged me to play the main role, which sort of catapulted me into a discovery of myself through a cultural experience." *In the Rock Garden* was about a young Asian American woman who had grown up in multi-ethnic Los Angeles and was coming to terms with who she was in a predominantly white East Coast college. Though she'd grown up in a very different environment, Miho's year at Amherst was also a time of coming into her own, and the character took hold in her. "Roberta's play ignited something in me that was not there before, and it propelled me to find out more about myself and about my history."

In the Rock Garden played for three days in May 1979 with great success. The next fall, the Third World Theater (later renamed New WORLD Theater) presented four plays. *Homeland*, by Selaelo Maredi and Steve Friedman, performed by Modern Times Theater, was the first of many international productions. The play connected racism in South Africa with racism in the United States. (As a result of student and faculty activism, UMass had become, in 1977, one of the first U.S. universities to divest itself of South African financial interests.).[11] Apartheid continued to be a major issue around the country and in the area, where a group of South African students had settled and continued to agitate for change until 1994, when the apartheid regime finally fell. That season also included *Prisms*, by Mascheri Chapelle and Jerome Robinson, an original production by a Smith College student that was based on her brother's letters from prison.

One goal of the Third World Theater series was to unite the atomized groups of students of color, partly because there was so little funding to go around, but also out of a desire to create a new type of community that found strength in difference. Still, at the start, it was hard to attract people to plays that weren't directly related to their own ethnic group. "I remember something we talked about a lot was 'Why would Ahora [the Latino students' group] tell their people to go to the play about Asian Americans? Why would they be interested?'" Lederer recalled. "It didn't happen a lot in the early years," Uno replied. "People went to their own thing." There was also a pervasive expectation that the theater should be making the communities it depicted look good. "Every single thing we did was under this microscope in the early days. People wanted us to be celebratory," said Uno. "We got a lot of complaints. The first year we did *Simpson Street* [by Eduardo Gallardo] and people said, 'Why are you hanging our dirty laundry? There's a whore in the play, and we don't all talk that way,' and we assured them that this wasn't the only play we'd ever do about Puerto Ricans."

At the start, the Third World Theater series was staffed by just three part-time work-study students: Karen Lederer, Derek Davis, and Miriam Carter Langa, as well as Uno. The budget was tight. "In our first ten years, we didn't get a single grant. It's not that we didn't apply for them," said Uno, noting that Dave Mazzoli, the grants administrator she later worked with at the Ford Foundation, used to sign her letters of rejection. She attributes the theater's sturdy identity to the fact that it didn't contort itself to fit funders' expectations. The team raised money creatively: it got small contributions from student groups, and the music department's famous faculty set the stage for the Bright Moments festivals. Inspired by a college trip to Cuba—where Uno had attended cheap, excellent cultural events, from Afro-Cuban music festivals to ballet performances—she believed that art should be accessible to the public, so she created an inexpensive outdoor summer concert series. They passed the hat until 1985, when they started charging $5 per adult. Bright Moments generated between $15,000 and $20,000 every year, which was reinvested into the theater. It featured the likes of Tito Puente, Sonny Rollins, Sun Ra and Fela Kuti, and attracted thousands of people.

Another key to the organization's early success was Uno's ability to attract and engage allies. Beth Nathanson was a theater major when she first encountered NWT in 1982. "I went to see a play and next thing I knew I was stage managing for Roberta. I don't know how she did it," said Nathanson, who went on to become NWT's "first real administrator," according to Uno. "When I graduated from UMass in 1984, she hired me and threw me into the fire. She got pregnant and left." Uno took two months off after the birth of her second child, and during our New York meeting, Uno and Nathanson reminisced about Uno breastfeeding during rehearsals for *The Dance and the Railroad*—definitely a new experience for some of the male actors. Nathanson wrote her first grant proposals at New WORLD Theater, and is now the director of planning and development at Playwrights Horizons in New York. She describes her time at NWT as formative. "I grew up right outside Boston in an upper-middle-class white Jewish neighborhood, and I was being exposed to cultures that I'd never been exposed to before in a very close-up-and-personal way. That was a big part of my education as well," she said.

Early staffers and volunteers note that over the first few years of NWT's existence, crowds weren't always flocking to its shows—there might be thirty or forty friends and friends of friends sprinkled around the cramped Hampden Theater, in the basement of a residence hall—but gradually the audiences grew. In the fall of 1983, when she directed *Do Lord Remember Me*, by James de Jongh, in collaboration with the gospel music scholar Dr. Horace Clarence Boyer, Uno remembers people calling the NWT office trying to pay with credit cards, which she had no means of processing. One night during its run, she recalled, when she looked out from backstage at an audience that included plenty of gray-haired white people, "That was when we knew we had reached beyond our community." At a time when the national discourse was less and less receptive to the presence of people of color in traditionally white spaces—President Ronald Reagan was doing all he could to dismantle affirmative action—at UMass, New WORLD Theater was putting down roots. Music professor Fred Tillis had become the head of the university's Fine Arts Center, and in 1984 he invited Uno to join the Center in its Department of Multicultural Programs. She brought with her New WORLD Theater, Bright Moments and the summer music workshop Jazz in July.

"Largely because of who Fred was as a person, and Fred's recognition by the institution, he carved out an independent niche for the Fine Arts Center, and when he saw NWT looking for a home, he said, 'Come,'" according to Lee Edwards, another UMass administrator who played a key role in NWT's history.

It was also in 1984 that the name was changed to New WORLD Theater in response to student and audience input. The name was inspired by Nina Simone's song "New World Coming." The theater's mission was twofold: to present touring professional companies and to create its own productions, drawing on the local Five Colleges community. In 1983 NWT established its own core ensemble, a multiracial group of actors from the area. Members of the ensemble were given actor-training workshops and were expected to work on all aspects of productions—from back of house to onstage—and to work on productions that focused on cultures other than their own. They also participated in script selection.

The town of Amherst was mostly white, the university was mostly white, and its theater department was all white. As a result, there were few opportunities for people of color to perform. In her oral history of the theater, Maya Gillingham, a Caucasian woman whom Uno had been teaching since she was in high school, writes,

> The experience of working with New WORLD Theater, as an ensemble member, staff or even as an audience member, was seeing complex, varied, living, thinking representations of people of color. Certainly that was not to be found in the UMass theater department—as expressed by the countless stories of discouraged actors who got cast as waiters and servants if they got cast at all. In the time I was there, there was an [American] Indian role played by a white person with a gigantic rubber nose and a feather, a stable boy role for Black actors, etc.[12]

In this context, New WORLD Theater created and nurtured a generation of performers and behind-the-scenes theater staffers. By the early 1990s, the ensemble had swelled to eighty people, including its eldest member, E. Jefferson "Pat" Murphy, an older white man who was the coordinator of the Five College consortium at the time. Celia Hilson and Ingrid Askew, African American actors in the NWT ensemble who also took Uno's classes in the theater department, talked about how important it was to be part of a company that gave them the opportunity not only to play a variety of roles onstage, but also to develop their skills offstage.

"New WORLD gave you all of these opportunities to fall flat on your face or to shine, and nobody thought any less of you," said Askew, who joined the theater in 1981. "There are a lot of theater companies in this country and this world that don't do that. They produce great theater, but they don't give people those opportunities." Hilson, an undergraduate in the theater department from 1985 to 1989, who was usually the only black student in her classes, describes being part of NWT as a process of self-discovery. "It opened my eyes," she said. "I was dealing with so much internalized oppression. It helped me to get to the core of who Celia is through the different stories . . . to step into the story and speak through the lens of other characters. It's really informed how I walk in the world. I walk with a different posture; I breathe different."

Both Askew and Hilson returned to NWT again and again through the years. In the 1990s, Hilson was an instructor in NWT's youth program. Askew's play *Crossing the Waters, Changing the Air* was to be produced in 2009, but the theater was shut down two months before the play's scheduled debut. Both have continued their commitment to theater. Askew founded her own theater company and now leads a cultural exchange program with South African youth. After teaching theater for many years, Hilson is now pursuing a master's degree in marriage and family therapy.

New WORLD Theater's relationship with the university that housed it was fraught: On the one hand, the university provided the theater with little economic support outside its residency at the Fine Arts Center; NWT had to raise the bulk of its programming funds from student groups and outside sources. On the other hand, UMass used the theater to recruit students of color. A 1979 photograph of the theater's founding staff—Uno, Derek Davis, Karen Lederer, and Miriam Carter Langa—was used and reused on the school's promotional materials for years. In 1984, the photo appeared on a poster that read "The University of Massachusetts-Amherst welcomes minority students."[13] (A copy of that poster hung in Uno's office at the Ford Foundation.)

The theater department was particularly challenging. "There had not been any person of color teaching in that department prior to me, and they really hated it years later when I would say, 'I desegregated this department because I was the first faculty of color here and I brought the first plays by writers of color to both the experimental theater and the main stage,'" said Uno, who started teaching in a lecturer position in 1984. She taught courses including Contemporary Playwrights of Color, Asian American Theater, Black Theater and Native American Drama.

"I believe that universities have a real responsibility to include the material in the curriculum, to start to correct history," Uno told Gillingham.[14] "Unless there's a demand for a certain type of theater, it won't be commercially viable. . . . And so where do you break that spiral? I believe that one of the first places is in the classroom."

Uno's courses were a haven for people of color, who made up the majority of her students. Most of the former UMass students I interviewed who had been part of New WORLD Theater had taken her classes, whether they were theater majors or not. Her courses were unusual both for their content, which was unique in the department, and for their guest lectures from artists who were performing at New WORLD Theater. "Pearl Cleage came in and did a playwriting workshop with us, and she said in that workshop, 'Playwrights either write their way into something or write their way out of something,'" said Joe Salvatore. "I tell my students that all the time, and I tell them I heard it straight from her mouth. . . . It was life-altering to have that kind of experience." Salvatore had arrived at UMass thinking that he would study classical theater, but working on NWT's New Works for a New World summer play-development workshop changed his mind. "I remember sitting in the rehearsals [of works by the Colorado Sisters, lê thi diem thúy and Sekou Sundiata] and thinking, 'These artists are working in a way that I've never seen before, but it really resonates for me as what I want to do,'" he said.

Uno credits Lee Edwards, the dean of the Faculty of Humanities and Fine Arts from 1991 to 2006, and Murray Schwartz, her predecessor, with helping her become a full professor in 2000, a post that enabled her to recruit the department's first black graduate students, and build her own curricula; it also stabilized New WORLD Theater's position within the university. "Fred Tillis created the administrative home for New WORLD Theater, and Lee Edwards created the academic home for the classes I taught," said Uno. For Edwards, who had witnessed the establishment of the Afro American Studies and Women's Studies departments when she was a young English professor, New WORLD Theater represented an opportunity. "The whole existence of an entity like New WORLD Theater inside an institution like the University of Massachusetts is challenging and interesting," said Edwards, who is now retired. "I always thought the trick would be, Can we institutionalize this? Can we make it happen, create a niche, as has happened with Afro Am, as has happened with Women's Studies, so that the institution will accept it as a natural part of itself?"

Some theater faculty members supported New WORLD Theater. Harley Erdman, who was chair of the department in the 1990s, required all students in the Theater 100 survey course to attend NWT productions, and Doris Abramson, a pioneering scholar of black theater, successfully advocated for students to receive academic credit for working on NWT productions. Still, many professors were resistant, despite the fact that their graduate students needed opportunities to work on shows. Many considered NWT a glorified community theater that produced inferior work. Others thought it was anti-white, despite the fact that since the theater's founding, Caucasians had always been involved. "We tried to figure out a way that there would be a joint production between [the] theater [department] and NWT every year," said Edwards. "Most of the energy was coming from the NWT side. . . . The department at best was always ambivalent, always jealous, always fearful that somehow the success of NWT would come at its expense." In 1994, Edwards resorted to hiring a mediator to address the conflicts between the department and New WORLD Theater. "She came highly recommended and at the end of half a day she was in my office in tears, saying 'I quit!! I cannot do it,'" said Edwards.

Instead, New WORLD Theater began to develop other types of collaborations, looking outside the ivory tower. Since the theater's 1979 founding, the demographics of the Pioneer Valley surrounding it had shifted. The population of Amherst doubled between 1980 and 2000, with a significant increase in both its Asian and Latino communities and in the proportion of families living at or below poverty level. "When I originally came to Massachusetts I felt uncomfortable being there, it was so white," said Uno "I had to bring my own rice from California; now there are lots of ethnic markets in the area." Nearby Holyoke was always more diverse than Amherst; by 2000, its black, Asian and Latino populations made up almost half of the total population there, of whom Latinos were the largest group. In Springfield, the area's largest city, almost a third of the population spoke a language other than English at home. These changes inspired the theater's decision, in 1995, to develop the Latino Theater Project, which brought two national theater companies together with local community organizations with the goal of increasing Latino participation in theater. Plays developed through the project were presented at local Latino festivals, reaching thousands of new audience members, and as part of NWT's seasons.

Evelin Aquino, who was a student at UMass-Amherst from 1994 to 1999, described participating in that project as one of the most important experiences she had while at college. "I worked in audience development, bringing young people to campus, and these young people represented me," said Aquino during the Amherst conversation. "They had never been on a college campus, they had never been to a play, so it was incredibly important to me." In 1996, NWT launched its Asian Theater Project, focusing on the Cambodian and Vietnamese refugee communities. Hung Nguyen, one of the artists who had a three-week residency at the Vietnamese-American Civic Association in Dorchester, was struck by the transformation in workshop participants.

> I remember one of the young men said to me on the first day that we met that he had no stories to tell. He repeated that he had "nothing" interesting to say. Two weeks later that same young man, standing in front of his peers and the audience, shared his memories of growing up in Vietnam and his journey to America. He danced as his voice moved with emotion. Much laughter and tears were shared during the process of sharing stories.[15]

As a Latina who had grown up in New York and Springfield, Aquino said that working on the project brought her closer to the struggles of other people of color, from Cambodian refugees to African Americans.

Quang Bao, who was then an assistant dean in Lee Edwards' office, became a supporter, and wrote grants to get the project funded. "I saw a group of youths performing that was incredibly moving; it was a movement towards self-possession," said Bao, a writer who is now co-director of SecondGuest and executive director of the Rema Hort Mann Foundation. "It was all the positive strokes of telling a person, 'That story is yours and it is true and it's part of America, too.' It wasn't like the kids were being educated. . . . The program relocated the stories inside of them."

The Latino and Asian theater projects evolved into a summer program called Looking In/To The Future, involving young people from Asian, Latino, and African American communities in the area. When the Census Bureau began projecting that the United States would be "majority minority" by 2050, New WORLD Theater reconceptualized its youth work as Project 2050, which became one of the theater's most beloved and nationally known programs.

For Steven Raider-Ginsburg, who had been part of NWT as a student and then became a student teacher assisting Celia Hilson in the youth program in Holyoke, the program changed his trajectory as an artist. "Learning from Celia was my crash course in devising, and that's what I do now. We worked with a Puerto Rican group in Holyoke and the performances were amazing," he said. "What Roberta was delivering . . . to the communities in the freedom of theater of place and theater of identity and how to create and have a voice of who you are, it was such a benefit to Holyoke." Joe Salvatore was impressed by Uno's approach to working outside of the university's walls. "Rather than saying, 'This is what NWT wants to do for your community,' you asked the community what they wanted to do. That lesson has never left me," he said.

In 2011, two years after the theater had shut down, New York University's Hemispheric Institute hosted a symposium celebrating the theater, and alumni from Project 2050 performed a short piece. Afterwards, they burst into tears in the hallway. The sense of loss after New WORLD Theater's suspension was expressed most clearly by those young people, but everyone I spoke with was in mourning. "I'm not sad for Roberta. I'm sad for the institution," said Lee Edwards. "I think NWT held a special place for a lot of people because it really was a gathering place to network and see themselves presented and reflected in a bigger way than you might encounter in a small town like Amherst," said Pam Tillis, Fred Tillis's daughter, an NWT intern and then staff member, who is now Director of Public Programs at the New School.

In many ways, NWT anticipated a future that is finally catching up to it. President Barack Obama was elected to a second term with significant support from the Latino community, already the country's largest minority. The nation's babies are already mostly non-white, but even as communities of color are flexing politically, the country has become more economically unequal and perhaps more politically and socially segregated. In response to Obama, there has been a resurgence of white supremacist activity.

Throughout the years that New WORLD Theater was active, racial strife continued to be a problem on campus. In 1986, after the New York Mets defeated the Boston Red Sox in the World Series, a brawl between mostly white Sox fans and mostly black Mets fans erupted in the college's Southwest dormitory complex, and a black student was beaten unconscious by white students with golf clubs and baseball bats. In 1988, two black students were beaten by five white students after a dormitory party. Students responded by occupying the campus's New Africa House.[16] "I was so moved that it was a really diverse group that came out. It wasn't all black students, it was all different kinds of students," Karen Lederer said of that sit-in. "So I felt like, wow, if you build these cultural institutions, they may have some effect."[17] Nine years later, Lederer took food to the students who were occupying UMass's Goodell Hall, demanding increased diversity on campus. Among them was Evelin Aquino, who rehearsed her lines for the NWT production of Edwin Sanchez's *Unmerciful Good Fortune* out the window of the occupied building; Uno took the rehearsal to her.[18]

New WORLD Theater created a context for responding to these incidents; it encouraged action. "Participating in New WORLD Theater, it was like learning how to become a global citizen, and it was experientially based," said Steven Raider-Ginsburg, who is now the co-founding artistic director of HartBeat theater ensemble in Hartford, Connecticut, during the Ford Foundation meeting. "You go sit in the theater and experience viscerally the stories that were brought there to Western Massachusetts and came from every aspect of the world, from all sorts of traditions." Uno agreed. "You're on to something when you say 'global citizen,' as opposed to now, I think it's a global consumer. Now it's very individual and easy and those who can afford to have access will have access," she said. "Those who can participate do so because they can charge it, go surf the Internet, and just kind of take things as opposed to when you actually sit in that space."

Not only did people sit in the theater and experience the stories; they incarnated them, as actors; they interpreted them, as directors and dramaturgs; they invested in them, as stagehands. New WORLD Theater offered experiences that changed its participants' lives and transformed its community. At the end of our conversation at Ford, Uno returned to *Quinceañera:* "I was thinking of that tension when it's that moment when the actors say to name your people that you've lost to the AIDS pandemic and you just start hearing people around you, and some people are silent, and some people say name after name and you have to negotiate all of that," she said. "That is the global citizenry of recognizing. And it's not easy."

Notes

1 "HIV and AIDS, United States, 1981–2000," *Centers for Disease Control*, http://www.cdc.gov/mmwr/preview/mmwrhtml/mm5021a2.htm#tab1, accessed December 2012; "A Timeline of AIDS," *US Department of Health and Human Services*, http://aids.gov/hiv-aids-basics/hiv-aids-101/aids-timeline/, accessed February 2013.

2 Quoted in Maya Gillingham, "There's a New World Coming: The Development of the New WORLD Theater at the University of Massachusetts, An Oral History Project," undergraduate thesis, University of Massachusetts Amherst, 1991.

3 "NWT Mission statement," 2000, http://hemisphericinstitute.org/hemi/es/hidvl-profiles/item/2199-ntw-mission, accessed February 21, 2016.
4 Unless otherwise indicated, quotations in this chapter are from transcripts of those group conversations.
5 Margalit Fox, "Kevin H. White, Mayor Who Led Boston in Bussing Crisis, Dies at 82," *New York Times*, January 27, 2012, http://www.nytimes.com/2012/01/28/us/kevin-h-white-82-boston-mayor-during-busing-crisis-dies.html?pagewanted=2, accessed July 6, 2016.
6 Mary Ann French, "The People's Professor," *Boston Globe Magazine*, September 12, 1999, http://cache.boston.com/globe/magazine/1999/9-12/featurestory1.shtml, accessed December 2012.
7 The Committee for the Collegiate Education of Black and Other Minority Students, mission statement, http://www.umass.edu/ccebms/Mission.html, accessed February 2013.
8 Gillingham, "There's a New World Coming," 17.
9 Donna Beth Aronson, "Access and Equity: Performing Diversity at the New WORLD Theater," PhD dissertation, Florida State University, 2003, http://diginole.lib.fsu.edu/cgi/viewcontent.cgi?article=1032&context=etd.
10 Ibid.
11 Lauren Yelinek, "South Africa Divestment," *Radical UMass*, 2011, http://blogs.umass.edu/radicalumass/histories-of-radical-actions-at-umass/south-africa-divestment/, accessed December 2012.
12 Gillingham, "There's a New World Coming," 48.
13 Gillingham, "There's a New World Coming," 77. In her oral history, Gillingham notes that in 1991, the staff of New WORLD Theater was on the cover of the Admissions Office recruiting brochure for students of color, and half of the quotes in the brochure came from NWT members.
14 Ibid., 33.
15 Aronson, "Access and Equity," 131.
16 Brian Canova, "Riot Police Disperse 1,500 Students at UMass-Amherst Following Super Bowl," *Masslive.com*, February 5, 2012, http://www.masslive.com/news/index.ssf/2012/02/riot_erupts_at_umass_amherst_f_1.html, accessed February 2012; Valeria M. Russ, "Sit-in Continues at UMass, Black Students Allege Racism On Campus," *Philadelphia Daily News*, February 17, 1988, http://articles.philly.com/1988-02-17/news/26240010_1_white-students-black-students-minority-students, accessed February 2012.
17 Gillingham, "A New World Coming," 61.
18 Yelinek, "South Africa Divestment."

Chapter 2

Steps towards a new world

Roberta Uno

I started New WORLD Theater when I was 23 years old; in many ways I grew up in it. I raised my children, Chinua and Mikiko, in the theater and grew a community around it—it was the world that I wanted for them, for us to live in. New WORLD Theater was a thirty-year experiment in cultural organizing, social paradigm shifting, and artistic questioning. I had the privilege of working with artists across a span of generations—from sages who have gone to dance with the ancestors like James Baldwin, Horace Clarence Boyer, Alice Childress, Gordon Heath, Errol Hill, Pearl Primus, Barney Simon, and Sekou Sundiata, to artists who have revitalized American theater and arts today, such as Jorge Cortiñas, Danny Hoch, Marc Bamuthi Joseph, Nobuko Miyamoto, Dipankar Mukherjee, lê thi diem thúy, Carl Hancock Rux, Mildred Ruiz and Steve Sapp and UNIVERSES, and so many others. I remember my toddler son playing with "Uncle Jimmy," my daughter being hoisted onto the back of a dancer during rehearsal with Pearl, Carl writing a poem about the two of them when they were teens, my daughter babysitting Steve and Mildred's son Kwest, and both of them performing in Project 2050 as they came of age. The story of New WORLD is the story of a community family farm that raised not just me and my children, but flourished under the labor of, and provided sustenance for, so many others—artists, students, organizers, administrators, educators, and our larger community. As its founder, I offer these reflections as a way of understanding the ethos of New WORLD Theater. What were NWT's overarching principles over the years? The eleven precepts below are neither prescriptive nor complete, but are considerations of revelatory moments and points of consistency through the decades I led the theater. I offer these stories about the past as ways to think about creating the future.

1. It's about difference

The drama started in the lobby. Arriving for a staged reading of *Blues for Mr. Charlie* by James Baldwin, the buzz was swelling in pockets of commotion as audience members encountered the two entrances, one marked "Whites Only" and the other beneath a "Colored" sign. A middle-aged white man refuses to go through the "Whites Only" door; he tells the usher, "I marched on Washington, it was wrong then and it's wrong now." He starts through the "Colored" entrance and a group of young black students stop him, "This is our door—yours is over there." They are laughing; his expression shifts from confusion, to hurt, to anger as he reconsiders the "Whites Only" door. A young white woman is reasoning with the usher at the "Colored" door, "My child is black, I've been shunned by the white community, I'm part of the black community because of him—I should sit in the black section." A black woman turns to her and says gently, "It's a play. And you can choose to be a white woman any other time, so why not for just a while now?"

Inside, the drama continues and the play has yet to begin. The audience is wrapped around the thrust performance area in an upside down horseshoe—and at the top, right in the middle, James Baldwin is sitting, watching, his large luminous eyes taking it all in. To his left is the "Colored" side, divided down the center; and facing it, the "Whites Only" side. The white audience members sit in quiet, nervous anticipation. But the colored side is boisterous, people greeting each other; somehow it's become a reunion. Yet as they settle in, small intergroup dramas erupt: a man from India is sidling down a row in the "Colored" section and a black man advises him that he should be sitting on the white side. Another black man cuts in with ironic laughter, "The man is darker than you—let the brother sit down!"

I was a young Asian American woman theater director who had been asked to work with James Baldwin to stage a reading of his dense and powerful drama. It had originally flopped on Broadway when it was staged by Burgess Meredith at the height of the Civil Rights struggle in 1964. In 1983, Baldwin was in residence at the Five Colleges and I knew him as a friend of my husband at that time; I had listened to him late into many nights "talking story" as we say in Hawai'i. To me he was Jimmy: elegantly kind, wickedly funny, wise, generous to a fault, and irreverent. Now we were working on the play together. I was pregnant and coping mightily with meetings in his favorite habitat, smoke-filled bars, where at least I could control his gregarious tendency to recast parts unauditioned. I learned from him that staging the play on Broadway in 1964 had been critical to him, urgent even. He could have put the play on anywhere else, certainly in Harlem, but he wanted it where Mr. Charlie could not ignore it. How fitting that two decades later, the invitation would come from Amherst College, to wake up Mr. Charlie's grandchildren.

I had been wracking my brain with how to make the play come alive for a contemporary 1983 audience and not be viewed comfortably from a twenty-year distance as a museum relic of the Civil Rights movement. The answer was in front of me, literally in the architecture of the venue chosen for the reading. Converse Hall at Amherst College is a lecture hall raked in a horseshoe around a postage stamp of an arena, with two entrance doors on either end facing a common lobby. As a reading there would be no props or set beyond chairs and the signs above the doors. The segregated audiences would face each other, mirroring the play's division between Blacktown and Whitetown. The black actors would sit in a row in front of the Blacktown audience side, the white actors on their side, each scene intermixing as they interacted, but always returning to their "tribe" as Baldwin put it. There was no theater lighting in the lecture hall, so the audience would remain unavoidably present to each other, watching each others' responses throughout.

My one anxiety about the two doors was not wanting to disrespect an elderly black person. I imagined an unheralded elder being offended and lost sleep wondering how s/he might react to this conceit. Would it be seen as making light of history? Would it provoke painful memories? But Baldwin liked the idea and thought we should try it. It might work because the staging made the audiences equals, rather than in a traditional proscenium, where blacks had sat behind or above whites during segregation, watching the stage through their filter. In this staging, they would never lose sight of each other throughout the play; they would have to watch each other bear witness, as Baldwin's writing had urged—we could not look away.

Difference, as opposed to the multicultural notion of sameness, was an ongoing, sometimes painful, often exhilarating exploration of New WORLD Theater. Multiculturalism's assumption had been that in celebrating our distinct identities, a common humanity would be engendered. Its limitations were reached at the blurred edges of reductive and essentialized identity categories, and in the complex refusal of narratives to conform to simple representation. At NWT the schisms and nuances of difference were grappled with on stage, in staff dynamics, and in the deepening of how the theater related to its community. In knowing that difference was continuously acknowledged, if not always understood, our audiences in time transformed into a community.

2. Getting out of the way

I recall director Nefertiti Burton's delighted surprise when I asked if she would like to direct Elizabeth Wong's *Letters to a Student Revolutionary*, a play inspired by events of the Tiananmen Square uprising. As an African American woman, she was used to being approached about "the black play," but didn't anticipate that an Asian American would offer this production to her. It made more sense to invite Nefertiti to direct, rather than to take this project on myself. At that point in my life, I hadn't been to China; even if I had, Nefertiti had years of experience as part of the U.S. China Peoples' Friendship Association and could bring far more knowledge, insight, and passion to the project.

I've never believed in matching productions to the race or ethnicity of a director, or the practice of sanctioning white directors to direct everything and pigeonholing directors of color to a diversity slot. And I've always been troubled by white, usually academic, directors who tell me they don't know if they have a right to direct work by playwrights of color—and yet they have no problem directing Chekhov or Churchill, but not writers from their own country. When asked for advice on how to build rapport with casts/audiences of color, I've advised that they take a step back—not only to examine their own social relationships, but to think about how to best position themselves within a project. Maybe they aren't the best fit for the material; and, instead of not staging it, can they move themselves to a producing or assistant directing position and raise the funds to bring in a guest director, or to give an opportunity to an emerging director? Thus at New WORLD I gave many emerging directors opportunities across racial categories, when they had a passion and vision for the material—Anna Dolan, an Irish woman, directed Puerto Rican playwright Estrella Artau's *Marine Tiger*; a Nigerian, Anna Ibe, directed the Trinidadian playwright Erroll Hill's *Moon on a Rainbow Shawl*; Cecelia Cavalcanti, a Brazilian, directed Cuban Pepe Carril's *Shango de Ima*, Joe Salvatore, a Caucasian American, directed *Quinceañera* by Beto Arraiza, Paul Bonin-Rodriguez, and Michael Marines, and so forth—while I supported their vision by raising resources, producing, and assisting behind the scenes.

When I chose projects to direct at NWT, it was because I felt I had insight to offer and that the work might mesh with my directing and dramaturgical process. But I also disciplined myself to step back and play a supportive role by creating the right environment, beginning with trust and belief in processes I wasn't leading. For example, Steven Sapp and Mildred Ruiz of UNIVERSES were my Artistic Associates for four years during which time they developed *Slanguage* with director Jo Bonney. While Steve and Mildred collaborated deeply with me on Project 2050 and the Intersections conferences, for *Slanguage*, the right decision was to give the artists the ideal conditions to produce their work. Simply put, to determine the best way to make it happen and get out of the way of the work.

3. Concentric circles and the further margin

New WORLD Theater was known by artists as having an extraordinary audience: large, appreciative, and eloquent; racially and ethnically pluralistic, multi-generational, integrated across class and education, and possessing a high level of cultural literacy. I have almost never seen this audience profile at mainstream theaters—even now, in my fifties, my husband will look around a New York mainstream theater audience and comment that I may be both the diversity and youth quotient. I was often asked how we built that community and who we considered our target audience; for whom were we making work? From the start, when we were very aware that we, as artists of color, were a minority in New England—I never wanted the theater to be a travel guide explaining "the other" to tourists. I believed the work should exist in concentric circles: at the center those of the play's cultural context, however the artists defined it. I felt if truth was at the core, then those sitting farther away might not understand everything, but they would certainly feel the reverberations. This was a different paradigm than the polarizing and limiting duality majority/minority, black/white cultural politics.

Another aspect of the concentric circles approach was an awareness of who was sitting at the furthest margin; whose stories weren't being told and what creative strategy could be developed. For example, in the early 1990s I was troubled that heterosexuality was the normative narrative we were presenting on stage. We were not engaging the reality of our staff, production and acting ensemble.

Queer artists of color were, for the most part, not being supported for their own work by Black, Asian American and other ethnically specific theaters, but finding homes in experimental, women's, and queer spaces. The staff agreed we needed to change, but before we could, we had to acknowledge the deep divisions between and within our communities and move forward without the pretense that we are all allies. We held a community forum with an unwieldy title, something like "Homophobia in Communities of Color and Racism in the Gay Community"—basically, we set up a microphone and a room full of people lined up and said anything they felt on the topic. It was heated, heartfelt, exhausting, and cathartic. We didn't bring in scholars or health professionals or create any artistic response. In retrospect, it wasn't thought through at all, but somehow it worked. The 1992–93 season followed, featuring work by the Pomo Afro Homos and commission of Marga Gomez. Rather than relegate queer work to a play laboratory, it was launched with full commitment and woven through our season, commissioning, youth work, and play lab.

4. Working with the given circumstances

In my directing studio seminar, I used to give my graduate students an early exercise: to respond to a given text by staging a scene anywhere in the immediate environment, except in a rehearsal room or on a stage. Champing to get on stage, they typically initially felt blown off—until the next class revealed the myriad possibilities in a stairwell shaft, atop piles of cable, a hallway of lockers, etc.

The first time I was invited to be part of a grant review panel for the Theater Communication Group directing fellowship awards program, I was struck by resumes of young aspiring directors, almost all conservatory trained with impressive credentials as assistant directors to a series of notable theater directors. And yet several didn't have a body of work themselves as directors. During the review panel discussions, I noticed a bias towards mainstream (implicitly white) spaces. A black woman director under consideration had two decades of productions in what some panelists were calling "community-based" theaters (translation: black and women's theaters). They wondered if she was "too junior," "too emerging," in contrast to other younger candidates who had far fewer or no productions under their sole direction, but impressive credentials of who they had assisted in recognized regional theaters. Making a career seemed to be of greater value to the review panel than actually making the work.

I believe a director directs, a writer writes—an artist makes art because that is the way s/he engages the world. Limitations—lack of a venue, production slot, budget aren't an excuse for not making the work; as artists of color, that's just part of the given circumstances. Beyond formal theater space, NWT appropriated space and made theater in public parks, school gymnasiums, community centers, parking lots, gay bars, and churches. A New WORLD artist leads with the art, finding possibility in every deficit, recognizing resources in people, and not waiting for, but continuously making, opportunity.

5. Taking small steps

The legendary choreographer Pearl Primus inadvertently gave me the metaphor for our basic work in the theater. It was at the first dance rehearsal for Wole Soyinka's *Lion and the Jewel*, a NWT co-production with the UMass Department of Theater that brought another legend of the American Theater, actor Gordon Heath, home from Europe after decades of absence, and featured a young student actor, Jeffrey Wright, who would go on to Tony award and feature film acclaim.

The dancers were anxiously awaiting Primus's arrival, eager to meet the "Grandmother of Black Dance," the dance ethnographer, the woman who in her prime had been featured in photographs, leaping her height. As she regally entered the room; warm-ups and stretching ended abruptly; all fell silent under her appraising eye. She warmly beckoned us to sit as she began the rehearsal. I thought she was going to give her insights into the text, talk about the Yoruba cosmology, or her research in Africa. All of that would come in time. Instead she asked us to cradle our bare feet. She said to look for cracks, to examine our nails, to look at the condition of the skin. And then she proceeded to explain step-by-step the proper washing, oiling, and caring for our feet. She advised us to care for ourselves and then extrapolated to the work at hand, "Your feet plant you on the ground—and that is the essence of African dance."

Aside from the profound cultural and spiritual orientation to African dance, I was stunned by Pearl's introduction because the norm in a dance rehearsal is to demand from the body, not to care for it, to delve into action, not reflect inwardly. As theater artists, as community organizers, we often forget to take care of ourselves or we demand more from our bodies than possible for the long haul. And as theater makers, we often put the artistic vision before all the initial work of community building that ensures our audience will go with us, even when we fail. Pearl taught us that there are small steps before leaping. I believe we took the small steps of earning community trust, which allowed for experimentation and urged greater rigor. But the small steps of caring for ourselves was the harder lesson as a constant all-hands-on-deck small arts organization with large ideas. Yvonne Mendez, NWT's design director, and I would joke that it took having a baby or a car accident to make us stop, and even that would be momentary. It's a lesson I still am learning.

6. Commitment to the unknown

It's often said that theater is a process of discovery and I believe in that revelatory process. But I also believe it requires deep commitment and even courage to delve into the unknown. And that means going to the unexpected.

In the mid-1980s, I wanted to push our artistic program to produce Native American Theater; previously we had presented touring works by artists such as Spiderwoman, Craig Kee Strete, and Hanay Geiogamah, but we had never produced a Native playwright work ourselves. We identified a production slot in the season, but quickly realized that it was too soon; in order for Native American dramaturgy to be integral to the theater, we had a lot of homework to do. I started by contacting playwright Hanay Geiogamah, who was teaching at UCLA and he graciously arranged a visit to the American Indian Studies Center archive to read plays. Returning armed with a trove of literature, I co-developed and co-taught a course on Native American theater with Donna Goodleaf, a Mohawk UMass graduate student and activist. We reached out to UMass-Amherst's Josephine White Eagle Cultural Center which helped us recruit a number of Native American students to the class. Parallel to that, with New WORLD Theater dramaturgy staff and interns, we started a script review process open to the community.

This would be our first production of a Native American play and it was important to me that we recruit and train actors locally. New WORLD Theater had started as a student organizing project; my goal had always been to activate our community, not just inspire or inform. So of course, I had a script in mind; it was a series of vignettes that would be easy to cast and train a number of novice actors. At the initial script review meeting, I got my first lesson. I was overjoyed that a lot of Native students and community members attended. But I wasn't prepared for everyone to speak—that we would go around the table and each person would give voice to their thoughts. The meetings lasted forever; yet, I was amazed that everyone read the texts and I deeply appreciated the insights and comments. Of course, I tried to steer towards the play that would be the easiest to stage; I wanted this initial project to be a success. And of course the group eventually chose a play that would be the most challenging as a first production.

Sneaky by William Yellow Robe Jr. is a play about three estranged Assiniboine brothers who come together after the death of their mother. Despite their deep differences, they decide to re-discover and carry out a traditional Assiniboine burial, where the body is nestled in a tree and burned. The play requires actors who can sustain a full-length drama. A body is stolen from a morgue. A tree is torched on stage. Oh, and did someone mention there is also a grandmother, a child actor, and a puppy? I loved this play, but didn't know if we could find an all-Native cast locally, carrying through with the commitment to cast within our community.

George Whirlwind Soldier (Lakota), John Cruz (Filipino Hawaiian), Scott Shepherd (Wampanoag), Sharon Smith (Mohawk) emerged from our community—I never announced that the rehearsals were open, but got used to people respectfully coming to observe; the support was palpable. On one break the Apache artist, Kitty Wagner, approached me and with a smile handed me something rolled in newspaper, one of her beautiful prints. And when the play opened, it was the Native community that gave the audience its bearings. Given the topic of death and conventional stereotypical images of Indians, non-Natives came with stoic expectations. The Native audience readily got the hilarity integral to the play's dramatic storytelling.

I reached out to find playwright Bill Yellow Robe of the Fort Peck reservation in Montana. When he came for the production, he told me that he was deeply touched because it was the first time a theater had committed to an all-Native cast, despite his having worked with regional theaters in Montana and Colorado. We had far less money than a regional theater, but we had the resource of time; we were willing to shift to what became a protracted process that led to discoveries of assets deep within our own community. When we had our cast party, we were surprised by Chris Pegram and the Youngblood Singers who had brought their drums from Shinnecock on Long Island. When they played an honor song for us, Bill and I were invited to link arms to dance together as everyone present passed to shake hands with us, joining an ever-widening circle.

7. Relevance

I've always disliked "political" theater that ends with actors, fists raised, calling for revolution. That dramaturgical cop-out is as lazy as ending a play by dragging audience members up to the stage to dance. What made these choices work for *Waiting for Lefty* or *Hair* is that they were: (1) original and (2) of their moment. In high school I was a student organizer for the United Farm Workers Support Committee and was inspired by the agit-prop theater I saw both spontaneously on the picket line and also in the brilliant plays of Luis Valdez's Teatro Campesino. The urgency of the cause and direct connection to the "audience" being spurred to action was immediate. Today I see that in the powerful work of Teatro Jornalero Sin Fronteras (the Day Laborers Theater Without Borders), performed at Home Depots, workers' centers and other sites where day laborers gather. And also in the movement of political theaters evolving this work in a complex way like Cornerstone Theater, the Foundry, Pangea World Theater, Sojourn Theater, Theater Offensive, Playback Theater, and others.

As Artistic Director, I never prescribed a singular aesthetic for the theater. Playwright Lorraine Hansberry said, "A classical people deserve a classical art." I felt that a complex community needed a complex array of genres and aesthetics to tell our stories—drama, solo performance, devised works, spectacle, melodrama, performance art, agit prop, satire, comedy, musical, hip-hop performance, ensemble performance, community collaborations, folk opera, and so forth—from canon works, to innovative new approaches. What mattered was relevance. We searched for material that had meaning, and could give context to our society. From its inaugural season, themes were presented that would continue to be complicated and explored over three decades. Some of the most prominent themes included:

- A feminist voice: NWT never identified as a feminist theater because of the marginalization of women of color within feminist organizing, but it activated feminism on its own terms. The majority of playwrights, directors, and production staff were women of color and women who multi-tasked, raised children of their own or of the community, taught or mentored, and made art. Over time, this enacted feminism manifested and linked an enormous span of artistic voices. And it created a culture markedly different than most theaters. A white woman set designer told me that in the mainstream theater, she never mentioned having children for fear of not being perceived as a professional artist. In contrast, she observed that working at NWT, children were omnipresent and beloved. She shared her revelation that "At New WORLD, having children seems to give women even greater credibility."

- Incarceration: Related to the feminist perspective, the first play produced in the debut season was Mascheri Chapell's *Prisms*, a choreopoem written by a Smith College student, inspired by her brother's letters from prison. This wasn't the expected narrative coming from a Seven Sister college; incarceration as a topic was re-examined through many different lenses from canon work like Miguel Piñero's *Short Eyes*, to Rha Goddess collaborating with Project 2050 youth artists to envision what would be considered a crime in the future.
- Segregation and inequity: NWT always had a global perspective, originally naming itself the Third World Theater Series, and aligning with international struggles, most prominently, the South African anti-apartheid movement. It related global struggles for human rights to domestic fights for equality through works like Modern Times Theater's *Homeland* by Steve Friedman and Selaelo Maredi, Barney Simon and the Market Theater's *Born in the R.S.A.*, *Asinamali* by Mbongeni Ngema, Alice Childress's *Florence*, and *Sheila's Day* by Duma Ndlovu.
- Re-visioning history: In many ways theater is a magpie art of borrowing, repurposing, and creating anew; filled with traps and expected choices. Conscious of the absence of our stories and histories, we sought to re-vision history, but not from a celebratory, Black/Asian American/Latino/Native American History Month/Week/Day, but to seek fresh ways of foregrounding these histories with innovative productions and presentations like Roger Guenveur Smith's *Frederick Douglas Now!*, *Dance and the Railroad* by David Henry Hwang, *Dark Cowgirls and Prairie Queens* by Carpetbag Theater, *Do the Riot Thing* by Chicano Secret Service, *Miss Ida B. Wells* by Endesha Ida Mae Holland and Pearl Cleage's *Flying West*, *The Return of Elijah, the African* and *Udu* by Sekou Sundiata, and *Ameriville* by UNIVERSES.
- Complex identities: While we rejected multiculturalism and asserted an anti-racism framework, finding accurate language for the work of NWT was an ongoing challenge. In hindsight, polyculturalism might best describe the work, but at the time we adapted the term "People of Color" to describe our artists. The theater was started by myself as staff and three students: Miriam Carter, Derek Davis, and Karen Lederer—Asian American, Panamanian/Jamaican, African American, and Caucasian—agnostic, Muslim, Christian, and Jewish. We never had to diversify or become inclusive; we were. The works of NWT would explore over time the dynamics and layered identities of race, ethnicity, gender, sexuality, and class.

8. Go there

Audience development was a huge buzzword of the 1990s. An aging subscription audience, the cultural shifts in media consumption, and changing demographics challenged theaters then and continue to challenge their relevance in the twenty-first century. After attending a theater conference session where theater administrators addressed the problem by suggesting enlarging the type size on programs, starting shows earlier, making performances shorter, and boosting sound levels, I wondered what would happen to these theaters after the demise of their aging patrons? I was also frustrated by a discussion about youth audiences. The speakers outlined strategies to introduce youth to culture. Unstated was a smug cultural superiority; they viewed young people as passive consumers at best or violent at worst, and that theaters could help bring them to civilization.

I'm convinced that theater will never die because even with a thousand television channels, people still crave the live moment of being in a room together, experiencing great performance and interaction. I'm also certain that creative expression is inherent to all people, but that we live in parallel universes, often oblivious to each other's worlds. My conviction that young people were making art, gathering of their own volition to express themselves led me to b-boy gatherings, ciphers, and hip-hop events; and later to poetry slams—places where I never failed to be the oldest person in the room. I remember going to an event organized by the Linwood B-boys from Compton; the emcee called out, "The chairs are reserved for the elders in the room—so if your name isn't Roberta Uno, get your butt out of the seats." I think I was 40 at the time.

The engagement of hip-hop produced unexpected tension within NWT when I asked our dramaturgy staff to go to these events. Two met with me and summed up their dissatisfaction, "We didn't get M.F.A.'s in theater to go to watch kids rapping. Why are we doing this?" Although much younger than me, they explained that they felt uncomfortable and out of place, that they wanted to return to reading texts and finding great plays. I responded that NWT had never been about being comfortable, that it's okay to be out of one's element, that's the beginning of discovery. Reluctantly, they came around and eventually fully embraced where the exploration led us. I've written elsewhere about Future Aesthetics, the term I eventually coined to capture a genre of work inspired by hip-hop aesthetics and approaches. But my point here is to make theater, it's important to go outside the theater, beyond its insular walls.

9. It's not about the money: lead with the art

New WORLD Theater started without money and ended with over a half a million dollars in its accounts.[1] After its thirty-year residency at the University of Massachusetts, following the disastrous economic meltdown of 2008, the Fine Arts Center Director, Dr. Willie Hill, a short-sighted bureaucrat, decided to suspend the theater's operations in 2009, effectively ending a program that had brought the University major national attention and significant community participation. The *Amherst Bulletin* reported that, "closing New WORLD is expected to save UMass $116,000, as the university attempts to close a $10 million budget gap by trimming expenses."[2]

At the time NWT started, because it was housed at a Massachusetts state institution, the by-laws of the Massachusetts Cultural Council prevented it from applying for their grants, which would be seen as "double dipping"—effectively the state funding the state. So while the Fogg Museum at Harvard University, one of the most richly endowed U.S. universities, was eligible, New WORLD Theater, based at an underfunded public university was not. Lacking state imprimatur, it wasn't seen as a viable candidate for National Endowment for the Arts (NEA) funding. NEA staff were gracious, but couldn't find a programmatic fit with their guidelines of that era. What they deemed strong multicultural work couldn't be funded by their Expansion Arts program, because the theater wasn't located in an urban center or rural area. And it didn't qualify for the NEA Theater program because it was university-based and worked with a combination of professionals, students, and community people. Without state and NEA funding, NWT couldn't approach national funders. Ironically, until I was invited for a job interview at the Ford Foundation, I had never been given a meeting there and had a file of Ford rejection letters. NWT did not receive any outside grants for well over its first decade.

Instead we turned to our community and found support in unanticipated places. A surprising disappointment was that the obvious academic allies (Theater, Women's Studies, Blacks Studies) were not initially responsive to the fledgling project. Rather it was the Dean of Students, William Field, who controlled discretionary funds from pinball (later video) and soda machine concessions, and took a risk by offering matching funds. I went to the various student organizations: the Afrik Am Society, Ahora, the Asian American Student Association, and others to leverage the first $10,000 that launched the program. During the summer, I started a free jazz music festival, the Bright Moments Festival, that attracted broad audiences, and which after expenses, brought concessions and donation revenue into the commissioning of new work. Finally, once I was invited to join its board, the Massachusetts Cultural Council eligibility criteria was changed. As NEA programs were reconceptualized, NWT was finally awarded funding, through its interdisciplinary and presenting programs.

I believe that the silver lining of being locked out of external funding, was that we were compelled to mine deep relationships at all levels of our community and to develop entrepreneurial thinking. Without external funding, we honed our artistic vision organically, instead of responding to funders' priorities. Significantly, artist peers who had worked at NWT over that decade began serving on grant review panels; they were able to validate and carry our vision and story to others. Through necessity we learned to lead with the art, not with need.

Ultimately money couldn't save the theater—unbelievably, the University had to return grants awarded by national foundations. Perhaps it was mistakenly thought by the administration that grant funding could be repurposed for other priorities within the Fine Arts Center. The key timing of the decision, during the summer while students and faculty were away, made it a foregone conclusion by the fall. Dissension among staff and tension in the community revealed fissures that precluded a united strategy of response; tragically the community organizing roots of the theater had been neglected. However, the precept of NWT's original vision was underscored: It's never just about the money. Money may impact the scale of work, but never the vision. And in the absence of clear artistic leadership, grounded in the theater's founding principle of community organizing, NWT ended.

The value of leadership is that one person can make a tremendous difference; the downside is that without that key individual, there is no change unless the institution has changed. New WORLD Theater was a project that found power and autonomy in the periphery, functioning best at times in the shadow of institutional neglect. But the fact that it was dismantled with relative ease is a testament to how it had failed to be institutionalized, despite great effort over three decades. Its end was also evidence of a change in institutional priorities following field wide developments weakening progressive gains of the Civil Rights era in higher education. It was the leadership of key individuals: William Field, former Dean of Students who took a chance and provided initial seed funds, Fred Tillis, a visionary Vice Chancellor and Director of the Fine Arts Center, who gave the theater an administrative home within the Fine Arts Center; and Murray Schwartz, Dean of the College of Humanities and Fine Arts, and his successor, Lee Edwards, who mentored me as an academic, protecting me within a fractious, territorial academic department. Once they retired and I left the University—and my successors were without the academic rank of the professorship that was coupled with my artistic position—there was no institutional foothold for response, especially in the absence of organized strategy.

10. Transforming space

New WORLD Theater was an experiment that was initially made possible because at the time the University had a unique and rare independent space: Hampden Theater—a 120-seat flexible theater, with a scene shop, renovated from a former dining hall. It was located in the heart of the Southwest Residential complex, an experiment in student housing whose vertical towers had concentrated students, producing tensions—it had been the site of racial violence and student riots. The staff, Robert Antil and Eugene Warner, provided exceptional artistic programming and significant open access to students and community members. Most important, it was unaffiliated with an academic department. It was unencumbered by the bureaucracy of faculty review, season selection committees, or curriculum requirements. Until it was closed in 1999, this unorthodox facility and its creative programmers allowed New WORLD to germinate and flourish. By that time, NWT was regularly presenting in larger venues, but it lost the invaluable rehearsal and production space that Hampden Theater had provided.

Subsequently, NWT produced and presented in a variety of venues, with numerous collaborators including the UMass Department of Theater and those of the Five Colleges. Amherst College Department of Theater was a gracious host to Project 2050 in the summers. NWT might have been characterized as a homeless theater; I thought of it as an itinerant theater, continuously appropriating and transforming others' spaces. We were the people who had invited ourselves in and who didn't conform to the status quo—in our production choices, in forging new curriculum, in bringing new partners and people into spaces they had never known existed. NWT was the house sitter who rearranged all the furniture, threw a fabulous party, and couldn't understand why the owner hesitated to hand over the keys again. But profoundly, NWT was a desegregation project. It brought the first writers and directors of color into many production spaces and at the University of Massachusetts, it brought public cultural access to facilities of a state university funded by public dollars. I would never forget that in 1982, before I joined the department as its first faculty of color, I approached the UMass Department of Theater and offered them an evening with Ozzie Davis and Ruby Dee at no expense. They merely had to identify a dark night in the theater where we could drop two microphones and a music stand in front of the act curtain. The Department had never produced a play by a writer of color in nineteen seasons and turned down the offer to host these two icons of the American theater. Instead of the mainstage of the Department, we presented the evening Ms. Dee and Mr. Davis in the much larger Student Union Ballroom, filling it to capacity.

Years later, once I had become a faculty member of the Department, I was able to bring the first productions by writers of color to the Department's main and second stages and to recruit the first black graduate students to the directing program. The moment that spoke to me most strongly of change was when I saw some graffiti by one of the Latino actors in our youth program on a concrete column in the scenic shop. Proudly underscored was where he was from: "Holyoke"—a former mill town, deeply challenged economically. I don't know why this moved me; something to do with how off-limits that scenic shop was, a very male, rock music and flannel shirt environment. And now it had been tagged, simple proof of the fact that we are here.

This struggle for space largely influenced my work at the Ford Foundation, where one of my initiatives supported a new generation of arts leadership and facilities that are firmly grounded in the communities in which they reside and that are models of artistic innovation, cultural equity, and social partnership. The issue of space isn't limited to conventional arts facilities development; it's also about virtual space, spiritual and mental space, and the larger public sphere. Many non-profit arts organizations have worked hard to build a building, only to find it becomes an albatross that weighs heavily on artistic experimentation as debt and depreciation impact artistic choices. Others are so focused on the four walls that they don't engage the surrounding neighborhood, maintaining a type of de-facto segregation evidenced by the difference between their audiences and the residents in the community or larger city surrounding the building. I see this issue of space as one of the unanswered questions raised by the Civil Rights struggle. We are still grappling with institutional racism, including inequality perpetuated by the built environment.

11. Imagine the future

New WORLD Theater was an experiment in imagining a collective future, in appropriating places we were never meant to occupy, and in artistically defining an unimagined space. Our work with youth through Project 2050 most vividly embodied that experiment. Whereas most theaters view youth work as service, educational outreach, or audience development—emphasizing the numbers served—I saw Project 2050 as a core artistic program. The adult/youth ratio was intentionally 5:1, recognizing that all were participants in the exploration. It brought together key potential stakeholders: youth, professional artists, community activists, and scholars in dialogue and creative visioning about the future. Policy discussions about the future are typically made without the participation of people who will live the consequences of decisions made. Working with youth was a chance to collaborate with people of the future.

The concept for Project 2050 was built on earlier work we had been doing with youth and professional artists in separate Western Massachusetts neighborhood-based projects with Latino teens from Holyoke, Cambodian youth from Northampton, and Vietnamese and African American youth from Springfield. These youth lived in pockets of geographical isolation; initially we worked separately with them to develop a primary voice and ensemble identity. Later we experimented with ways to bring them together cross culturally. We were partnering with various local community-based organizations that specialized in youth organizing, to community health, and social service.

One of the most powerful works from that era was called *Simultaneous Histories*. We brought together our separate Latino, Cambodian, African American, and Vietnamese groups in a series of cross cultural encounters that culminated in a week retreat exploring various themes. In *Simultaneous Histories*, youth were asked to identify key dates including: a date before their lifetime that affected who they are now and a date in the future they hoped to impact. The result was fascinating, for example they chose 1975: noting key social phenomena like the invention of Microsoft. For the Vietnamese youth, the war with America had ended and they were in the throes of being refugees, the Cambodian genocide was in process; and for the Latino and African American youth, their fathers and uncles were returning veterans, many with post-traumatic shock, struggling to find jobs and adjust to their families.

These markers of time suddenly provided larger social context for individual experience, often missing from much youth theater. Most powerful and unexpected was the date the youth chose to imagine the future: 2061, the return of Halley's Comet. It was electrifying to hear their voices refracted from decades to come—these were unexpected missives from people who often wouldn't speak about their lives beyond the next trimester.

We brought scholars and activists into the mix to provide a framework of knowledge, activism and ideas, with a historical and social framework. While I couldn't think of a date as poetic as the return of Halley's Comet, I thought that 2050, the year that demographers had predicted Caucasians would be eclipsed by people of color in the United States, would provide fertile context. Originally, I called it The 2050 Project. But when one of the youth showed me a T-shirt design he created, I pointed out he had written the name incorrectly as Project 2050. He didn't hesitate in answering, "But shouldn't it be a verb and a noun?" Indeed.

This ability to flip a noun into a verb, to produce a performance without a stage, to create new aesthetics from reclaimed materials, and to create a collective imaginary is what I see as New WORLD Theater's cultural contribution to the American theater. Its continued relevance is evident in the persistence of the social inequities and divides it attempted to redress. These divisions are seen in the polarized and vitriolic terms of national political debate, the ever-growing gap between rich and poor, and continued racial inequity in terms of access and opportunity. The distribution of arts funding has yet to create a level playing field. The 2011 report on cultural equity by the National Committee on Responsive Philanthropy concluded that,

> The majority of arts funding supports large organizations with budgets greater than $5 million. Such organizations, which comprise less than 2 percent of the universe of arts and cultural nonprofits, receive more than half of the sector's total revenue. These institutions focus primarily on Western European art forms, and their programs serve audiences that are predominantly white and upper income. Only 10 percent of grant dollars made with a primary or secondary purpose of supporting the arts explicitly benefit underserved communities, including lower-income populations, communities of color, and other disadvantaged groups.

Clearly, there is much work to be done.

New WORLD Theater began in a context of social unrest and ended in an era of economic upheaval; its most significant contribution was a dynamic and continuous remapping of a new America. To me, while the end of NWT was heartbreaking and perhaps avoidable, I always questioned whether it was an institution that should last forever. In the early years, I optimistically dreamed that the institution and the society would change around it as the margins became the center of a changing nation. As I mourned the end of NWT, my husband Andrew, in his calm wisdom told me, "Thirty years is a good round number—think of all the legacies out there, the artists New WORLD touched." And a friend expanded on this saying, "Some organizations sunset—and then there are those that supernova and create new universes." I'm certain there are scores of New WORLDs out there, not waiting for, but making change.

Notes

1 At the time of its closing, the University of Massachusetts Fine Arts Center had received grants from the Ford Foundation, Surdna Foundation, and Nathan Cummings Foundation totaling over $500,000 for the New WORLD Theater. These funds were subsequently returned or grants modified to support the archiving of key holdings of the theater.

2 Kristin Palpini, "Curtains for Novel Theater: Funding Problems Shut 30-Year UMass Venture," *Amherst Bulletin*, July 24, 2009.

Chapter 3

"Imagining" and "restaging" otherwise

New WORLD Theater, memory work, and multiculturalist critique

Cathy J. Schlund-Vials

> When I founded New WORLD Theater in 1979, I wasn't aware of the term multicultural. I became uneasily familiar with the term, as a hegemonic discursive site to which I was assigned, by funders, scholars, journalists, and some members of the public. Often the expectation of us, as a multicultural organization, was an art that minimizes difference, that celebrates common human experience, and that provides representation in often rigidly defined slots.
>
> (Roberta Uno)[1]

> the problem of the twenty-first century . . . is the problem of the colorblind [in which we] are led to believe that racism is a prejudicial behavior of one party against another rather than the coagulation of socioeconomic injustice against groups.
>
> (Vijay Prashad)[2]

Deep in the heart of the Pioneer Valley in Western Massachusetts,[3] about an hour or so away from the hustle and bustle of Northeast metropolises like New York, Boston, Providence, and Hartford, New WORLD Theater would become, at the turn of the twenty-first century, a significant New England hub for artists and playwrights of color. A multi-ethnic, multi-racial, and multi-generational enterprise, New WORLD Theater (originally called Third World Theater) was founded in fall 1979 as a company-in-residence within the Fine Arts Center at the University of Massachusetts-Amherst. Faced with budget cuts, institutional non-support, and the university's increased "austerity" measures, the company would—despite public outcry and protest—inauspiciously close in 2009.[4]

Notwithstanding these contestations, over the course of its thirty-year run—and ironically, given its geographic location—New WORLD Theater was an incontrovertible artistic and epistemological pioneer. Envisioned by founding artistic director Roberta Uno as an anti-racist creative refuge, cutting-edge performance venue, and innovative playlab, New WORLD Theater was ahead of its time with regard to its attention to divergent viewpoints. The company was likewise prescient, via its imaginings of future aesthetics and changing demographics and its activist stance against interlocking modes of discrimination (race, gender, class, and sexuality). Perhaps most important, New WORLD Theater was at the intellectual forefront of Ethnic Studies vis-à-vis its consistent critique of mainstream multiculturalism.

To be sure, this multiculturalist critique organically emerged as New WORLD Theater's reputation as a leading multi-ethnic, multi-racial theater company grew. As the opening epigraph makes clear, while Uno wasn't initially "aware of the term multicultural," she nevertheless became "uneasily familiar" with it over the course of her tenure as artistic director (1979–2002). Ostensibly suggestive of multiplicity, representation, and cultural complexity, "multiculturalism"—which operates in close tandem with "diversity" as an institutional value—has become an oft-used catchword among politicians, teachers, and university administrators as a superficial means of inclusion.[5] Even so, as Uno rightly observes, the term "multicultural" is by no means neutral, and remains inextricably bound to "a hegemonic discursive site" intent on "minimize[ing] difference," "celebrat[ing] common human experience," and "provid[ing] representation in often rigidly defined slots."[6] On a global/national level, Uno's criticism of a homogenizing multicultural racial project underscores a problematical universalism that seems in especially dire need of deconstruction in this post-Obama, allegedly post-racial, age. Within recent memory, such declarations of "post" tolerance uneasily coexist with accounts of anti-black vigilante violence (e.g., Trayvon Martin), police brutality in Fergusson Missouri and beyond, and reports of nativist attacks against immigrants of color (in Arizona and Wisconsin).[7]

More immediately, these still-relevant evaluations undeniably foreground the scholarly stakes of this chapter, which contemplates, calibrates, and resituates New WORLD Theater's multivalent legacy (redolent in its mission, programming, and publishing) via an anti-multiculturalist, anti-hegemonic politics. These cultural, social, and racial politics, rooted in performance, drama, and criticism, potently remind those within and outside the academy that bodies of color have historically, politically, and socially been tactically integrated and opportunistically co-opted in service of U.S. exceptionalism. If a dominant reading of the nation-state as a classless and raceless space of democratic virtue is central to U.S. exceptionalism, then people of color are, to paraphrase W.E.B. Du Bois and echo the work of critical race theorists, both the problem and the solution.[8] While discrimination, subjugation, exclusion, and oppression remain legible keywords in Ethnic Studies (inclusive of Asian American, African American, Native, and Latino/a Studies) and Women's, Gender, and Sexuality Studies, they are nonetheless dismissed in amnesic characterizations of "America" as an imagined teleological space of capacious possibility and liberal tolerance.

As a company dedicated to producing and developing work by artists of color, whose respective experiences and histories made (and continue to make) visible the failure of U.S. exceptionalism, New WORLD Theater was from the beginning a racially progressive, politically driven venture. Set perpendicular to violently forgetful frames, New WORLD Theater's epistemological legacy—which continues long after its doors closed in 2009—encapsulates a form of performance-oriented "memory work." Drawing on James Young's productive notion that the efficacy of Holocaust memorials is mapped according to the degree to which they instantiate debate, New World Theater's "memory work" (epitomized in its various archives and apparent in its performance history) is unquestionably grounded in a distinctly artistic subversion of state-sanctioned exceptionalism.[9] From Chinese exclusion to Jim Crow segregation, from indigenous self-determination to immigrant identification, from South Africa to Argentina, and from the Global North to the Global South, New WORLD Theater's programming unfailingly explored all-too-real terrains of racism, classism, nativism, sexism, and homophobia—at times in the same season. In so doing, the company militated against a mode of exceptionalism consistent with what Jodi Melamed productively characterizes as "the liberal race paradigm" at work in mainstream U.S. discussions about race and racism. Such a paradigm "recognizes racial inequality as a problem, and it secures a liberal symbolic framework for race reform centered in abstract equality, market individualism, and inclusive civic nationalism."[10]

Admittedly, New WORLD Theater's institutional status as a "multicultural" theater company in residence at the University of Massachusetts is seemingly consistent with the university's (and by extension, the state's) rather superficial recognition of "racial inequality" through Melamed's above-mentioned "liberal symbolic framework." However, in the face of structural realities and emplacements, which repeatedly attempt to classify such work via limited diverse agendas, New WORLD Theater's lasting pedagogical impact brings to light an indubitably resistive and progressive politics. These cultural politics tirelessly recognize the persistence of racial inequality through the dialogic and syncretic negotiation of multivalent difference.[11] Correspondingly, this chapter continues its remembering of New WORLD Theater's "memory project" using an epistemologically imaginative schema. I then shift to how this remembrance militates against prevailing notions of multicultural "colorblindness" via the 2002 publication of *The Color of Theater*, which utilizes a pedagogic practice that is at the forefront of Comparative Ethnic Studies. I conclude with a brief reading of *The Color of Theater* alongside Barack Obama's re-election in 2012 as a way to monumentalize New WORLD Theater's political legacy and signal its increased epistemological relevance vis-à-vis an *intersectional* critique of multiculturalism.[12]

The terms through which I remap and restage New WORLD Theater's critical multiculturalist imaginary not surprisingly arise from the company's purposeful mission: to "promote cultural equity and a social justice vision of a 'new world.'" Such social justice vistas productively intersect with Avery Gordon's provocative assertion to "imagine otherwise." Situated adjacent Third World liberation struggles, domestic civil rights, and international human rights, Gordon notes that such thinking encompasses a "folk theoretical statement," redolent of a new and revolutionary episteme: "We need to know where we live in order to imagine living elsewhere. We need to imagine living elsewhere before we can live there."[13] Gordon's imaginative notion, which involves local, national, and global movements, intersects with past/present moments of resistance. Indeed, first wave feminism imagined a world of political empowerment in the face of voter disenfranchisement. The rise of Third World liberation, the Civil Rights movement, and the second wave women's movement in the 1960s imagined social equality and freedom notwithstanding its antitheses: colonialism, discrimination, and patriarchy. Recently, Ethnic Studies and Women's, Gender, and Sexuality scholars have had to imagine places of peace and equality in the face of the ongoing "war on terror," the neoconservative rise of the Tea Party movement, and legislative assaults against immigrants, gay marriage, and reproductive rights.

This idea of "imagining otherwise" is at the forefront of New WORLD Theater's founding, which occurred alongside the formation of Ethnic Studies programs across the country and the rise of ethnically specific theater companies during the late 1960s and early 1970s.[14] Yet the notion of "otherwise imagination" is perhaps most textually evident in *The Color of Theater* anthology, which features essays, interviews, and original work developed in the company's summer playlab series, "New Works for a New WORLD," begun in 1996. While acknowledging the breadth of New WORLD Theater's play archive, forged over the course of the company's thirty-year history, I strategically focus on *The Color of Theater* as a blended literary/performance anthology. I maintain that the collection instantiates a comparative Ethnic Studies critique of multiculturalism, which dialogically situates African American, Asian American, Latino/a, and Native American histories and perspectives in conversation with one another. This comparative critique commences with a deconstruction of particular categories of power and specific classifications of difference. As literary critic Werner Sollors maintains, "the literature customarily filed under labels such as immigration, race, regionalism, and ethnicity provides a unique testing ground for exceptionalist interpretations of America." Correspondingly, the creative work of playwrights of color—rooted in asymmetrical histories and experiences of exclusion and incorporation—makes feasible (and renders necessary) a multifaceted evaluation of race, class, gender, and sexuality.[15]

This reading of *The Color of Theater*—as a critical site of intersectional and comparative cultural politics—figures keenly in this retrospective analysis, which in part reflects my own relationship to the company and the academy. With regard to the former, I was fortunate to work for New WORLD Theater as its literary manager/program curator from 2000–2004, a time that coincided with the publication of *The Color of Theater*. In terms of the latter, I very much "came of age" academically while at New WORLD Theater as a graduate student trained in English, Ethnic Studies, and American cultural studies; indeed, my current location as a comparative Asian Americanist is directly attributable to my intimate connection with the company. Notwithstanding these personal registers, I return to *The Color of Theater*, which at once captures New WORLD Theater's pedagogical mission and functions a literary embodiment of the company's "memory work."

Equal parts archive, manifesto, theater history, and performance text, the book's overriding political agenda renders identifiable what Gary Okihiro argues is the central point of comparative ethnic studies, which engages the productive "study of power, and its locations and articulations around the axes of race and ethnicity, gender, sexuality, class, and nation."[16] As a closer evaluation of *The Color of Theater* underscores, the very politics that brought the collection "into being" cohere, on the one hand, with Gordon's evocative call to "imagine otherwise." On the other hand, these imaginings—reflected in artist interviews, scholarly evaluations, and original performance texts—militate against what Prashad notes in the opening epigraph as a profound twenty-first-century problem of multicultural "colorblindness." A rather common medical condition, "color blindness" refers to the pathological inability to see color or perceive color differences. Prashad's indexical manipulation of the disease as a means to encapsulate U.S. multiculturalist politics inadvertently presages the multiculturalist critiques contained in *The Color of Theater*.

Divided into four sections (comprising an introduction, critical essays, artist interviews, and performance texts), *The Color of Theater* reproduces a literary imaginary "where artists, intellectuals, and community members interact; where race, gender, and generation are neither tokenized nor represented but are fully present, unmediated and uncensored; where the discourse is between us, not about us."[17] In stressing "interaction," "between-ness," and "presentness," Uno and Burns revise the flattened scripts at play in multiculturalism, which is fixed to Prashad's characterization of the "problem of the colorblind." Such a polemic problematically eschews the "coagulation of socioeconomic injustice against groups" in favor of individualized characterizations of racism, sexism, and homophobia. This colorblindness, to paraphrase Prashad, denies the ongoing existence of systemic oppression and instead emphasizes a now-achieved imaginary of overriding equality exemplified in the conservative interpretation of Martin Luther King's 1963 "I Have a Dream" speech, wherein we as Americans are presently judged "by the content of our character" and not by the "color of our skin."[18] With regard to mainstream cultural production and literary canonization, "colorblindness" strategically fails to "see" politicized differences at the forefront of work produced, created, and performed by artists of color who refuse facile multiculturalist categorization.

If what's at stake in comparative ethnic studies is a multivalent "study of power," then *The Color of Theater* serves as a text upon which to map the shifting terrain of so-called "identity politics" at the turn of the twenty-first century. Indeed, the anthology's very title reinforces its racial politics insofar as "color" occupies a prominent position. Rooted in asymmetrical histories and experiences of exclusion and incorporation, which traverse "over here" politics (i.e., homophobia and nativism) and "over there" modalities (e.g., war and relocation), *The Color of Theater* makes necessary a comparative evaluation of racialized, gendered, sexualized, and classed artistic formations. These artistic formations are concretized in the following works: *Quinceañera* (by Alberto Antonio Ariaza, Paul Bonin-Rodgriguez,

Michael Marinez, and Danny Bolero Zaldivar), *the bodies between us* (by lê thi diem thúy), *BORDERscape 2000* (by Guillermo Goméz-Peña and Roberto Sifuentes), and *Elijah* (by Sekou Sundiata). From queer Latino masculinity to Vietnamese refugee subjectivity, from contested Mexican migration to unreconciled histories of African slavery, these plays, developed in New WORLD Theater's summer playlab, resist easy classification as Latino/a, Asian American, and African American works respectively. They likewise involve two-person ensembles, solo performances, and more "traditional" dramatic formations.

In sum, the creative works featured in *The Color of Theater* choose to move beyond singular classifications of race, gender, sexual, or ethnic identity. Correspondingly, what links each of these works is the multiplicity that is part and parcel of New WORLD Theater's larger project of "desegregating" institutional spaces and epistemological places by bringing into focus multiple peripheries and variegated centers.[19] This desegregation project extends beyond the plays and is evident in interviews with La MaMa's Ellen Stewart, La FOMMA's Petrona de La Cruaz and Isabel J.F. Juarez Esponisa, Jesusa Rodriguez, Brian Freeman (of Pomo Afro Homos), Great Leap's Nobuko Miyamoto, Muriel Miguel (of Spiderwoman Theater), Chay Yew, and Chuck Mike. Essays by Thulani Davis, Rustom Bharacha, Diana Taylor, Jaye T. Darby, Velina Hasu Houston, Harry J. Elam, Jr., and Cherrie Moraga reinforce the anthology's intended scholarly aim to engender intersectional discussions "between" artists and theater practitioners from a multitude of social backgrounds.

These interstitial dynamics are most evident in an account that opens and closes the collection's introduction. Expressly, *The Color of Theater* commences with a heated discussion about lê's *the bodies between us* involving multiple scholars, artists, and practitioners of color. The setting for this volatile conversation was New WORLD Theater's conference/play festival, "New Works for a New World: An Intersection of Performance, Practice, and Ideas," which took place at the University of Massachusetts on October 8–11, 1998. In particular, lê was called to task by some of those in attendance (specifically a Chicana playwright, a Caucasian audience member, and an African American woman artist) on the grounds that her piece—concentrated on forced refugee relocation and the American War in Vietnam—is ethnically non-specific and politically abstract. Characterized as a "critical melee," Uno notes that the discussion, which "catalyzes and encapsulates this volume," was "an extraordinarily raw, complicated, honest, and revealing session that spoke to issues of race, gender, culture, generation, ethnicity, identity, expectation, perception, media representation, artistic approach, cultural authenticity and critical authority."[20] Such "rawness," indicative of multiple "otherwise" locations, underscores variegated sites of power that require comparative approaches and methodologies; moreover, this "rawness" destabilizes a multiculturalist regime which insists on divergent sameness. Accordingly, the representational tension between art, authenticity, and authority functions as the basis for a multiculturalist critique embedded in the collection.

This multiculturalist critique, epitomized by a comparative turn towards radical politics, engenders a concluding consideration of New WORLD Theater's ongoing relevance—notwithstanding its closure—in the so-termed "Age of Obama." To clarify, in the 2012 presidential election, Barack Obama defeated Republican challenger Mitt Romney by a healthy margin of 4,683,793 popular votes and 126 electoral votes.[21] The forty-fourth president triumphantly averred the following characterization in his post-election victory speech:

> What makes America exceptional are the bonds that hold together the most diverse nation on earth. . . . It doesn't matter whether you're black or white or Hispanic of Asian or Native American or young or old or rich or poor, able, disabled, gay or straight, you can make it here in America if you're willing to try.[22]

To be sure, Obama's celebration of unmatched diversity, directly linked to "the American dream," eschews radical agendas and coheres with a now-familiar multiculturalist, tolerance-based politics; such declarations also "make sense" in light of his successful re-election bid, which (as media outlets repeatedly asserted) relied heavily on traditionally marginalized groups: women, GLBT, Latino/a, African American, and Asian American voters.

In the face of utopic coalitional politics, the election night remarks of one Fox News commentator function as a potent reminder of why such multiculturalist declarations—which disremember difference, elevate political like-mindedness, and remain fixed to an overly optimistic belief in "America"—are, within a racialized imaginary, problematically premature. Expressly, as electoral returns were announced, conservative stalwart Bill O'Reilly dramatically asserted that "the white establishment is now the minority. . . . The demographics are changing. It's not traditional American anymore."[23] O'Reilly subsequently reiterated the death of "traditional America" in a November 19, 2012 commentary, wherein the outspoken pundit ominously opined:

> a coalition of voters put the president back into the oval office. That coalition was non-traditional, which means it veered away from things like traditional marriage, robust capitalism, and self-reliance. Instead, each constituency that voted for the president—whether it be single women, Hispanic Americans, African Americans, whatever—had very specific reasons for doing so. . . . Traditional American voters . . . believe in American exceptionalism.[24]

Set adjacent to Obama's victory address, O'Reilly's comments divergently underscore the racist parameters that undergird vehement characterizations of "traditional America." This sensibility, evident in hyperbolic and reactionary articulations of white loss, foregrounds an "us versus them" divisiveness that remains despite multiculturalist classifications of democratic virtue and pronouncements of a united nation. As present-day secession petitions, legislative threats against Medicare, cuts to Ethnic Studies and Women's Studies programs, and ongoing political partisanship bring to light, class-, gender-, ethnic-, race-, and sexuality-based identity politics still matter, for these bodies are currently under hegemonic attack. What is even more necessary in these increasingly volatile times is what New WORLD Theater untiringly engendered via its attention to the contested and politicized contours of "traditional America," and what *The Color Theater* eloquently expounds: a comparative multiculturalist critique that disallows wholesale declarations of tolerance, takes seriously the problematical project of U.S. exceptionalism, instantiates radical vocabularies of difference, and imagines new spaces vistas for resistance.

Notes

1 Roberta Uno, "Introduction," *The Color of Theater: Race, Culture, and Contemporary Performance*, ed. Uno with Lucy Mae San Pablo Burns (London and New York: Continuum, 2002), 9.
2 Vijay Prashad, *Everybody Was Kung Fu Fighting: Afro-Asian Connections and the Myth of Cultural Purity* (Boston: Beacon Press, 2002), 38.
3 The "Pioneer Valley" is a familiar colloquialism for the Connecticut River Valley in Western Massachusetts. Major cities and towns in the region include Springfield, Holyoke, Northampton, and Amherst.
4 According to Andrea Assaf, New WORLD Theater's third artistic director, on July 14, 2009 she was "informed that due to significant budget cuts at the University, the Fine Arts Center would no longer be able to support New WORLD Theater." *Valley Advocate*, July 16, 2009, www.valleyadvocate.com/blogs/home.cfm?aid=10179, accessed November 20, 2012. It should be noted that the company had just received a two-year $100,000 grant from the Surdna Foundation.
5 To illustrate this point, I draw upon my own institutional affiliation as Professor in English and Asian American studies and as the director of the Asian American Studies Institute at the University of Connecticut (Storrs). UConn currently awards graduate students of color a "multicultural award"; in the university's academic plan (2009–2014), diversity and multiculturalism are stressed; and, in various conversations about the Asian American Studies Institute, what is stressed is our location as a "multicultural" unit.
6 Uno, *The Color of Theater*, 9.
7 In 2010, the Arizona state legislature passed SB 1070, which allowed law enforcement to racially profile those deemed possible undocumented immigrants. On February 26, 2012, while visiting his father in Sanford, Florida, 17-year-old Trayvon Martin was shot by George Zimmerman on the grounds that he posed a threat (even though the teenager was unarmed). The case received much press, due to the fact that Zimmerman wasn't initially arrested following the shooting. Zimmerman was found not guilty of manslaughter and second degree murder. And, on August 5, 2012, in Oak Creek, Wisconsin, Wade Michael Page, an avowed white supremacist, opened fire in a Sikh temple and killed six worshippers.
8 In *The Souls of Black Folk* (1903), Du Bois recounted the "problem of the color line" via the oft-asked question, "How does it feel to be a problem?" Vijay Prashad revises this to address the model minoritization of Asian Americans (particularly South Asian Americans) in *The Karma of Brown Folk* (Minneapolis: University of Minnesota, 2001) by asking, "How does it feel to be a solution?"
9 James Young, *The Texture of Memory: Holocaust Memorials and Meaning* (New Haven: Yale University Press, 1993). I use Young's notion of "memory work" as the basis for a

Cambodian Americanist critique in my book *War, Genocide, and Justice: Cambodian American Memory Work* (Minneapolis: University of Minnesota Press, 2012). Notwithstanding the connection to state-authorized mass violence that undergirds both Young's work and my own, I use the term as a way to address systemic racial violence.

10 Jodi Melamed, "The Spirit of Neoliberalism: From Racial Liberalism to Neoliberal Multiculturalism," *Social Text* 89, 24 no. 4 (Winter 2006): 2.

11 The notion of "tireless recognition" is built upon Lisa Lowe's provocative assertion that Asian American literature and Asian American studies is fixed to a "tireless reckoning" with past/present histories of war, relocation, dislocation, and exclusion. See her *Immigrant Acts: On Asian American Cultural Politics* (Durham: Duke University Press, 1996).

12 In *Represent and Destroy: Rationalizing Violence in the New Racial Capitalism* (Minneapolis: University of Minnesota Press, 2011), Jodi Melamed considers *This Bridge Called My Back* in a chapter titled "Counterinsurgent Canon Wars and Surviving Liberal Multiculturalism." While I do not analyze this text, Melamed's observation of intersectionality and radical politics is influential.

13 Avery Gordon, *Ghostly Matters: Haunting and the Sociological Imagination* (Minneapolis: University of Minnesota Press, 1997).

14 Following the longest student strike in U.S. history, at San Francisco State College, the first Ethnic Studies department was established at the University of California, Berkeley on March 20, 1969. Analogous programs were established at San Francisco State College and the University of California, Los Angeles. Shifting from higher education to theater, the late sixties also witnessed the rise of the Black Arts and Chicano arts movements.

15 Werner Sollors, *Beyond Ethnicity: Consent and Descent in American Culture* (London: Oxford University Press, 1986).

16 Gary Okihiro, "The History of Ethnic Studies," *Columbia Spectator*, October 15, 2007, http://www.columbiaspectator.com/2007/10/15/history-ethnic-studies, accessed September 12, 2012.

17 Uno, *The Color of Theater*, 5.

18 As exemplified by far-right-wing commentators Glenn Beck, Bill O'Reilly, and other Fox News pundits, the amnesic use of Martin Luther King's "I Have a Dream" speech ignores the revolutionary politics of the larger Civil Rights movement, which sought to dismantle racist institutions. Indeed, as the rise of the Black Power movement and King's subsequent "War on Poverty" campaign illustrates, integration ceased to be a wholesale goal.

19 Ibid., 7.

20 Ibid., 3–4.

21 To elaborate, Obama won the popular vote by a margin of 3.7 percent; he also won 332 electoral votes. His challenger, Mitt Romney, won 60,781,275 popular votes and 206 electoral votes.

22 Barack Obama, "Election Night Speech," *Detroit Free Press*, November 7, 2012, http://www.freep.com/article/20121107/NEWS15/121107007/Barack-Obama-s-speech-aft, accessed December 8, 2012.

23 Quoted in Mackenzie Weinger, "Bill O' Reilly: 'The White Establishment Is Now the Minority,'" November 6, 2012, www.politico.com/blogs/media/2012/11/bill-oreilly-the-white-establishment, accessed December 8, 2012.

24 *The O'Reilly Factor*, November 19, 2012. O'Reilly was responding to John Stewart's critique of his "traditional America" characterization; Stewart's criticism appeared in a November 16, 2012 episode of *The Daily Show*.

Chapter 4

Third World studies

Gary Y. Okihiro

In his revolutionary anthem, *The Wretched of the Earth* (1961), Frantz Fanon described the spaces created by European colonizers. Their cosmos or order, Fanon observed, segregated the colonizer and colonized into different worlds, separate and unequal. That divide and hierarchy of race and class involved white, capitalist invaders from the First World over colored, native workers of the Third World. The former were humans and individuals while the latter, non-humans and the masses. Because of those conditions of colonialism, Fanon wrote, Third World decolonization is necessarily a revolutionary process, replacing a certain "species" of men with another "species" and changing the consciousness of both the colonizer and the colonized.

That transformation of the world order is not merely destructive, Fanon explained. It is also a work of creation. The revolution produces "new men" with a "new language and a new humanity." We, the colonized, Fanon urged, must "change our ways" from a "nauseating mimicry" that copies the European example and pattern. "Leave this Europe," he exhorted, move "in a new direction," fashion "the whole man," and thereby, as Third World peoples, begin "a new history of Man."[1]

The New WORLD Theater, originally the Third World Theater, had Fanon's idealism in mind in forging "a new humanity" and scripting "a new history of Man." The Third World Theater, through its programming, scholarship, and community outreach, strived to promote social justice and greater equality, envisioning "a new world" that embraces all peoples. Set against a colonizing culture that ignored, debased, and tried to assimilate and thereby blunt the revolutionary potential of works by artists of color, the New WORLD Theater sought to decolonize and liberate the consciousness of both the colonizer and the colonized. The Theater's astute founders knew that recuperation of culture, "a new language" in Fanon's words, was a crucial first step in the formation of "a new humanity," aligning their project with the Third World liberation movement.

Third World Studies

At the century's start in 1900, W. E. B. Du Bois famously declared: "The problem of the twentieth century is the problem of the color line."[2] His prophetic announcement was delivered, fittingly, in London, the seat of the British Empire that at the time spanned the globe. Race or more accurately racializations constituted the pivot for social relations primarily because of the saturation of imperialism, which closed the nineteenth century and its counter, the decolonization struggles of Africa and Asia, which ushered in the twentieth century. The "problem" for racists like Lothrop Stoddard, a Harvard history PhD and a journalist, was "the rising tide of color" that threatened to swamp white supremacy worldwide.[3] For anti-racists like Du Bois, the "problem" was European colonial rule and the need for Third World self-determination and the eradication of racism, the ideology that propped up the edifice of colonialism.

That contest across the essentializing color line survived the white, fratricidal aspects of "world" wars one and two, and after the latter, emerged alive and well under colonialism and neo-colonialism. The "Third World," conceived about mid-century and comprised of Africa, Asia, and Latin America, was, in the words of Frantz Fanon, a project by the periphery to solve the core's problems of imperialism, wars, and systems of bondage.[4] And the Third World's historic turn, Indonesian President Ahmed Sukarno told the 1955 Bandung conference of newly independent African and Asian states, was directed at "the liberation of man from the physical, spiritual and intellectual bonds which have for long stunted the development of humanity's majority."[5] Indeed, the Third World's rise and with it the end of European empires marked a turning point in some four hundred years of world history. The achievement was revolutionary.

That was what the students of the Third World Liberation Front at San Francisco State College had in mind in 1968 when they demanded a "Third World curriculum." The Third World Liberation Front, its founding statement declared, consisted of "Third World students" in solidarity with "Third World people." "We adhere to the struggles in Asia, Africa, and Latin America," the document explained, "ideologically, spiritually, and culturally." Because of racism in the US, the Front declared, "we have decided to fuse ourselves with the masses of Third World people, which is the majority of the world's peoples, to create, through struggles, a new humanity, a new humanism, a New World Consciousness. . . ."[6]

That "New World Consciousness" drew from anti-colonial intellectuals like Fanon and Albert Memmi who denounced the erasure of the colonized from history and their resulting "cultural estrangement" from self and society. Colonization "disfigures," wrote Memmi, and requires a restoration of "a whole and free man"; Fanon urged the creation of "a new humanity . . . a new humanism."[7]

Moreover, like Fanon in his call for a Third World revolution, students of the Third World Liberation Front explained:

> We offer a positive program. We are not anti-white; we are anti-white-racist-oppression and it is this powerful and just determinant that is the genesis of our movement, but the growth of the movement is affirmative; an affirmation of our humanity, our strength, our beauty, our dignity and our pride. Our programs are working programs. Our direction is revolutionary. Our method

is organization. Our goal is Third World Power. Our essence is a New World Consciousness of oppressed peoples.[8]

Across San Francisco Bay at the University of California, students organized Berkeley's Third World Liberation Front to demand Third World Studies on that campus. Their influence can be seen in a 1971 foundational text edited by a collective drawn from a course on Asian women at the University of California, Berkeley. A prominent section was devoted to "Third World women." The editors, in selecting chapters for that section, observed the connections among women in North America and Asia forged by the common threads of resistance and liberation against oppression and exploitation. Central was the Indochinese Women's Conference held in Vancouver, Canada in April 1971 that brought together Third World and women's liberation concerns and engaged over 150 Canadian and U.S. activists with a six-woman delegation from Viet Nam. "As Third World people," a conference report asserted, "we share similar struggles in fighting racist conditions and attitudes in our communities and our everyday lives. Our people—Blacks, Chicanos, Asians, Native Americans, and Native Hawaiians—have had our land ripped off by the whites, our women raped, our homes plundered, and our men drafted to further this country's imperialist ventures into Third World countries." Accordingly, "we see a need for learning about each other's history as Third World people and of informing each other about our movements for self-determination."[9]

That declaration of a global solidarity with the liberation struggles of Third World people, "the problem of the twentieth century," was trivialized and derailed by faculty and administrators who had the power to rename the "Third World curriculum," calling it the "Program of Ethnic Studies" at San Francisco State and later, at Berkeley. That move from "Third World" to "ethnic studies" not only domesticated an international alliance and movement; it reduced its revolutionary potential and power by grafting it onto the trunk of assimilation as espoused by sociology at the University of Chicago.

Ethnic studies

At base, Chicago sociology's twin tracks of "ethnic studies" and "race relations" were designed to distinguish American from European sociology by focusing on social processes deemed unique to the American experience. Moreover, Chicago sociology sought to advance the field through the new concept of "ethnicity" in addition to "race," which had dominated U.S. sociology from the late nineteenth century pioneered by sociologists such as George Fitzhugh, Henry Hughes, William Graham Sumner, and Lester Frank Ward. They saw race as a natural state and racial hierarchies as permanent and necessary for social order.

American sociology, according to a study, emerged from a mix of factors in the late nineteenth century. Urbanization and immigration from southern and eastern Europe and their attendant problems, including housing, sanitation, poverty, ethnic and labor strife, social disorganization, and crime and juvenile delinquency prompted the rise of the social gospel and various reform movements. The first courses in sociology in the US offered during the 1880s and 1890s addressed the pathologies of contemporary American society as studies directed at problem solving.[10] Sociology was thus a science of society and its management.

Robert E. Park, a central figure in establishing an American brand of sociology at the University of Chicago, was especially concerned with the "Negro" and "Oriental" problems as samples to test his general propositions about American modernity. As he observed:

> The study of the Negro in America, representing, as he does, every type of man from the primitive barbarian to the latest and most finished product of civilization, offers an opportunity to study . . . the historic social process by which modern society has developed. The Negro in his American environment is a social laboratory.[11]

The consequences of Chicago sociology were both far-reaching and paradigmatic. Its students and faculty, notably Park and William I. Thomas who had recruited Park to Chicago, conceived of race relations and its subjects—problem minorities, as case studies to understand and offer cures for the ills of urbanization. The focus, thus, was on U.S. cities and modernization broadly, and African and Asian Americans, like European ethnic groups, were mere transients and experimental subjects in the advance of progress.[12] Chicago sociologists, thereby, saw their studies as a subset of urban and spatial orderings of individuals and groupings. Additionally and importantly, Franz Boas and his colleagues and students had separated race from culture,[13] and ethnicity thus bore the prospect of problem solving and social change through cultural assimilation.

Within that flattened world of the modernizing, homogenizing city, ethnicity or culture displaced race, and European ethnic, immigrant groups constituted the model for the progressive cycle of immigration, contact and interaction, competition and conflict, and accommodation and assimilation. African Americans from the rural South and Asian migrants in the agrarian West were like Polish peasants in urban centers in the North, according to the Chicago school. The urban environment and its civilizing modernity dissolved the affiliations of race, enabling a single frame of reference and direction for disparate peoples.[14] That optimism was ultimately diminished by the durability of racism, called "racial prejudice," evident in the experiences of African and Asian Americans, and in the light of stark, contrary evidence.

Perhaps pivotal in that regard was the Chicago race riot of July 1919 that lasted over a week and resulted in the deaths of fifteen whites and twenty-three blacks, injuries to 537, and left over 1,000 homeless. The Chicago riot was the worst of several instances of racial violence during the summer of 1919 in which 120 people died. In the wake of the Chicago riot, the state's governor appointed a commission to study its causes and make recommendations for remediation. An African American graduate student in the University of Chicago's sociology department, Charles S. Johnson, led the commission's research staff and was the principal author of the commission's report, *The Negro in Chicago*.[15] Although the Chicago school's ethnic cycle of migration, contact, competition, conflict, and assimilation formed the organizing framework of the report, *The Negro in Chicago* documented the persistence and deleterious effects of racism on African Americans revealed in inferior housing, schools, and recreational facilities, poverty, and unstable family life. It was clear to the report's authors that the African American experience in Chicago failed to fit the European ethnic model.

The 1924–26 Pacific Coast survey of race relations headed by Robert Park similarly tested the applicability of the ethnic cycle to non-European groups. The assumption was that the problems of Europeans in the cities and Asians in the West differed but were similar enough to sustain comparison. Instigated by the Institute of Social and Religious Research in New York City, the survey sought to ascertain the causes of anti-Japanese hatred on the Pacific Coast. Instead, Park conceived of the project as a study in assimilation, especially of second-generation Japanese Americans. As was shown in later studies, however, notably by Emory Bogardus, a former Chicago student, social distance and discriminatory laws intervened in assimilation's advance, resulting in amalgamation but also in segregation. Even the so-called assimilated second generation among Chinese, Japanese, Filipinos, and Mexicans, Bogardus found, were partially alienated from both America culture and that of their immigrant parents, resulting in the marginal man.[16]

As Park himself came to acknowledge, "Japanese, Chinese, and Negroes cannot move among us with the same freedom as the members of other races because they bear marks which identify them as members of their race." That fact of race isolates them. Segregation and isolation leads to prejudice and prejudice to isolation and segregation.[17] Because of their "racial badges," Park went on to explain, "Negroes" and "Orientals" were unassimilable; "the chief obstacle to assimilation of the Negro and Oriental are not mental but physical traits." They accordingly posed the "Negro problem" and "Oriental problem."[18]

Exceptional, then, were African and Asian Americans to the primacy and general rule of ethnicity, the ethnic cycle, and eventual triumph of assimilation.[19] They belonged to the field of "race relations." European immigrants, by contrast, affirmed the ideas of "ethnic studies." They sustained the foundational narrative of the US as a nation of immigrants. African and Asian Americans, by contrast, could not assimilate with whites because of their color and white race prejudice, which, Park held, was "a spontaneous, more or less instinctive defense-reaction." Segregation and even slavery, accordingly, were "natural" solutions to "the race problem," because under slavery and Jim Crow, both groups, masters and servants, knew their places. But when racialized minorities claimed democracy's promise, demanding equality with whites, they became "problems" for the normative majority.[20]

Sustaining those ideas of "natural" and "instinctual" responses to racializations was the Chicago school's analogy of social relations with evolution, natural selection, and biological competition, procuring the vestment of science. Thus, in the language of ecological succession, the "invading race," according to Park, whether black or brown posed the problem and not white supremacy or the ideology and material conditions that sustained it.[21] Biological determinism was a key feature of race relations and racialized discourses. Accordingly, human nature rather than human institutions held the answer to the race problem.

Colored subjects did not constitute problems when they supplied efficient, pliant labor for white masters, but they caused apprehension, even dread when they aspired to full equality and a measure of self-determination. "One speaks of race relations when there is a race problem," declared Robert Park. To illustrate, he wrote of the "race problem" in South Africa where "the African does, to be sure, constitute a problem."[22] Of course, from the San, Khoikhoi, Nguni, or Sotho stand point, the invading Dutch and British were the problem.[23] Race relations as a field thrived in the US especially during the interwar period of the twentieth century, and it took turns particular to the US and Britain.[24] On the eve of World War II a "state of the field" U.S. race relations conference cautiously diagnosed an obvious condition, "the world seems to be reorganizing to some extent along racial lines."[25]

As a field of study, race relations sought to understand and better manage colonized and dependent peoples, and thereby solve the problem of the twentieth century and forestall the prospect of a "race war."[26] Its purpose was to study "racial tensions" and "racial conflicts" as social problems with an eye toward ameliorating those conditions. Called racial "adjustments," those solutions were evolutionary and designed to preserve the status quo, and assimilation was in a single direction, toward and in conformity with the majority group.[27]

In the US, accordingly, the Institute of Race Relations was charged with studying "native peoples" to install "effective government" and thereby continue their subjugation, and the Institute of Pacific Relations, established in 1925, had as its prime objective, "to prevent a possible Oriental-Occidental war arising . . . out of an increasing bitterness over racial, religious, economic and political differences."[28] That "bitterness" was not, in reality, generated by "differences," but by the power politics of oppression, exploitation, and dependence.

When colonized, Third World subjects claimed the "universal" human rights of the European Enlightenment, including equality, freedom, and self-determination, imperialists hastened to extinguish those aspirations as premature and undeserved. As British Prime Minister Winston S. Churchill explained to the House of Commons in early 1942, the Atlantic Charter's provisions were not "applicable to [the] Coloured Races in [the] colonial empire, and that [the phrase] 'restoration of sovereignty, self-government and national life' . . . [was] applicable only to the States and the Nations of Europe."[29]

"Race thinking," it appears, fell out of favor when Third World elites not only assumed the claims of European humanism but also emulated their white supremacist rulers by crafting racial identifications and solidarities such as in the decolonization struggles in Africa and Asia and their demands of "Africa for Africans" and "Asia for Asians," which threatened to disrupt the extant racial regime and world order. Japan's 1905 victory over Russia, the first defeat of a white by a nonwhite nation in modern warfare and its call to decolonize Asia from European bondage were particularly potent in this regard. Moreover, white supremacy and its eugenicist "final solution" taken to its logical, obscene end by the Nazis during World War II spelled the final demise of race relations and the turn to ethnicity.

Chicago sociology's crafting of "ethnic studies" and "race relations" exerted their discursive powers in the misnaming of Third World studies. While the students of the Third World Liberation Front at San Francisco State demanded a "Third World curriculum," college faculty and administrators made a distinction between African American studies, which they classified as "race relations" and Asian, Mexican, and Native American studies, as "ethnic studies." African Americans were thereby racialized, while the others they rendered as ethnic or cultural groups. The former were accordingly unassimilable, the latter, assimilable. At the time, the late 1960s, Asian Americans had become assimilated, "model minorities," unlike African Americans. The "Negro problem" remained; the "Oriental" problem had been solved, according to the dominant discourse. The students insisted on their solidarity with and as "Third World peoples" but also uncoupled the "Black Studies Program" from the "School of Ethnic Studies"; the faculty and administrators named them all, as people of color, "ethnic studies."[30]

Social formation[31]

Perhaps because the transnational color line at the twentieth century's start narrowed into nationalist struggles in Africa and Asia by the century's midpoint, Third World or ethnic studies, which began amidst that nation building, lost its bearings in the thicket of nationalism and national culture, as was advocated by, among others, Fanon.[32] Black power and its permutations, an effective antidote to the poison of a colonized mentality and a radical declaration for self-determination, also bore the stain of white identity politics and programs of national and manly reconstitution.[33] Patterned on nationalisms abroad and racialized identity politics at home that promoted homogeneity and punished difference for the sake of solidarity, U.S. cultural nationalism among peoples of color pursued that same policing of the racialized borders of the original together with the nation-state's patriarchal and heterosexist temperaments.

Social formation builds upon without vacating the premises of the U.S. racial formation.[34] Third World or ethnic studies, led by men, erred when it chose race, patriarchy, and nationalism as its subject matters. Albeit creations of the imaginary, racializations persist because white racial politics mandates them. We also witness the power of racializations in how they have structured our lives and circumscribed our life's chances. They have material, palpable effects. We see these in the correspondences of race with income, education, health and wellness, and social mobility. But our resistance against white racial politics need not be solely or even principally colored racial politics. We must find alternative, radical ways to free ourselves from the bonds of white supremacy and our choices of the past.

The insufficiencies of racial formation were clearly evident for those who experienced multiple, intersecting forms of oppression. A journalist and teacher, Elise Johnson McDougald, described the condition of black women in Alain Locke's *Survey Graphic* in 1925. Although possessing disparate experiences, McDougald noted, black women as a whole were subjected to the handicaps and indignities of race, gender, and class. "Like women in general, but more particularly like those of other oppressed minorities," she wrote, "the Negro woman has been forced to submit to over-powering conditions. Pressure has been exerted upon her, both from without and within her group. Her emotional and sex life is a reflex of her economic station." But, she observed, "feminist efforts are directed chiefly toward the realization of the equality of the races, the sex struggle assuming a subordinate place."[35]

That inferior position of gender equality changed with a new wave of African American feminists like Frances Beale, a former NAACP (National Association for the Advancement of Colored People) youth leader and a member of SNCC's (Student Nonviolent Coordinating Committee) international affairs commission. At a 1968 SNCC meeting in New York City, Beale presented a paper on the impact of racism and sexism on the lives of African American women, and proposed a black women's caucus to explore those particular concerns. Capitalism, she pointed out, exploits all workers but white workers can subscribe to a false consciousness of racial superiority and black men, a feeling of dominion over black women. Moreover, the state's sterilization campaigns exert control over black and Puerto Rican women's sexuality, and the white women's movement, largely a middle-class project, excludes the masses of black women whose struggles are against gender but also class, racial, and sexual oppressions.[36]

Beale formed with others the Black Women's Liberation Caucus, which split from SNCC in 1969, and changed its name to the Black Women's Alliance (BWA). Widening its purview and circle with the recognition that, in Beale's words, "the complexities of intersecting oppressions [were] more resilient than the distinctions of the particular groups," the BWA established solidarity with other women of color, including American Indians, Asians, and Latinas. That outreach led to BWA renaming itself the Third World Women's Alliance, which stated as its goals, "to make a meaningful and lasting contribution to the Third World community by working for the elimination of the oppression and exploitation from which we suffer" and to create a socialist society free from "the pressures of racism, economic exploitation, and sexual oppression."[37]

Perceiving a similar marginalization from the civil rights and women's liberation movements, African American women formed the Combahee River Collective in 1974. Sisters Beverly and Barbara Smith, with Demita Frazier, crafted the statement that articulated most persuasively the case for what became theorized as intersectionality. As Barbara Smith recalled years later, "we wanted to integrate a race/class analysis with an antisexist analysis and practice. And we didn't just want to add on racism and class oppression like white women did."[38] The statement begins with an explication of the Collective's politics, which it described as:

> we are actively committed to struggling against racial, sexual, heterosexual, and class oppression, and see as our particular task the development of integrated analysis and practice based upon the fact that the major systems of oppression are interlocking. The synthesis of these oppressions creates the conditions of our lives.[39]

The ideologies and practices of the Third World Women's Alliance and Combahee River Collective worked at the intersections of race, gender, sexuality, and class, unlike other African American women's organizations that might have stressed race and gender, but glossed sexuality and class.[40] The interlocking systems of oppression, their synthesis, became a basis for legal scholar Kimberlé Crenshaw's foundational 1989 essay, "Demarginalizing the Intersection of Race and Sex" in which she named the "multidimensionality of Black women's experience" "intersectionality." "Because the intersectional experience is greater than the sum of racism and sexism," Crenshaw wrote, "any analysis that does not take intersectionality into account cannot sufficiently address the particular manner in which Black women are subordinated."[41] Other African American scholars expanded upon the intersections of gender, race, and nation like the sociologist Patricia Hill Collins,[42] and other women of color deployed the intersections of race, gender, sexuality, class, and nation,[43] but few have theorized fully the articulation.

Perhaps the most thorough exposition is found in sociologist Evelyn Nakano Glenn's *Unequal Freedom: How Race and Gender Shaped American Citizenship and Labor* (2002) in which she describes genderings and racializations as "linked identities" that are "relational." Also, she notes, gender and race comprise ideologies that constitute individuals and groups and supply mobilizing tools for political work. Moreover, those discourses of race and gender are mapped onto the U.S. economy as a central axis of the labor (class) system and the nation-state wherein property, whiteness, and manhood constituted freedom and defined the "citizen worker" and his entitlements.[44] Power, Glenn proposes, is "a" factor in those relational identities at both the micro and macro levels.

Social formation theory draws from that intellectual geneaology of Third World women, but holds, unlike Glenn, power to be "the" organizing principle, and thus its locations and articulations, the central objects of analysis. Those expressions of power comprise discourses, not mere identities, and they are made real in the material and social relations. As historical, social formation attends to the forms of society and their passage and changes through space and over time. For Third World or ethnic studies, then, the social structure is conceived and cultivated by power and its articulations around the bearings of race, gender, and sexuality, economy, polity, and the social as discrepant and intersecting constructions. Constituting a system, the formations of and relations in society are designed by their creators to function as a whole to achieve certain ends. But because of human agency and ceaseless contestations, the social formation is neither self-regulating nor is its path or destination predetermined.

Social formation, in sum, attends to the multiplicity of forces at work in the locations and exercise of power. It demands a complexity in our thinking and politics to ascertain how social categories overlap, interact, conflict with, and interrupt each other. Social formation is not solely the intersections or cumulation of oppressions; it involves those intersections but it also accounts for their resistances (and accommodations) and the mutually constituting and shifting relations between discourses (language and ideology) and the material conditions. Finally, it provides a rubric for unions among racialization, feminist, queer, Marxist, and critical theories, and for political coalitions among peoples of color and among and across created divides of socially constructed expressions of power.

Third World or ethnic studies must rethink its strategy for educational and social transformation beyond national culture and the racial formation. In 1966, when SNCC turned from multiracialism to black power under the influence of Stokely Carmichael's (Kwame Toure) call "to reclaim our history and our identity" for racial self-determination and black liberation—entitlements demanded by Third World or ethnic studies—Bayard Rustin and Harold Cruse warned against what they saw as an introspective turn toward another kind of chauvinism. They argued that black racial politics would elide class oppressions and de-couple black poverty from white privilege. The black struggle, they proposed, should transform blacks, but also whites. Relevant, too, is the realization that Carmichael's black power was modeled after white power and the ethnic politics of the Irish and Jews.[45]

What George Lipsitz observed about the 1960s generally applies, I hold, to Third World or ethnic studies, another feature of the decade. The counter-culture, he astutely noted, more closely resembled the system it claimed to be overturning than opposed it, replicating rather than resisting the status quo.[46] Race-based ethnic studies is essentially conservative intellectually and politically. Adrienne Rich's criticism of U.S. feminism applies equally to ethnic studies. Rich scored feminism's retreat to "versions of female oppression which neglect both female agency and female diversity, in which 'safety' for women becomes valued over risk taking, and woman-only space—often a strategic necessity—becomes a place of emigration, an end in itself." Instead, she proposed, feminists should advance and carry on "a conversation with the world."[47]

And that global engagement should be enjoined with the twin recognition of the falsity and reality of race. Although a fiction, we know that race structures self and self's choices. I am not calling for an end to race thinking; what I am advocating is the reorientation of our field away from U.S. "race relations" and "ethnic studies" to Third World studies and social formation—a shift not only in name but also in substance. If the problem of the twentieth century was the problem of the color line, it was because white and its opposition, colored racial politics made it so. By contrast, the opportunity, not "problem" of the twenty-first century for those of us in the newly constituted field of Third World and social formations will be "to create, through struggles, a new humanity, a new humanism, a New World Consciousness." The struggle continues. . . .

Notes

1 Frantz Fanon, *The Wretched of the Earth*, trans. Constance Farrington (New York: Grove Press, 1961), 35–36, 311, 315.
2 As first published in W.E.B. Du Bois, "The Freedmen's Bureau," *Atlantic Monthly* 87 (March 1901): 354. See the statement from the first Pan-African Conference in London, 1900, "To the Nations of the World," in *W.E.B. Du Bois: A Reader*, ed. David Levering Lewis (New York: Henry Holt, 1995), 639. See also W.E.B. Du Bois, *The Souls of Black Folk* (Chicago, IL: A. C. McClurg, 1903), 10; and "The Color Line Belts the World," *Collier's Weekly*, October 20, 1906, 30.
3 Lothrop Stoddard, *The Rising Tide of Color Against White World-Supremacy* (New York: Charles Scribner's Sons, 1920).
4 Fanon, *The Wretched of the Earth*, 314.
5 As quoted in George McTurnan Kahin, *The Asian-African Conference, Bandung, Indonesia, April 1955* (Ithaca, NY: Cornell University Press, 1956).
6 *The Daily Gater*, San Francisco State College, May 22, 1969.
7 Albert Memmi, *The Colonizer and the Colonized* (Boston, MA: Beacon Press, 1967), 147, 153; and Fanon, *The Wretched of the Earth*, 246.
8 *The Daily Gater*, May 22, 1969.
9 *Asian Women* (Berkeley, CA: Asian Women, 1971), 79, 80.
10 Fred H. Matthews, *Quest for an American Sociology: Robert E. Park and the Chicago School* (Montreal: McGill-Queen's University Press, 1977), 90–91.
11 Quoted in Winifred Raushenbush, *Robert E. Park: Biography of a Sociologist* (Durham, NC: Duke University Press, 1979), 50. For a review of the Chicago school of sociology, see Andrew Abbott, *Department & Discipline: Chicago Sociology at One Hundred* (Chicago, IL: University of Chicago Press, 1999).
12 See, for example, William I. Thomas and Florian Znaniecki, *The Polish Peasant in Europe and America: Monograph of an Immigrant Group*, 5 vols. (Chicago, IL: University of Chicago Press, 1918–20); and Henry Yu, *Thinking Orientals: Migration, Contact, and Exoticism in Modern America* (New York: Oxford University Press, 2001).
13 Franz Boas, "Introduction," *Handbook of American Indian Languages*, Bulletin 40, Bureau of Ethnology, Smithsonian Institution (Washington, DC: Government Printing Office, 1911), 1–85; and George W. Stocking, Jr., *Delimiting Anthropology: Occasional Inquiries and Reflections* (Madison, WI: University of Wisconsin Press, 2001).
14 Stow Persons, *Ethnic Studies at Chicago, 1905–45* (Urbana, IL: University of Illinois Press, 1987), 34–35. Another Midwestern idea was the frontier hypothesis that proposed the American frontier as the leveler of ethnic and class distinctions. See Frederick Jackson Turner, *The Frontier in American History* (New York: Henry Holt, 1920).
15 Chicago Commission on Race Relations, *The Negro in Chicago: A Study of Race Relations and a Race Riot* (Chicago, IL: University of Chicago Press, 1922).
16 Emory S. Bogardus, "A Race-Relations Cycle," *American Journal of Sociology* 35:4 (January 1930), 612–617; and Robert H. Ross and Emory S. Bogardus, "The Second-Generation Race Relations Cycle: A Study in *Issei-Nisei* Relationships," *Sociology and Social Research* 24:4 (March–April 1940), 357–363. See also E. Franklin Frazier's version of Park's cycle in his "Theoretical Structure of Sociology and Sociological Research," *British Journal of Sociology* 4:4 (December 1953), 293–311. Robert Park coined the term "marginal man" in "Human Migration and the Marginal Man," *American Journal of Sociology* 23:6 (May 1928), 881–893.
17 Robert E. Park, "Introduction," in Jesse Frederick Steiner, *The Japanese Invasion: A Study in the Psychology of Inter-Racial Contacts* (Chicago, IL: A. C. McClurg, 1917), xvi.
18 See, for example, Robert Park, "The Nature of Race Relations," in his *Race and Culture* (Glencoe, IL: Free Press, 1950), 81–116; and "Racial Assimilation in Secondary Groups with Particular Reference to the Negro," *American Journal of Sociology* 19: 9

(1914), 610–611. See also Stanford M. Lyman, "Race Relations as Social Process: Sociology's Resistance to a Civil Rights Orientation," in *Race in America: The Struggle for Equality*, ed. Herbert Hill and James E. Jones Jr. (Madison, WI: University of Wisconsin Press, 1993), 370–401.

19 Cf. the resuscitation of ethnicity and assimilation in Richard Alba and Victor Nee, "Rethinking Assimilation Theory for a New Era of Immigration," *International Migration Review* 31: 4 (1997), 826–874.

20 Park, "Introduction," xiii, xiv.

21 Ibid., xv.

22 Park, *Race and Culture*, 82. For a "state of the field" affirmation of Park's views specific to the U.S. South, see Edgar T. Thompson, ed., *Race Relations and the Race Problem: A Definition and Analysis* (Durham, NC: Duke University Press, 1939).

23 As put by Fanon, the Third World must "resolve the problems to which Europe has not been able to find the answers." Fanon, *The Wretched of the Earth*, 314.

24 See, for example, Michael Banton, *Race Relations* (New York: Basic Books, 1967); and Robert Miles, *Racism After "Race Relations"* (London: Routledge, 1993).

25 Edgar T. Thompson, ed., *Race Relations and the Race Problem: A Definition and Analysis* (Durham, NC: Duke University Press, 1939), vii; Hugh Tinker, *Race, Conflict and the International Order: From Empire to United Nations* (New York: St. Martin's Press, 1977), 12–14, 42–48; and Frank Füredi, *The Silent War: Imperialism and the Changing Perception of Race* (London: Pluto Press, 1998), 2, 7.

26 Tinker, *Race, Conflict*, 12–14; and Füredi, *Silent War*, 2, 27–28, 34.

27 Milton M. Gordon, *Assimilation in American Life: The Role of Race, Religion, and National Origins* (New York: Oxford University Press, 1964), 60–83.

28 Füredi, *Silent War*, 34, 50, 86–87.

29 As quoted in Penny M. Von Eschen, *Race Against Empire: Black Americans and Anticolonialism, 1937–1957* (Ithaca, NY: Cornell University Press, 1997), 26.

30 See, for example, "Demands and Explanations," [n.d.], Folder 164, Box Third World Liberation Front, San Francisco State Strike Collection, University Library Archives, San Francisco State University; and Robert Smith (San Francisco State College), "President Smith's Statement on Black and Ethnic Studies," *On the Record* (San Francisco State College official newsletter), Nov. 4, 1968.

31 For fuller explanations of what I mean by "social formation," see Gary Y. Okihiro and Elda Tsou, "On Social Formation," *Works and Days* 24 (2006), 69–88; and my "Theorizing Social Formation," an unpublished paper.

32 Fanon, "On National Culture," in *The Wretched of the Earth*, 206–248.

33 Stokely Carmichael and Charles V. Hamilton, *Black Power: The Politics of Liberation in America* (New York: Random House, 1967).

34 Foundational is Michael Omi and Howard Winant's *Racial Formation in the United States: From the 1960s to the 1980s* (New York: Routledge & Kegan Paul, 1986).

35 Elise Johnson McDougald, "The Struggle of Negro Women for Sex and Race Emancipation," in *Words of Fire: An Anthology of African-American Feminist Thought*, ed. Beverly Guy-Sheftall (New York: New Press, 1995), 81–82.

36 Frances Beale, "Double Jeopardy: To Be Black and Female," in Guy-Sheftall, *Words of Fire*, 146–155.

37 Kimberly Springer, *Living for the Revolution: Black Feminist Organizations, 1968–1980* (Durham, NC: Duke University Press, 2005), 45–49, 185.

38 From an interview in Springer, *Living*, 60.

39 "The Combahee River Collective Statement," in *Home Girls: A Black Feminist Anthology*, ed. Barbara Smith (Latham, NY: Kitchen Table Women of Color Press, 1983), 26.

40 See, for example, Kristen Anderson-Bricker, "'Triple Jeopardy': Black Women and the Growth of Feminist Consciousness in SNCC, 1964–1975," in *Still Lifting, Still*

Climbing: Contemporary African American Women's Activism (New York: New York University Press, 1999), 49–69.

41 Kimberlé Crenshaw, "Demarginalizing the Intersection of Race and Sex: A Black Feminist Critique of Antidiscrimination Doctrine, Feminist Theory and Antiracist Politics," *University of Chicago Legal Forum* (1989), 139, 140

42 Patricia Hill Collins, "It's All in the Family: Intersections of Gender, Race, and Nation," *Hypatia* 13:3 (Summer 1998), 62–82; and "Gender, Black Feminism, and Black Political Economy," *Annals of the American Academy of Political and Social Science* 568 (2000), 41–53. See also Angela Y. Davis, *Women, Race, and Class* (New York: Random House, 1981); and Leith Mullings, *On Our Own Terms: Race, Class, and Gender in the Lives of African American Women* (New York: Routledge, 1997).

43 See, for example, Cherríe Moraga, *Loving in the War Years* (Cambridge, MA: South End Press, 1983); and Evelyn Nakano Glenn, "Racial Ethnic Women's Labor: The Intersection of Race, Gender and Class Oppression," *Review of Radical Political Economics* 17:3 (1985), 86–108.

44 Evelyn Nakano Glenn, *Unequal Freedom: How Race and Gender Shaped American Citizenship and Labor* (Cambridge, MA: Harvard University Press, 2002).

45 Clayborne Carson, *In Struggle: SNCC and the Black Awakening of the 1960s* (Cambridge, MA: Harvard University Press, 1981), 220, 227–228.

46 George Lipsitz, "Who'll Stop the Rain? Youth Culture, Rock 'n' Roll, and Social Crises," in *The Sixties: From Memory to History*, ed. David Farber (Chapel Hill, NC: University of North Carolina Press, 1994), 224, 227.

47 Adrienne Rich, "Living the Revolution," *Women's Review of Books* 3:12 (September 1986), 3.

Chapter 5

All the stage's a world

The organization of international, multicultural, and global theater companies in the US

Esther Kim Lee

When in 1979 Roberta Uno founded the Third World Theater (later renamed New WORLD Theater) on the campus of the University of Massachusetts in Amherst, the emphasis on the "world," was both deliberate and specific. At a time when most of the new theater companies in the US focused on regional identities and repertories, Uno's group began with an ambitious mission aimed at creating a different, better world. In the context of theater history, there are many examples of using the "world" as an abstract concept to describe a theater company's mission. Numerous variations of the Latin idea of *theatrum mundi* ("All the World's a Stage") have inspired theater artists throughout history to connect the world to theater. As in the case of the Globe Theater of the English Renaissance, the theater space has often been promoted as a microcosm of the "world." Stage settings, costumes, props, and actors' bodies have functioned as tropes to project what the audience might imagine as the "world."[1] In each incidence, however, the specific ways in which "world" was defined and used differed. This chapter examines the New WORLD Theater in comparison to two other theater companies in the US that have also used the framework of the world to explain the main purpose of their artistic mission in the second half of the twentieth century and the early twenty-first century. The two companies are: La MaMa Experimental Theater Club (New York City) and Silk Road Rising (Chicago, IL; originally named Silk Road Theater Project). The three companies serve in this chapter as case studies for examining how the concept of the world has been incorporated and contested in American theater.[2]

The three companies selected for this study are examined comparatively in order to provide an interpretative history of how the idea of the world has been defined by theater artists as both a cause for celebration and a call for change in contemporary U.S. theater history. At the same time, the primary lens through which the comparison is made in this chapter is Asian American theater. All three companies have had an extensive influence in all sectors of American theater, but Asian American theater provides a unique focal advantage. Asian American theater is often situated in the blind spots of widely used conceptions of "world theater," "intercultural theater," or "American theater." Artists of Asian American theater have had to negotiate what Karen Shimakawa calls "national abjection" against the desire to be unequivocally accepted as part of American theater.[3] Asian American theater has traversed the cultural landscapes of both international and domestic and as well as intercultural and multicultural. How the three companies examined in this chapter have dealt with Asian American theater, therefore, raises questions that can expose the potentials, contradictions, and fault lines in using the idea of the world as a way to define their mission.

The International: La MaMa Experimental Theater Club

Ellen Stewart founded La MaMa ETC in 1961 in lower Manhattan's East Village in New York City in a one-room basement café with the goal to promote international theater. For Stewart, the term international was the vocabulary of choice to explain her approach to the intersection of theater and the world. In a 1989 interview, Stewart stated, "[C]ross-pollination is something I've believed in strongly for a long time. It relates to internationalism, and La Mama has been international from its very beginnings."[4] As an African American woman leading an off-off Broadway theater, Stewart was unlike any other in American theater. Especially after her death in early 2011, her legacy as a pioneer of internationalization of American theater has been wisely accepted, and the *New York Times* describes her in the obituary as a "theatrical missionary, scouting new talent abroad and planting La MaMa seeds wherever she went."[5] According to Stewart, the initial motivation to promote international theater was practical. She wanted to get playwrights produced at La MaMa, published, and their plays reviewed by critics.[6] The location of New York City also aided in the internationalization of the company. Before the company's first trip to Europe, Stewart had worked in New York City with artists from Colombia, Korea, France, Japan, India, Peru, Finland, and Poland.

Ellen Stewart deserves the credit that she has received for internationalizing American theater, and if it was not for her, many influential theater artists may have never found an opportunity in New York City and elsewhere. However, what Stewart meant by international theater was not as original as what she did with it. The term "international theater" can be traced back to the early twentieth century, but the way Stewart used it specifically has its roots in 1948 when UNESCO's sub-committee on Arts and Letters created the International Theater Institute (ITI).[7] According to the ITI website's description, it did not take long for the sub-committee to realize that Theater was one of the best ways to promote the goals of UNESCO, which came into being in 1946. A sub-committee on Arts and Letters, which included distinguished writers and dramatists, met at its First General Conference. It soon became clear that there was a need for an international clearing-house for theater arts, a non-political, non-commercial association in which theater artists and administrators of all countries could work out a practical program to facilitate exchange and circulation of play scripts, current theater information, performing companies, and young artists. The first ITI Congress met in Prague in June 1948, with twelve centers in operation: Austria, Belgium, Brazil, Chile, China, Czechoslovakia, France, Italy, Poland, Switzerland, UK and USA.[8] Since 1948, the ITI has grown to be the world's largest performing arts organization for theater and dance with over 100 centers around the globe.[9] In 1961, the year La MaMa was founded, the term "international theater" was already being widely used, and various forms of artistic and educational exchanges involving the performing arts were occurring in both governmental and non-profit sectors.

Like the ITI, La MaMa celebrated the artistic synergy that occurred when theater artists around the world encountered theatrical forms that were different from theirs. The approach to international theater sought by both the ITI and La MaMa emphasized the commonalities amongst theatrical cultures. Despite the vast differences between Japanese Kabuki and Shakespeare, for instance, the promoters of international theater in the 1960s argued, "Theater does indeed serve international understanding."[10] Theater, as part of a larger spectrum of cultural expression, was seen as a tool to achieve the UN's goal of world peace, and the ITI's emphasis was on what was common amongst all forms of theater around the world. Ellen Stewart speaks about international theater in basically the same way. In defending the need for diversity in American theater, Stewart states: "[T]he key to art in the Theater is universality. There may be opposite styles of working, but each has the possibility of universality: how you express and explore is your individual art form."[11]

The most universal elements in theater, for Stewart, were non-verbal actions. More specifically, she believed that physical movements, dance, music, gestures, and images were more effective and entertaining onstage than spoken dramas. Such form of performance has now become La MaMa's signature style, the influence of which can be seen in works by Robert Wilson, Lee Breuer, Philip Glass, and many others who found artistic home in Downtown New York in the 1960s and the 1970s. While La MaMa's goal was aesthetic experimentation and the ITI's ultimate purpose was political, both organizations saw international theater as a utopic space for the world. ITI provided Ellen Stewart a definition of international theater as well as frequent opportunities for collaboration on productions, exchange of artists, and organization of international theater festivals.

While La MaMa's international outlook has had a profound impact on domestic theater, its push for an international vision of theater garnered opposition in unexpected places. According to Stewart in an interview with Alvin Eng, both The Negro Ensemble and the Black Panthers found her and La MaMa suspicious and downright antagonistic to "blacks" as they defined the racial group because her company was not a black theater. Stewart herself rejects what she calls "a Black box," a label that limits who she is as a person:

> Some people keep trying to put me in a "Black box" and I tell them, "you can't put me in a 'Black box.'" I told them that a thousand times. It's very racist, I think. The only people, who I guess you could say, wanted to put me in a box were people who have nothing to do with La MaMa.[12]

When asked by Alvin Eng, who is Asian American, why The Negro Ensemble and the Black Panthers would be against what she was doing, Stewart answered, "It was because of you," meaning that helping non-blacks was perceived as betraying the black cause.[13] Ellen Stewart's inclusive view of theater may have been rejected by some in the black theater community, but it was welcomed by those who, like Stewart, disagreed with the black and white binary stipulation of theater in the US.

Stewart's international vision directly benefitted Native American, Latina/o, and Asian American theater. The artists and groups she supported domestically were those who did not fit into the niches of white-dominated mainstream theater nor the hyper-masculine black theater of the late 1960s. She rightly claimed that she started Asian American theater in New York City by supporting Tisa Chang (who founded Pan Asian Repertory, the first self-described Asian American theater company in New York City) and Ping Chong (who is one of the most prolific Asian American theater artists).[14] Many Asian American theater artists were made aesthetically and culturally legible in the US through Stewart's efforts toward international theater. Conversely, La MaMa found domestic support from minority artists who had to navigate the racially volatile yet artistically exciting period in lower Manhattan in the 1960s. Stewart's international vision of theater translated to a multicultural one in the US, and Asian American theater benefitted from the new cultural identifier in terms of funding and audience base.

The multicultural: New WORLD Theater

One of the many theater artists Ellen Stewart inspired and influenced was Roberta Uno, who founded the New WORLD Theater (NWT) on the campus of University of Massachusetts in Amherst in 1979. NWT started at the closing of the decade that saw the founding of many minority theater companies in the US such as the Asian American Theater Company (San Francisco), the Negro Ensemble (New York City), and El Teatro Campesino (San Juan Bautista). Most of these companies specialized in one racial or ethnic group, and there were very few companies that focused on multiracial and multiethnic topics. Growing up in Los Angeles, Uno was exposed to a cultural environment that included Asian Americans, African Americans, and Chicanos, and she wanted to see them represented onstage.[15] At the same time, she encountered student protests at the University of Massachusetts where students of color made up only 5 percent of the student population. Many students demanded diversity on campus, and Uno believed that a theater program for students of color could play a key role in helping to make diversity materialize.

Uno and other members of the new group saw themselves as part of the Third World Movement that called for the end of apartheid in South Africa and the war in Vietnam. Locally, they fought for desegregation and racial equality. The theater group was initially called Third World Theater, and the first production was a play by a South African playwright.[16] Describing themselves as "very political" with a "global perspective," participants of the new group used theater to align themselves with the larger political changes that were occurring both in the US and around the world. The Third World movement sought liberation of Third World countries and minorities from western domination in all sectors of society, including the arts. Uno did not want to organize a theater company that only focused on domestic U.S. issues; rather, what was happening in the US was seen as part of a worldwide struggle for equality and justice. The "world" represented by the New WORLD Theater in its beginning was defined racially and culturally in the Third World movement context.

In the early 1980s, the name of the company was changed to New WORLD Theater as a way to signal a move away from the rhetoric of the Third World movement and to suggest a more inclusive and hopeful connotation. According to its mission statement in 2009:

> New WORLD Theater has presented seasons of innovative, contemporary theater by artists of color in order to foster creative communities that exist at the intersection of artistic practice, community engagement, scholarship and education; and to promote cultural equity and the vision of a "new world"—one that embraces diverse cultural backgrounds, interdisciplinary approaches, widespread geographic roots, and a commitment to justice.[17]

The language promoting a "new world" that embraces diversity and interdisciplinary approaches echo the mission of the International Theater Institute (ITI) and La MaMa ETC, but at the same time, the focus on social justice and racial equality in the statement emphasizes the company's roots in the Third World movement of the 1970s. Moreover, the use of the phrase "artist of color" also reflects the company's acknowledgement of the minority theater movement in the US.

Writing in 1989, ten years after the founding of NWT, Roberta Uno describes NWT as part of "the multicultural theater movement," which she traces back to the very beginning of American theater history and defines as having "revitalized the American theater" in the 1980s.[18] The way she describes the first ten years reveals much about how broadly she envisions multicultural theater:

> Ten years of New WORLD Theater have been marked by nearly 100 productions of the theater of the African diaspora, Asian America, Native America and Latin America presented side by side. They are often unified by themes, but more often strikingly disparate in their range of artistic styles, aesthetic sensibilities, and social concerns. The New WORLD Theater's artistic vision has included a wide spectrum of dramatic styles and structures—melodrama to performance art, drama to Yoruban folk opera, comedy improvisation to dance theater. The Theater has sought to present each cultural expression as distinct, emerging from separate cultural traditions—leaving the audience to make comparative analysis and draw thematic and cultural relationships.[19]

Uno's inclusive and celebratory language referencing the world is similar to that of Ellen Stewart and the ITI, but there is one crucial difference between NWT and the other two entities. Because NWT was founded on a state university campus, its productions were seen by many—especially the campus administrators—through the lens of multicultural education in an academic context. The way Uno defined multiculturalism was broad, historical, and anti-racist but the campus used the concept more narrowly befitting the political rhetoric of the 1980s and 1990s.

In those two decades, multiculturalism connoted both a sense of universal need for equality and what Charles Taylor calls "the politics of recognition."[20] The two paradoxical agendas—one toward demand for equal worth of all cultures and another toward special recognition of each culture—led Taylor to describe multiculturalism as having severe problems. The most critical problem for Taylor is deciding which standard to make judgments about equal recognition. He warns, "even if one could demand it of them, the last thing one wants at this stage from Eurocentered intellectuals is positive judgments of the worth of cultures that they have not intensively studied."[21] Others have also identified liberal politics that promote multiculturalism as perpetuating Eurocentric views of culture in ways that are damaging and sinister. Taylor rhetorically asks whether there is a "midway between the inauthentic and homogenizing demand for recognition or equal worth, on the one hand, and the self-immurement within ethnocentric standards, on the other."[22] Is there a way to define multiculturalism without using Eurocentric definitions of culture and without perpetuating balkanization of individual ethnic and racial groups?

Roberta Uno, in writing about New WORLD Theater, addresses Taylor's inquiry with what she calls three different kinds of contexts. The first context, for Uno, is illustrated by those companies that bring "color" to their productions by using multiracial casting in European or Euro-American plays. The Gutherie Theater in Minneapolis produced in 1991 a production of *Death of a Salesman* directed by Sheldon Epps with black actors in main roles. With the production, the Gutherie claimed to promote multiculturalism and diversity through color-blind casting.[23] As Charles Taylor warns, however, the production's measure of standard was Eurocentric judgment of worth valorized, in this case, by Arthur Miller's play. For Uno, such practice necessitates the reactive definition of "minority cultures" as different from the "dominant culture," which is assumed as the norm. Needless to say, Uno rejects the assumption that minorities need to find standards in reaction to the dominant culture. The second context Uno identifies is an ethnically and racially specific definition of multicultural theater in which African American, Native American, Chicano, and Asian American theaters work separately. At its worst, separate minority theaters would resist anything that challenges the way they narrowly define themselves. Some black theater artists, for instance, would reject multiracial or queer topics in their repertory and claim that such topics do not represent the black experience. At its best, on the other hand, the separation of minority theaters allows the rare opportunity for specific ethnic or racial actors to be represented onstage and share with the audience a strong sense of cultural bonding and common story. No one can deny the fact that the East West Players in Los Angeles catered to predominately Nisei (second generation Japanese Americans) in the 1980s and provided a profoundly positive cultural resource to the community.

Roberta Uno does not deny the advantages of separate minority theaters, but she wants to work beyond the limitations of cultural separatism. Uno prefers a third context and feels "compelled by how the nature of theater has changed and how the world is changing."[24] The world, for Uno, is heading towards the year 2050, the projected time in which Caucasians will become a minority in the United States. What is predicted to happen in the US will have ramifications around the world with increased globalization and migration across nations and cultures. The demographic change has already occurred in major cities in the US, and the national change may come earlier than 2050. The undeniable fact is that the racial and ethnic composition in the country is growing more complex and diverse, and some of the categories will become irrelevant in a few decades. Uno uses the projected view of the US to explain her artistic vision of the New WORLD Theater and her political vision of the world. It is the projected future of the world that defines her agenda and the third context. According to Uno, the third context creates a place of desegregation and dialogue.[25]

The New WORLD Theater aimed to promote the kind of multiculturalism that would avoid the "politics of recognition" that Charles Taylor identified by supporting initiatives, festivals, and conferences to encourage innovation and conversation. Instead of advocating for a project that celebrates cultures as discrete, homogenous, units, NWT created mechanisms that fostered intercultural exchanges. A key term used by the company throughout the 1990s was "intersections," and a number of events were created to support various forms of artistic, cultural, and political intersections. Participants of the events included artists, scholars, and community members who explored new forms of performance and community outreach. The anthology Roberta Uno edited with Lucy Mae San Pablo Burns entitled *The Color of Theater: Race, Culture, and Contemporary Performance* is a culmination of the conversations New WORLD Theater has led since its beginning. Uno ends her introduction to the anthology with an invitation to enter "an immense space, the unrecognized" to continue the exchange and learning of the unfamiliar. Again, it is her vision of the unknown future that provides the foundation for her definition of the world and her vision of theater in the US.

The anthology features a solo performance piece entitled *bodies between us* by thúy lê, a Vietnamese American writer and performer, and Uno showcases it as a representative form of performance for her company. The piece provokes a new narrative of migration and displacement, and its author embodies the new face of U.S. demography. Instead of promoting lê as a new Asian American artist, which would have been the case for Asian American theater companies or regional theater companies, the New WORLD Theater described her as an unlabeled writer and performer who can complicate the conversations and interactions between artists. A new artist such as lê is not forced into a niche but put into the center of what Uno calls "an extraordinarily raw, complicated, honest, and revealing" interaction between artists of different backgrounds.[26]

As it has been widely reported in the theater community, the New WORLD Theater was forced to suspend its operations in 2009 by the administrative leaders of the University of Massachusetts-Amherst. In suspending the company, the University of Massachusetts cited the economic recession and budget problems, but many have wondered why the decision had to be made quickly without any consultation with the management team of the company. It may be that the resignation of Roberta Uno from the position of artistic director in 2002 was the beginning of the end. Many theater companies often shut down after the charismatic founding leader steps down. The closing may have also been caused by campus politics or mismanagement. Most likely, a combination of many reasons led to the closing of the company. However, questions remain unanswered about the sudden suspension and why the campus leaders did not think that NWT belonged to the future of the university.

Many colleges and universities in the US are actively promoting global education befitting the twenty-first century, and the University of Massachusetts cites "international reputation" as a core value in the twenty-first century.[27] Why, then, would the campus not support an organization that strived to make the campus more international? The suspension can partly be seen as a result of how Charles Taylor's notion of "politics of recognition" was played out on the campus. Taylor's warnings about the paradoxical agendas of multiculturalism built up over thirty years despite the efforts of Uno and others to transcend them. The NWT attempted to redefine the "world" through theater by approaching it as part of the university's education on multiculturalism, and for many years, the campus and the company mostly agreed on how best to diversify the student experience and the curriculum. But ultimately, the university controlled how it would define multiculturalism, and the NWT depended on the agenda of whoever was in charge of the campus. To borrow Taylor's description, the NWT was founded with the support of "Eurocentered intellectuals" who had "positive judgments of the worth of cultures that they have not intensively studied."[28] As an organization, the NWT had an advantage in receiving support from the university, but it also had a disadvantage because the support could be pulled literally overnight, as was the case in 2009. While Uno's vision of multiculturalism was historical and progressive, the University of Massachusetts administrators saw it pragmatically and reactively.

In the late 1990s and the early twenty-first century, multiculturalism as an academic agenda began to lose appeal and urgency, and globalization replaced it as part of many universities' strategic planning. It is quite clear that the University of Massachusetts's vision of the "world" is inconsistent with the NWT's use of the term. While the NWT continued to focus on social justice and equality, leaders of higher education in general moved towards envisioning a world in which commercial globalization led by technological innovation, free markets, and entrepreneurship would be a major component of educating future world citizens. The value of the NWT's agenda was no longer consistent with the university's standards for higher education. Or, perhaps, the university gave "positive judgments of the worth" to the mission of the company as long as it could fit its multicultural education goals. Instead of giving the company the opportunity to reformulate their agenda to fit the university's vision, it was unfortunately dismissed as an organization that would not belong in the twenty-first century, at least in Amherst. It must be emphasized that Robert Uno rejects the university's narrow definition of multiculturalism that promoted a balkanized and apolitical education model. Instead, Uno's vision of multiculturalism was foremost anti-racist, and she wanted to broaden the very definition of multicultural theater. Under her leadership and beyond, the two different views of multiculturalism often clashed, but the legacy of the New WORLD Theater could not have been possible without the strategically symbiotic relationship between the campus and the company.

The global: Silk Road Project

Silk Road Theater Project in Chicago was founded in 2002 with the goal to become "Global Theater for Global City." The co-founders, Malik Gillani and Jamil Khoury, have cited the attacks of September 11, 2001 as the "spark" that led them to start the theater company.

> [Gillani and Khoury] felt galvanized to respond to the anti-Arab and anti-Muslim sentiments that swept the US in the aftermath of the attacks, and to challenge arguments surmising a "clash of civilizations." Their hope was to counter negative representation of Middle Eastern and Muslim peoples with representation that was authentic, multi-faceted, and grounded in human experience. That theater would be the medium in which they'd "create change" was a given.[29]

The initial idea led them to include a much larger geographical location, beyond the Middle East, to the diasporic communities of the Silk Road region. According to Gillani and Khoury, there are over 1.5 million diasporic people from the Silk Road territories in the Chicago metropolitan area and yet they are rarely represented in Chicago's theater. They claim that the company became the "nation's first ever Theater company dedicated to representing such a diverse grouping of peoples and cultures."[30]

In some sense, the Silk Road Rising began with a mission similar to that of the New WORLD Theater. Both companies were explicit about their commitment to social justice and equity, and diversity and outreach functioned as the core values in reimagining the cartography of the world in American theater. However, there is one major difference between the two companies. New WORLD Theater focused on supporting individual artists and groups by bringing them to Amherst for the company's established audiences, but Silk Road Rising's main goal has been to increase Chicago's theater audience base. In fact, Silk Road's mission statement states that the company aims to "expand the theater community's discourse on race and ethnicity."[31] It seems that for the Silk Road Rising, the expansion involves both the re-defining of race and ethnicity and the active reaching out to all Chicagoan theatergoers.

As an example of the goal, in the 2010 season, the company produced *The DNA Trail: A Genealogy of Short Plays about Ancestry, Identity, and Utter Confusion*. The description of the production reads:

> Theater meets science when a diverse group of playwrights each agree to take a genealogical DNA test and revisit their assumptions about identity, politics and the perennial "who am I" question. Self, family, community, and ethnicity are all up for grabs.[32]

The playwrights who participated in the DNA test were Asian Americans: Elizabeth Wong, Velina Hasu Houston, Lina Patel, Jamil Khoury, Shishir Kurup, David Henry Hwang, and Philip Kan Gotada. Each short play dealt with identity issues that have become overly familiar in ethnic theaters, but the premise of the production, with its focus on "scientific" DNA test, generated interest amongst general Chicagoan theatergoers.[33] The company also made a decision early on to support playwrights. Whereas La MaMa ETC and New WORLD Theater commissioned many performance artists and alternative theater groups, Silk Road's production history demonstrates preference for a much more conventional theater with written plays performed by Equity actors. Perhaps because Jamil Khoury is himself a playwright, the company's choices have been relatively well-known plays produced at regional theater companies in the US. One of the first plays the company produced was *Tea* by Velina Hasu Houston, which is one of the most revived Asian American plays. In the 2011 season, the company produced *Yellow Face* by David Henry Hwang. The production was co-produced with the Goodman Theater, the most visible theater in Chicago.

The production history of Silk Road resembles those of Asian American theater companies such as the East West Players with plays by Philip Kan Gotanda, Julia Cho, Shishir Kurup, and David Henry Hwang. One major difference is that Silk Road has also produced plays about the Middle East with plays such as *Pangs of the Messiah* by Motti Lerner in 2009. Chicago has been home to a few of ethnic-specific companies targeting Asian or Asian American themes. Pintig Cultural Group has focused on Filipino American themes while Rasaka Theater Company has been described as the first South Asian American theater group in Chicago. In the 1990s, Angel Island Theater was the primary company that produced Asian American works in Chicago, but it did so intermittently. When Silk Road was founded in 2002, there was no active theater company that regularly produced Asian American plays. As the "second city" in the US with a major theater community, the lack of Asian American representation was an obvious void. If Asian American theater is a niche in American theater, the co-founders of Silk Road could have filled it by calling itself an Asian American theater company. Moreover, many Asian American theater companies founded in the 1990s focused on specific ethnicities: Ma-Yi Theater (New York City) started out as a company for Filipino Americans and Lodestone Theater (Los Angeles) was founded by Korean Americans in Los Angeles. Moving against the trend, the founders of Silk Road Rising decided against emphasizing "Asian" as a descriptor for their company. They have destabilized the geographical term "Asia." The decision, instead, to call the company by the historical trading route that connected Asia to Mediterranean and European regions signaled new connections and possibilities.

It remains to be seen whether the company will indeed expand discussions of race and ethnicity and find a wider audience for plays about what the company calls "Silk Road people." Thus far, it has succeeded in introducing major Asian American playwrights to Chicagoan audiences. The 2011 season's co-production of *Yellow Face* with the Goodman Theater was part of what was advertised as "Summer of David Henry Hwang: One Great Playwright, Three Great Plays" in Chicago. The Goodman Theater's production *Chinglish* received extensive media attention as a play that was Broadway-bound. It also remains to be seen how the broad use of "Silk Road" as an epistemological category will affect Asian American and other ethnic theaters in the US. Is the company paving a path towards a new form of cosmopolitan and global theater? Or is it reiterating a familiar success model by showcasing such writers as David Henry Hwang, who is still the only Asian American playwright to have been produced on Broadway? What does a "global theater for a global city" look like?

The company's name change in 2011 to Silk Road Rising provides an answer to the questions especially in the way it wishes to grow as an organization in the future. In explaining the change, Gillani and Khoury see the Internet and global multimedia communication as a way to expand both what they do and how they do it. They use the term "polyculture" to articulate their vision of interconnected cultures, and the Internet becomes an essential method to expand both form and content. Moreover, by not limiting itself to live performance and written plays, they have changed the very definition of a theater company. The newly created website for Silk Road Rising describes the company as an organization that "creates live Theater and online videos that tell stories through primarily Asian American and Middle Eastern American lenses." The mission statement continues, "In representing communities that intersect and overlap, we advance a polycultural worldview."[34] In echoing Vijay Prashad and Robin Kelley, Gillani and Khoury use the term "polycultural" to move beyond the balkanized model of multiculturalism toward overlapping and interrelated view of cultures.[35]

Conclusion

The three companies examined in this chapter began in response to the realities of different historical moments: Ellen Stewart founded La MaMa ETC in 1961 because opportunities lacked for minority artists in both New York City and international venues; Roberta Uno founded New WORLD Theater in 1979 as a way to protest racial and social inequality in higher education; and the Silk Road Rising was founded at the beginning of the twenty-first century in response to the September 11, 2001 attacks and to expand the audience base of the Chicagoan Theater. The responses necessitated the envisioning of theater as a critical site to connect with different cultures, and the concept of the world was reimagined in the process of articulating and advocating each company's defining mission. While the three case studies have been presented in a chronological order, this is not to suggest an evolutionary model or superior efficacy of one theater company. Rather, all three interpretations of the world have co-existed and have influenced all sectors of theater in the US. The three companies have exemplified different ways to use the stage as a real space of representation and exploration of the world.

Notes

1 For an overview of theatrum mundi, see the Introduction in Tracy C. Davis and Thomas Postlewait, eds., *Theatricality* (Cambridge: Cambridge University Press, 2004).
2 It should be acknowledged that there are a number of other companies that could have been included in this study. Pangea World Theater in Minneapolis, for instance, was founded in 1995 with the goal to address the "fundamental paradigm of diversity in our world," http://pangeaworldtheater.org/about, accessed May 30, 2012. Mo'lelo in San Diego is another example that deserves a study in further exploring the relationship between the concept of the world and theater.
3 See Karen Shimakwa, *National Abjection* (Chapel Hill, NC: Duke University Press, 2004). Shimakawa uses Julia Kristeva's concept of abjection to explain how Asian Americanness has been made "not-American" and uses examples from theater and performance to illustrate the process of abjection. According to Shimakawa, "if [paraphrasing Kristeva] the nation must abject itself within the same motion through which it claims to establish itself, it does so by abjecting Asian Americanness, by making it other, foreign, abnormal, *not-American*" (17).
4 Bev Ostroska, "Interview with Ellen Stewart of LaMama Experimental Theater Club, Dec. 9, 1989," *Journal of Dramatic Theory and Criticism* (Fall 1991), 100.
5 Mel Gussow and Bruce Weber, "Ellen Stewart, Off Off Broadway Pioneer, Dies at 91," *The New York Times*, January 13, 2011, http://www.nytimes.com/2011/01/14/theater/14stewart.html?pagewanted=1&_r=1&sq=ellen%20stewart&st=cse&scp=1, accessed February 24, 2012.
6 Ostroska, "Interview with Ellen Stewart," 100.
7 One of the first uses of the term "international theater" can be traced to the 1931 International Festival/Conference of Worker's theaters in Russia. See Valleri J. Hohman, *Russian Culture and Theatrical Performance in America, 1891–1933* (New York: Palgrave Macmillan, 2011).
8 International Theater Institute, Organization for the Performing Arts, "History of the ITI," http://www.iti-worldwide.org/history.php, accessed February 27, 2012.

9 For a discussion on ITI, see Charlotte Canning, "'In the Interest of the State': A Cold War National Theater for the United States," *Theater Journal* 61 (2009): 417, and "Teaching Theater as Diplomacy: A U.S. Hamlet in the European Court," *Theater Topics* 21.2 (2011): 151–163.
10 Rosamond Gilder, "The Theatre and the International Theatre Institute," *Educational Theatre Journal* 14.2 (1962): 113–119, 115.
11 Ostroska, "Interview with Ellen Stewart," 105.
12 Alvin Eng, "Some Place to Be Somebody: La MaMa's Ellen Stewart," in *The Color of Theater: Race, Culture, and Contemporary Performance*, ed. Roberta Uno with Lucy Mae San Pablo Burns (London and New York: Continuum, 2002), 137.
13 Ibid., 138.
14 Stewart also gave artistic home to Cecile Guidote and Filipino American theater during the Marcos dictatorship. Others she supported include SLANT and Mia Yoo, a Korean American who became her successor. Many thanks to Roberta Uno for pointing out these facts.
15 Information on Roberta Uno is based on an interview conducted by the author on June 27, 2000. Also see Uno's Introduction in *The Color of Theater*.
16 For details on New WORLD Theater, see *A History of Asian American Theater* (Cambridge: Cambridge University Press, 2006), 97–101.
17 The NWT website is no longer available, but this mission statement can be found in the press release for the company's thirtieth anniversary exhibit on February 12, 2009 at the University of Massachusetts Amherst library, http://www.library.umass.edu/about-the-libraries/news/press-releases-2/new-world-theater-s-30th-anniversary-a-retrospective-exhibit/, accessed May 31, 2012.
18 Roberta Uno, "Preliminaries," *MELUS* 16 no. 3 (1989): 1.
19 Ibid.
20 Charles Taylor, *Multiculturalism and "The Politics of Recognition"* (Princeton, NJ: Princeton University Press, 1992), 70.
21 Ibid., 70.
22 Ibid., 72.
23 For a discussion of the production, see William Sonnega, "Beyond a Liberal Audience," *African American Performance and Theater History: A Critical Reader*, ed. Harry J. Elam Jr. and David Krasner (Oxford: Oxford University Press, 2010), 88–93.
24 Uno, *The Color of Theater*, 6.
25 Ibid., 7.
26 Ibid., 4.
27 http://www.umass.edu/umhome/about/history.html, accessed May 30, 2012.
28 Taylor, *Multiculturalism and "The Politics of Recognition*," 70.
29 http://www.srtp.org/aboutus.html, accessed May 30, 2012.
30 Ibid.
31 http://www.silkroadrising.org/about, accessed August 17, 2016.
32 http://www.srtp.org/history/productions/dnatrail.html, accessed May 31, 2012.
33 In the production I saw, which was a matinee, the vast majority of attendees were non-Asian Americans.
34 http://www.silkroadrising.org/about, accessed May 31, 2012.
35 For discussions of polyculturalism, see Vijay Prashad, *Everybody Was Kung Fu Fighting: Afro-Asian Connections and the Myth of Cultural Purity* (Boston, MA: Beacon Press, 2002); Robin Kelley, "People in Me," *ZSpace* (July 5, 2003), https://zcomm.org/znetarticle/people-in-me-by-robin-kelley/.

Chapter 6

Homes at the ends of the WORLD

Repertoires of access and agency out of New WORLD Theater (1979–2009)

Paul Bonin-Rodriguez

In 1979, the same year that New WORLD Theater opened, cultural historian and poet Lewis Hyde published a widely read book about art-making, *The Gift: Creativity and the Artist in the Modern World.* Elucidating gift transactions across cultures, *The Gift* argues that "works of art exist simultaneously in two 'economies,' a market economy, and a gift economy," of which, Hyde notes, only the latter is essential. Not surprisingly, given its thesis, the book happens upon a riddle central to a beleaguered arts and creative sector: if, as Hyde asserts, works of art are made trivial when assessed solely on commercial terms; then, conversely, how are artists trivialized when their works are not considered on professional terms?[1] A perfect answer to the riddle would likely address the appropriate amount of giving required of one's gift. The answer might also illustrate a new world for artists, one in which artistic laborers anticipate adequate social, political, and financial capital reward. Given New WORLD Theater's commitment to artists marginalized by color, as well as class, gender, sexuality, and aesthetic, the answer to those questions also models equity and access emerging in an arts infrastructure that has historically supported largely white, hegemonic "high-art" forms.[2]

It is easy to draw a line between *The Gift* and New WORLD Theater, not only in terms of the book's focus on a cultural economy and its progressive politics, but New WORLD's place in Amherst, Massachusetts. In his opening chapter, Hyde introduces the concept of an "Indian gift" as a gift that grows through repeated exchange. As Hyde notes, upon receiving gifts, the English had done the unthinkable and turned their gifts into commodities. Their failure to give back and give more generously, effectively keeping the cycle going and growing, prompted the native people to ask for their original gifts to be returned.[3]

As one of a team of artists creating a work about Latino men and AIDS at New WORLD Theater in 1997, one of my collaborators, Michael Marinez, kept challenging us to consider how we might include Jeffery Amherst's proposed "gift" of smallpox-infested blankets to the Native Americans after the Pontiac Rebellion in 1763.[4] For Michael, the poisoned gift and killing off a colonized people was an apt metaphor for the delayed response to AIDS of the Reagan Administration. In his assertion of the role of Amherst, after whom the town was named, my colleague embodied the mission of New WORLD, the one in which difficult questions were asked, cultural challenges addressed, and artistic solutions offered through professional relationships as well as gift and gifted exchanges of art and politics.

This article demonstrates how New WORLD Theater's relationship with artists represents a significant and early intervention in U.S. cultural policies and practices, then and now. To accomplish this task, I articulate how New WORLD Theater negotiated and balanced both gift and professional transactions through its production operations and the politics of space. Borrowing from Diana Taylor's notion of a "repertoire" as an embodied practice in which "people participate in the production and reproduction of knowledge by "being there,"[5] I believe New WORLD Theater catalyzed "material repertoires" of agency for artists. For Taylor, repertoires explain how performances, in their many forms, "function as vital acts of transfer, transmitting social knowledge, memory, and a sense of identity."[6] Through programs such as New Works for a New World, Project 2050, and Future Aesthetics, as well as the Intersections conferences, New WORLD staged not only performances, but performances *about* the field of performance, through which artists, scholars, and arts organizers imagined and enacted a more just cultural future. This volume's call for submissions suggested that the legacy of NWT largely resides in its "commitment to artistic practice, community engagement, scholarship, and social justice." Here I suggest that we also include artist professionalization and policy development as part of that legacy.

As this anthology and Roberta Uno's *The Color of Theater* demonstrate, a significant number of artists of color and allies developed unique practices and voices at New WORLD. In the process, these artists became what I define as "artist-producers," individuals who have the ability to make work and make its conditions possible, and who recognize their relationship to the spaces that host them as performances of equitably shared leadership and responsibility. Playing the role of artist-producer alongside the host spaces allows productions to emerge from shared decision-making processes about aesthetics and substance, but also marketing, community engagement, and even documentation, to name a few. As artist lê thi diem thúy observes, "New WORLD Theater" nurtured a kind of openness to what is possible. An openness grounded in vision and the vision allows you to take risks."[7] This openness was made manifest through its visionary programming, which anticipated significant shifts that would come to arts and creative sector.

My method for this cultural policy analysis is the stories of artists who have worked at New WORLD Theater—including lê thi diem thúy, Danny Hoch, and myself—juxtaposed to the policy concerns of an era. As an artist who studies cultural policy development, I believe that the answers to long-held concerns about artist sustainability, particularly among artists marginalized by identity, aesthetics, and tradition, can be found in the stories we share about artists and arts organizers working *as partners*. Such interactions represent ongoing artist-producer and host space negotiations over practices and investments addressing artistic work, institutional and artistic identity, and audience or community makeup.

These conversations, effectively transactions of social, political, emotional, and material gifts and rewards, are in fact iterations of a cultural policy development in situ. I identify artistic practice as a form of policy development for two very important reasons: to signal the organizational role artists play through their work, and to recognize the capacity anticipated by organizations today.

The fields of performance and cultural policy development share a methodological and theoretical relationship through "the argumentative turn" in public policy analysis and policy making, a movement that emerged in the academy in the early 1990s. Rejecting previous, "neopositivist" methodologies that presumed policy could be the direct application of social science theories and data analysis, policy analysts turned to more performative ones. Over two decades, argumentative policy's strategies expanded to include "practical argumentation, policy judgment, frame analysis, narrative storytelling, and rhetorical analysis, among others."[8] Argumentative frame analysis and performance analysis alike avail themselves of meta-analytical assessments, taking into account the core assumptions and power relations informing approaches, judgments, and decisions in pursuit of social justice.[9] As writer, performer, and actor Danny Hoch notes, New WORLD positioned artists marginalized by identity and aesthetics as "central to American culture, not on the margins."[10] Consequently, New WORLD's own policy development work anticipated America's changing demographic and modeled a progressive form of artist engagement.

At some point in 1996, on behalf of myself and two colleagues, Beto Araiza and Michael Marinez, I called Roberta Uno and asked if we might create a show at New WORLD, to be called *Quinceañera*—a celebration of survival for the fifteen years of the AIDS pandemic for U.S. Latino gay men, derived from the coming-of-age celebration for Latina girls. I had met Roberta at a National Performance Network (NPN) meeting, and the theater's mission seemed appropriate to what we wanted to do. Roberta responded openly and constructively to my rushed, nervous phone pitch. She asked for a proposal and some form of budget, which Beto, Michael, and I submitted. Together with her input—which included budget adjustments and narrative taming—we began to look for resources to support the show. When early fundraising met with mixed results, she asked us to consider working with Joe Salvatore, an MFA student in dramaturgy and directing at the University of Massachusetts Amherst (UMass), so she could access instructional resources. Although he was not Latino and much younger than we, and by his own account, largely unfamiliar with our direct experiences of loss during the AIDS crisis, he appeared to us an additional resource and proved a devoted member of the team.[11] In February 1997, after numerous, self-financed meetings among Michael, Beto, and me, we arrived in Amherst with a few scenes, a few costume ideas, a few props, and a few songs for a ten-day development period as part of New WORLD's commissioning program, New Works for a New World. Our residency activities included multiple community engagements, meals with staff designers and crew, art-making workshops at an AIDS crisis center and with a Latino gay men's group, as well as an interview on a Spanish-language radio program. It also included an open rehearsal during which a theater class watched as we composed and shaped, from some notes we had put together, one of the most critical moments of the show, "The Creed," which asserted our beliefs and affirmations forged through grief.[12]

Beto was already an accomplished writer-performer and arts organizer, as was I; Michael had a long history of working with the advocacy group ACT UP and a skill for generating material and relationships from community engagement work.[13] A somewhat competitive, creative spirit among us allowed us to improve on each other's ideas and to gather constituents who would respond well to our various ways of doing things. Our days and evenings were spent in these meetings and in rehearsal; our nights and early mornings were spent rewriting or assembling props. We also went through costume fittings, sound checks, tech rehearsal, and final dress at a time when the show was just shy of being fully scripted. We worked with a dramaturg, UMass graduate student Lucy Mae San Pablo Burns. At a critical moment just a few days before opening, she and Joey, as a dramaturgical team, helped us restructure the scenes and the arc of the show. The professional crew was kept entertained by Michael, who mixed a "theatah" affect with old Bette Midler concert shtick and disarmingly referred to the production team as "my fellow theater wizards!" While Michael entertained the crew, Beto, Joey, and I focused on edits, as well as lighting and sound cues. On the night before we opened, Roberta, who had been a constant and calm presence, asked me how I thought it would go. After I had shared my concerns, she responded, "If you were absolutely confident, I would be worried."

Roberta's comment destabilized my fear that she, as a "patron," expected a perfect outcome, and reframed my understanding of the organization as a "partner" in both the risk and the reward. I had launched into touring as a solo artist with already-formed scripts and a spirited performance in the absence of a polished one. I worked in the theater, but I considered myself a "performer," since I relied more on instinct and background in dance than formal theater training that Beto had.

The idea that I could open a production that was not complete, but with so much support, was also counter to the codes of acculturation under which I had been brought up. Difference was silenced at home and in public; permission and access were not presumed, but would have to be earned by charm, harder work, craftiness, or obstacles endured. José Esteban Muñoz's theory of "disidentification" describes how minoritarian subjects construct identities in resistance to "the cultural logistics of heteronormativity, white supremacy, and misogyny—cultural logics that . . . undergird state power."[14] Drawing on the work of performers including Marga Gomez, Carmelita Tropicana, Vaginal Creme Davis, Muñoz frames "disidentifactory" performances as out-loud responses to an individual's recognition of her exclusion from social, political, and economic power structures. New WORLD's engagement with our development process offered Michael, Beto, and me an alternative space to state power, invested in us as artists and as people. Our coopting of the Latina coming-of-age ceremony to explore our experiences of AIDS amounted to a disidentificatory performance; however, the organization's insistence that we had something important to say, and that a team was at hand to participate, lateralized our relationship to the theater. Moreover, the development support that New WORLD and, later, San Antonio's Jump-Start Performance Co. procured under the NPN Creation Fund served as risk capital to help us begin touring under our own leadership after our appearance at the first Intersections conference in 1998.

Echoing our experience, thúy explained how her development process for *the bodies between us* for New Voices for a New World expanded her capacities as an artist:

> I don't think I would have found, and certainly wouldn't have been able to afford, on my own, such an extensive level of support for my work. I felt like Roberta was saying, "You need to develop a number of different strengths in order to embody and deliver this work. How can we help you do that?"[15]

That same year, thúy's first solo authored piece, *Red Fiery Summer*, was presented at UMass and the International Women's Playwright Festival in Galway, Ireland. To the *bodies* commission, which was directed by Roberta, thúy brought a prose script with chapter headings, but no concrete idea of how to set the work. She credits New WORLD for matching her with scenic designer Miguel Romero, who constructed the play's central net structure, based on a dream she had about the show. A multi-disciplinary artist without an extensive theater background, thúy was also paired with a voice coach, choreographer Maura Nguyen Donohue, and Max Palar, a member of the Double Edge Theater ensemble in Ashfield, Massachusetts, who taught her White Crane, an Indonesian martial arts discipline that focuses on a grounded stance and hand gestures. Resisting the idea that she co-produced the show with New WORLD, thúy nevertheless concedes that her work at New WORLD helped her take a leadership role when she created her third performance work in Marfa, Texas, some years later.[16]

Two other New WORLD initiatives also illustrate the theater's visionary approach to allying artists as partners to an arts organization. Project 2050, a youth-centered artist-development program, addressed New WORLD's embrace of "the principles of racial visibility, access, autonomy, within the context of coalition and community-building" in anticipation of the year "when Caucasians will become a minority in the United States."[17] And Future Aesthetics supported the development of innovative, cross-disciplinary approaches to theater and performance embodied by the hip-hop phenomenon.[18] Danny Hoch recalls bringing two shows to New WORLD Theater, *Some People* (1994) and *Jails, Hospitals, and Hip-Hop* (1997) before being invited to develop new material in dialogue "with many theater artists who were blazing new trails or breaking new ground in these kinds of polycultural aesthetics that were also the center of my work," including UNIVERSES' Stephen Sapp and Mildred Ruiz, Will Power, Marc Bamuthi Joseph, Claudia Alick, and others:

> For those programs, we got to be in the same room together. If we weren't working together, then we were working on our own projects in the same place and at the same time. New WORLD offered us a place to discuss and develop our work, and our political and artistic visions. Those discussions reinforced the work we were doing as individual artists and as part of a community. . . . Just by virtue of being in a room, a big room, and having these conversations, that gave us a sense of empowerment. I might not have been thinking, "Hey I could go start a hip-hop theater festival" had I not been there with other artists who were sharing and strategizing their artistic visions.[19]

For Hoch, the convenings had the effect of not only promoting the development of an aesthetic and testing the bounds of a genre, but tasking artists to be organizers of a cultural future. For him, New WORLD's work in these programs represented a radical re-imagining of artists' professional repertoires a decade later, one still not taken up by regional theaters who are still focused on subscriber-based economic models "and audiences who are over sixty and white."[20]

The experiences of deep artistic, organizational, and community engagement shared by thúy, Danny, my collaborators, and me occurred at the same moment and even anticipated the findings of a critical juncture in U.S. arts and culture policy development. In 1997, the 92nd American Assembly convened on the subject of "The Arts and the Public Purpose." Bringing together "artists, arts executives, critics, business men and women, foundation officers, academics, politicians, and policy makers" from across the political spectrum and across the country to discuss "The Arts and the Public Purpose." The convening drew on contemporary policy issues, ongoing economic and social research, and the nation's cultural history to diagnose the nation's arts and culture infrastructure crises and to establish a sustainable "policy paradigm." The meeting's four key themes addressed the role of art on national identity, quality of life and economic growth, lifelong education, and individual expression.[21] The culture wars of the early 1990s, the cutting of the budget of the National Endowment for the Arts (NEA), and a referendum in publicly funded art in general, had put a spotlight on a nonprofit infrastructure in crises. The growth of the NEA and the nonprofit sector during the "Ford era" of funding produced a bloated nonprofit infrastructure by the end of the 1980s. Many arts organizations found themselves precipitously balancing their own sustainability concerns with political- and mission-based commitments to artists.[22] The theory of "cost disease"—the idea that successful arts organizations generally grow to exceed their capacity to fundraise for their ongoing work—has been around since William Baumol and William Bowen first diagnosed it in the 1960s.[23] Within the broad diagnostic and prescriptive agenda of "The Arts and the Public Purpose," artists and arts organizations would have to take equal shares in supporting a healthy arts economy.

The comprehensive approach of "The Arts and the Public Purpose" set forth a policy agenda in which artists were positioned as part of a larger project, even as they were understood as critical to its genetic makeup. It is important to note that in the report's final recommendations, artists are explicitly mentioned only three times. Their absence from the list may be connected to a culture-wars tarnish on artists' image, the broader ecosystemic goals pursued at the convening, or perhaps the failure of the policy sector to identify where its findings would lead it. Two mentions in the report's numbered recommendations put artists alongside, rather than within, the nation's arts infrastructure: along with "arts institutions," artists are called to identify and pursue "public purposes" (#1); public and private funders are tasked to ensure "financial stability for serious artists and arts organizations" (#3); and the report recommends the recognition of "artists as critical to America's artistic heritage" under the rubric of "preservation efforts" (#5).[24]

All of these approaches were already being put into place by New WORLD's programming. The organization's public purpose addressed "community and coalition building efforts."[25] New WORLD had established the means to support financial stability specifically by modeling it, but also by recognizing artists as co-producers of their work and of a cultural future. New Works for a New WORLD had already recognized artists as critical to America's diverse heritage. Within a very short time, New WORLD would take a lead in *artist* cultural policy development through paradigmatic programs like the 1998 Intersections conference, Project 2050, and Future Aesthetics.

Other recommendations in "The Arts and the Public Purpose" report address the repertoires already being cultivated by New WORLD and gesture toward more artist-led cultural policy development. The report's call for "partnerships among the commercial, not-for-profit, and unincorporated arts sector" (#2) can be said to hail artists for reasons both organizational and political: artists can only work as for-profit professionals or community-invested volunteers. Also, as the culture-war examples of photographer Andres Serrano and performers Karen Finley, John Fleck, Holly Hughes, and Tim Miller demonstrated, artists embody the public purposes of the spaces where they work.[26] On those same terms, the recommendation that "public and private funders, and commercial arts entities"—an organizational distinction that can include artists, since artist generally "fund" work through an equation that includes donated labor—create work in "geographically disadvantaged communities" (#4) was taken up equally by the artists who engaged in community activities beyond the campus.[27] Finally, New WORLD staged convenings through which artists actively worked to imagine and construct the conditions for their professional futures.

From its beginnings as "a student-organizing project" at UMass to its evolution as a "presenting, producing, commissioning, and play development"—and, I would argue, artist-producer-development program—New WORLD Theater emerged as an innovator in its field, artistically and organizationally. As dance historian Sally Banes has written, universities have long played a role in supporting artists who work outside of a cultural mainstream.[28] Despite its placement, or perhaps because of it, New WORLD's approach to avant-garde work embraced what was being performed and who was performing it through its radical assertion of theater by people of color as legitimate. Although we might have used the word "pampered" to explain the comparatively extreme supportive environment my colleagues and I faced, in truth, we were more "energized" and called to meet up as eye-to-eye partners in our process. For many artists, the recognition of how radical New WORLD's imagining of its artists was has been borne out over time, through subsequent shows and processes. Says Hoch:

> I don't think I thought about what I took from NWT at the time. I just went forward. I know I took the knowledge that it wasn't just me that was trying to do this work, which I think I knew already. And I took the vision that it was actually possible for me to gather all of these fellow artists of my generation, many of us who were working in bubbles, and bring us together under one roof.[29]

The legacy of New WORLD Theater can be found in the ongoing work of its artists, many of whom have widened their "bubbles" and played organizational roles, establishing new programs and new practices, like Hoch, or who have just continued working, like thúy, whose novel *The Gangster We Are All Looking For* was published in 2003. It can also be found in the ArtChangeUS: Arts in a Changing America, a new initiative led by Roberta Uno that "seeks to explore and understand the dramatic demographic transformation of the United States and its profound impact on arts and culture."[30] As these examples demonstrate, the work of *organizing for the work* is a project now shared, or rather co-produced, by artists and organizers alike.

Notes

1 Lewis Hyde, *The Gift : Creativity and the Artist in the Modern World*, 25th Anniversary ed. (New York: Vintage Books, 2007), xvi, xix.
2 See Holly Sidford, "Fusing Arts, Culture, and Social Change," *National Committee for Responsible Philanthropy*, 2011. http://www.ncrp.org/files/publications/Fusing_Arts_Culture_Social_Change.pdf. For a history of the development of New WORLD Theater's mission, see Roberta Uno, "Introduction," in *The Color of Theater: Race, Culture, and Contemporary Performance*, ed. Uno with Lucy Mae San Pablo Burns (London and New York: Continuum, 2002), 3–17.
3 Hyde, *The Gift,* 3–5.
4 Howard Zinn, *A People's History of the United States* (New York: Harper Perennial, 1980), 86.
5 Diana Taylor, *The Archive and the Repertoire: Performing Cultural Memory in the Americas* (Durham, NC: Duke University Press, 2003), 20.
6 Ibid., 2–3.
7 Interview with the author, June 11, 2012.
8 Frank Fischer and Herbert Gottweis, "Introduction," in *The Argumentative Turn Revisited: Public Policy as Communicative Practice*, ed. Frank Fischer and Herbert Gottweis (Durham, NC: Duke University Press, 2012), 1–3.

9 Joni Maya Cherbo and Margaret Jane Wyszomirski, "Mapping the Public Life of Arts in America," in *The Public Life of Arts in America*, ed. Joni Maya Cherbo and Margaret Jane Wyszomirski (New Brunswick, NJ: Rutgers University Press, 2000), 8.
10 Interview with the author, July 11, 2012.
11 Joe Salvatore, "Collaboration/Celebration: Introduction to *Quinceañera*," in *The Color of Theater*, 257–259.
12 The script of *Quinceañera* is reproduced in *The Color of Theater*, 261–301.
13 Alberto Antonio Araiza, communication with the author, May 31, 2012.
14 José Esteban Muñoz, *Disidentifications: Queers of Color and the Performance of Politics* (Minneapolis, MN: University of Minnesota Press, 1999), 5.
15 lê thi diem thúy interview.
16 Ibid.
17 Uno, "Introduction," 10.
18 Uno, "The 5th Element," *American Theater* (April 2004): 85.
19 Hoch interview. The artist adds, "Maybe Claudia Alick wouldn't have been thinking about making waves in diversified programming at Oregon Shakespeare Festival. I haven't talked to her about it, so I don't know."
20 Says Hoch, who served on the Theater Communications Group's board of directors, "I've seen on the TCG board, when they say, 'How do you see the Theater being diversified?' they're just humoring you. They're not changing. Roberta actually expected results. You were invited to the gathering because you were expected to create a result [to model change]. She really believes in changing the old guard, not just the people, but the whole system." See also Todd London, Ben Pesner, and Zannie Giraud Voss, *Outrageous Fortune: The Life and Times of the New American Play* (New York: Theater Development Fund, 2009).
21 "The Arts and the Public Purpose: Final Report of the Ninety-Second American Assembly" (New York: American Assembly, 1997), 6. See also Cherbo and Wyszomirski, "Mapping the Public Life."
22 For a description of the "Ford Era," the period during which the nonprofit grant model was developed and institutionalized, see John Kreidler, "Leverage Lost: Evolution in the Nonprofit Arts Ecosystem," in *The Politics of Culture: Policy Perspectives for Individuals, Institutions, and Communities*, ed. Gigi Bradford, Michael Gary, and Glenn Wallach (New York: New Press, 2000), 147–168. See also Bill Ivey, *Arts, Inc.: How Greed and Neglect Have Destroyed Our Cultural Rights* (Berkeley, CA: University of California Press, 2008); and Cherbo and Wyszomirski, 11.
23 See William J. Baumol and William G. Bowen, *Performing Arts, the Economic Dilemma: A Study of Problems Common to Theater, Opera, Music, and Dance* (1966, repr. Millwood, NY: Krauss Reprint Co., 1978).
24 "The Arts and the Public Purpose: Final Report," 7–8.
25 Uno, "Introduction," 7.
26 See Michael Brenson, *Visionaries and Outcasts: The NEA, Congress, and the Place of the Visual Artist in America* (New York: New Press, 2001).
27 For a discussion of "discounted labor," see Kreidler, "Leverage Lost," 148–149.
28 Sally Banes, "Institutionalizing Avant-Garde Performance: A Hidden History of University Patronage in the United States," in *Contours of the Theatrical Avant-Garde: Performance and Textuality*, ed. James Harding (Ann Arbor, MI: University of Michigan Press, 2000).
29 Hoch interview.
30 http://artsinachangingamerica.org/.

Chapter 7

Imagining a "New WORLD"

Asian American women playwrights' archives in western Massachusetts

Lucy Mae San Pablo Burns

In the early 1990s, Roberta Uno, founding artistic director of New WORLD Theater, instituted the Uno Collection of Plays by Asian American women playwrights at the University of Massachusetts-Amherst.[1] Housed at the W.E.B. Du Bois Library, this extraordinary collection currently holds over 200 plays as well as supplementary materials documenting the work of Asian American women playwrights. While the collection contains the writings of many contemporary playwrights, such as Alice Tuan, Jeannie Barroga, and Velina Hasu Houston, it also houses rare materials by early writers, including those of Gladys Ling-ai Li, a Hawai'i based playwright whose play was staged in New York as early as 1924.[2] My discussion of the emergence of this particular archiving project is embedded in multiple understandings of the term "archive" and of the processes of "archiving" within the specific context of Asian American women playwrights. I use "archive" and "archiving" here to mean the gathering of objects, in this case plays by Asian American women, for preservation and centralization of access. I deploy these terms to equally refer to the process by which an institutional entity emerges as a source of and material site for plays by Asian American women. Such a history of the Uno Collection is thus grounded in an understanding of archival projects as always already engaged in entangled structures of poetics, power and politics.[3]

The Uno Collection is unique in that it is one of few institutions that specifically archives the plays of Asian American women playwrights.[4] Of crucial importance here is that it is directly attached to a theater company and a university.[5] The works of Asian American women playwrights may be found in other collections, such as the East West Players (housed at UCLA) and the Asian American Theater Company (housed at UCSB). These companies' official archives primarily store scripts of plays that have been produced in their season productions while individual theater companies usually oversee and fund their own preservation and documentation processes.[6] Centralized archiving institutions such as the New York Public Library's Performing Arts Library have, over the years, equally amassed a formidable collection of diverse dramatic materials. A repository of plays/performance texts by Asian American women, I will suggest, figures the very dynamics of archival formation, not simply as a site of preservation but rather as a venue for theorizing processes of production, dissemination, and appropriation. I analyze the emergence of the Uno Collection primarily through an engagement with debates around archivization in Asian American Studies and Performance Studies. To do so, I delineate a strategic overview of the contents of this archive, highlighting a few key works and artists. Such an effort moves beyond the language of summary to signal the "discursive construction and proliferation" of "Asian American women playwrights" made possible through the creation of the Uno Collection (Kang 12). This categorical formation, "Asian American women playwrights," makes apparent a community otherwise effaced within the vastness and whiteness of American theater. My chapter closes with a set of provocations that emerge from the formation and institutionalization of archives such as the Uno Collection.

The management of race in American theater

In order to understand the significance of the Uno Collection of Plays by Asian American playwrights, I briefly consider how a project like New WORLD Theater is situated within and without reparative racial policies and practices in American theater in the last three decades of the twentieth century. American theater has struggled with its own history of racism, which includes overt exclusionary practices that denied theater artists employment based on their race, lack of source materials on stage that conveys a fuller and complex representation of different racialized communities that make up the United States, and histories of blackface, yellowface, redface, and brownface. Attempts to correct these racist institutional practices can be seen in the establishment of the Actor's Equity, the formation of Non-traditional Casting Project which includes color-blind and race-neutral casting. These reparative projects grapple with the disconnect between liberal notions of theater as an institution and a practice rooted in ideals of a "neutral body" and how the racialized performing body challenges this notion. Within these ongoing attempts and experiments by different constituencies of American theater, through its policies, initiatives, and creative/artistic endeavors to contain, manage, alleviate, and confront its own racism and the racialized performing body on stage, how do we make sense of the New WORLD Theater?

What does it mean to manage race? Is race manageable? Manage suggests handling, administering, disciplining, coping, and controlling; it also implies a way of neatly approaching a difficult task or subject that privileges data gathering towards compliance. I articulate the task of dealing with the "problems" posed by the topic of race and the presence of racialized bodies in the institution of theater here as "managing race" to point to the limits of policies and initiatives that sought to reconcile the ever-shifting grounds of race in the US, treating race as problem that can indeed be reconciled. "Managing race" refers to the material ways that race and racialized bodies were handled through various cultural policies which were attempts to address exclusionary practices in casting, in hiring artistic, administrative, and technical staff. Policies and other like-initiatives also worked to address what plays were getting produced. Connected to all hiring and what is being produced on stage, "management of race" sought to reflect the racial diversity of the American society with who occupied theater seats. For example, initiatives such as audience development programs provided the avenue to slot in plays by and about people of color. Such management strategies were meant to address the multi-dimensional problem of race in American theater.

I take this opportunity to think through the creative experiment of New WORLD Theater, as an attempt to take a more critical approach that confronts the fundamental and profound erasure of racialized peoples in American theater, while also acknowledging the impossibility of a complete confrontation and salvation. NWT begins with the premise that racialized peoples and the shifting relations of power that "race" represents deserve and require attention, a stage of its own, not as additive or after-thought. Imaging race, as opposed to managing race, sought to confront the challenges of the shifting grounds of relations of power and representational structures. Furthermore, New WORLD Theater began with a premise that the institution of American Theater is constitutive of race relations and racialized difference. The task therefore is to acknowledge, remember, and explore therefore imagining its possibilities, including its limits and failures. It is through this understanding of New WORLD Theater as a construct within the racial discourse in American Theater that I proceed with my discussion of the Uno Collection of Plays by Asian American Women playwrights.

Genealogies, archives, politics

While this chapter tells the story of the specific emergence of the Uno Collection, I make sense of this project through the question of "archive" in both Performance Studies and Asian American Studies. In doing so, my goal is to frame the story of the Uno Collection within and outside the politics of established archival practice. The foundation of the Uno Collection extends and complicates such inherited genealogies of archival formation in Asian American and Performance Studies. The emergence (temporally and spatially) of the Uno Collection in western Massachusetts foregrounds the archival convergences and divergences of Asian American Studies and Performance Studies. I am especially interested in some of the shared archival preoccupations of these two fields and their intersection with a community-based project such as the Uno Collection. As Performance Studies scholar Diana Taylor writes, "What makes an object archival is the *process whereby it is selected, classified, and presented for analysis.*"[7] For Taylor the emergence of an object as "archival" is an active and conscious undertaking that involves deliberate classification, selection, and presentation. Taylor's insistence on the active, embodied, and historical practices of archival formation is key here to my concerns on the practice of archiving and its relationship to performative expressions of community and self-identity. As I hope to demonstrate, the process of building the Uno Collection, and by extension any archive, is one of calling up a community into being.

Archiving practices in the fields of Theater and Performance Studies and Asian American Studies have elaborated common concerns around what and who gets archived. In Theater and Performance Studies, the question of what constitutes archival objects is complicated by performance and embodiment that are not captured in text-based materials. Taylor's critically acclaimed *The Archive and Repertoire* propels debates on archive and performance within Theater and Performance Studies. She critiques the process that led up to the dominance of texts as *the* objects that make up the archive. She proposes the "repertoire" as an alternative concept for the archival formation, underscoring the embodied and textured forms of recording and performing history. Useful here is Taylor's emphasis on how the social relations produced by historical conditions directly influence what gets constituted as archival objects. More specifically, Taylor has provocatively argued that European colonialism (as historical condition) produced domination and hegemony as determining social relations that naturalized the written text and writing as objects worthy of archiving. That is, the colonial archive's privileging of text-based materials routinely suppressed other forms of expressions. By offering the idea of the repertoire, Taylor proposes an alternative that shifts a text-based paradigm towards the inclusion of embodied expressions of self- and community identity.

Such a shift in archival practices has been prominent in Asian American Studies, a field formation preoccupied with the (re)collection of silenced and lost voices, disappeared and distorted by racism in U.S. society. More generally, Asian American Studies has vigorously promoted a "community-based" first-voice perspective that prioritizes the point of view of Asians in America. Academics play a key role in the recovery and constitution of archives as they can be made to mobilize the resources of the University to support the community. Asian American Studies encourages projects that break down the hierarchical relationship between academia and community, that are driven by community needs, and that make a recognizable impact on the community. Scholarship production within Asian American Studies must be understood as a transformative project that should be accessible and relevant to the community. As the field of Asian American Studies dynamically changes and adjusts, its commitment to recovery projects and to community continues even as it struggles to account for what Lisa Lowe calls Asian America's "heterogeneity, hybridity, and multiplicity."[8] At stake here is a sustained interrogation of the ideological entailments that fuel and fracture Asian American Studies' historical attachment to the very idea of the community and the archive. Any invocation of the Uno Collection must thus necessarily engage its situatedness at the cusp of multiple archival initiatives: a performance studies project that focuses on the inclusion of embodied self and community expressions and an Asian American Studies project that attempts recovery amidst the detritus of historical racism and elision.

The Uno Collection provides a key instantiation of the force of multiple archival logics. As I elaborate later, the Uno Collection disrupts, even transforms, what Asian American Studies historian Stephen Sumida has termed the hegemony of the "Californic-paradigm" or the "Pacific-dominated" paradigm within Asian American Studies.[9] Sumida's description of Asian American Studies' earlier trajectory productively critiques the dominance of scholarship and institutional formations that "originate" in California, the unmarked point of origin for the Asian American Studies imaginary. His formulation challenges Asian American Studies scholars to closely examine privileged intellectual and political constructs such as the concept of community, so key to any teleology of minority development. Sumida's call for a re-imagining of Asian American Studies de-links location, majority, and longevity as primary categories for the composition and emergence of community. Within such re-imaginings, the concept of community becomes primarily a space of the imagination, anchored to narratives that may or may not be attached to more conventional geographies of Asian migration.

The Uno Collection is an artist-centered archiving process in which the artists determine the contents of the collection. It is an exemplar of the multiple forms through which a community chooses to record (or disappear) itself. Here, the artist chooses what she submits to the archive, thereby maintaining partial control of the archiving process and what it might mean to her. It is also thus a vivid and strikingly "living archive."[10] In this context, this "living archive" refers to how these materials are attached to a place of production. The allusion to "liveness" foregrounds the continued process of archival evolution (if you will), and the life of the works archived in it. Of equal significance is that the Uno Collection is directly connected to a theater-producing institution, one that supports and manages the "liveness" of the archive. From its inception, the Uno Collection was designed to expand and remain active. The Uno Collection's affiliation with an educational institution that incorporates the contents of the archive into the curriculum clearly authorizes some of the frames through which the works and the artists in this archive, and the archive itself, may be understood and interpreted. In other words, the Uno Collection is housed within a structure that can produce knowledge about itself, even as it continues to emerge as a space of knowledge formation. In what follows, I detail Uno Collection's histories of emergence within a multi-racial theater company and an Asian American-led organization in New England.

A New WORLD, a new archive: global theater in rural Massachusetts

to have my work archived means

i have a voice beyond myself

to have my work archived

with other Asian American women writers means

i am part of a community of women

diverse in experiences, cultures, generations

and artistic expressions

to have my work archived means

it is possible that some distant day

a young sister struggling for her voice,

might stumble upon us and realize,

hey, these women have lived and found a way to tell their stories

i can do it too

to have my work archived means

my voice is part of the colorful, unruly, eurythmic choir that is Americana

(Nobuko Miyamoto)[11]

I imagine my words blending among sister playwrights, as safe as a locket, as independent as stone. My daughters and my daughters' daughters will move on, but I smile knowing they have a glimpse of who I once was.

(Louella Dizon)[12]

Any discussion of the Uno Collection of Plays by Asian American women must include an understanding of the organization that formed and coordinated this project in process. Other chapters in this collection already provide details about how this theater organization came into formation and its eventual closure. As mentioned earlier, this archive project was initiated and established by the NWT's founding director Roberta Uno. One may well ask, what is a nearly 30-year-old-theater by, about, and for people of color doing in the hinterlands of western Massachusetts? Perhaps such a question no longer needs to be asked, but in 1979, when playwright-director Roberta Uno had just dreamed up the idea of a multi-racial, global theater company, it was one that did not seem to belong in a rural western Massachusetts town.[13] From its inception, New WORLD Theater—originally named Third World Theater—filled a lacuna in the academic curriculum, as well as asserted narrative and aesthetic points of view that were underrepresented and directly excluded in the canon of American theater. NWT's mission exceeded strict university boundaries. After all, those who worked at the university belonged to other social networks outside of the university. Hence, this artistic organization serviced and found its support from those in the local community who sought and believed in the labor of culture in calling up a community.

In its early years, NWT productions primarily operated within the politics of inclusion through representation. In other words, they staged plays to present stories and experiences of people of color not typically dramatized on the American stage. Their productions confronted and defied racism in the larger American society and in its microcosm, American theater. An artistic team of actors and designers, who were students as well as non-university theater artists living in western Massachusetts, usually made up NWT's artistic, technical, and administrative staff. Yet from the very beginning, Uno was clear that the NWT project was not primarily about *integration*. She did not see this project as solely about claiming its rightful place within an existing canon or caliber of standards in American theater. As Uno elaborates,

> New WORLD Theater, as a theater of artists of color, was never an *integration* project, we were a *desegregation* project—and that is an important distinction. We never intended to join the existing structure of American theater or higher education. Nor did we aspire to reform those structures. Our goal was, as artists, to gain access to the means of production, however temporally, and transform the environment. We knew we were the people who weren't supposed to be there in the first place. And we have been creating "guerrilla" transformations of spaces—formal theater space and informal community space—for twenty-two years.[14]

NWT was focused on setting its own sets of standards that accounted for what mainstream white American theater did not. It was a project of paradigm transformation, and thus was not an exclusionary project. NWT supported all theater artists who imagine a new world, who offer a vision of transformation. True to its desire to disrupt standards, the renaming from Third World Theater to New WORLD Theater signaled a forward-looking and more capacious politics. While "Third World" described the politics that imagined the emergence of NWT, "New WORLD" signified a dynamic politics of always imagining new ways of being, creating, and relating.

NWT's multi-dimensional programming commitments that included producing and presenting theatrical works simultaneously involved collecting play scripts and supplementary materials and occasionally artists interviews.[15] Artistic director Uno taught University of Massachusetts-Amherst courses—such as "Third World Theater," "American Theater and Race," and "Contemporary Plays by Women of Color"—that integrated the theater's season productions into the course curriculum. These courses were laboratories for theorizing a radical genre of work, where frameworks and approaches included inquiry into modes and means of production and circulation. NWT also presented touring works by artists, in addition to producing and developing new works.[16] Hence, visiting artists gave classroom lectures, offering the students an opportunity to engage with the performance, dramatic literature, and aesthetic in the works of contemporary artists of color. It also trained students in skills such as oral history by assigning, for example, artist interviews that become part of the archival collection. At a personal level, I directly benefited from this pedagogical practice as a student and a teacher in training. Our intellectual and artistic training urged us to re-imagine the archival process as one of transparency and collaboration, as opposed to one of surveillance and cataloguing.[17]

Initially, Uno had reservations about establishing an archive of this significance in western Massachusetts. She had been collecting scripts and did not necessarily have a consistent system of storing these materials. She was also working on her first anthology of plays by Asian American women, *Unbroken Thread*. Uno considered sending the scripts to a place where the materials would be more accessible in a geographical and institutional center that had a large, established Asian American community, as well as an academic institution that already supported Asian American Studies.[18] Ultimately however, Uno's choice to build this archive at the University of Massachusetts-Amherst is a statement about Asian American community formation in the US: "We are everywhere, and such spaces [the university, western Massachusetts, the archive] belong to us as well."[19] Thus the Uno Collection is not only archiving an emergent culture—the practice of theater making by Asian American women; it is also a cultural practice in itself. The creation of the Uno Collection not only accessed and showcased Asian American communities in marginal locations, but in doing so, also creates future communities of alliance through its collection of Asian American writings.

As noted earlier, formations such as the Uno Collection, the East of California Caucus, and Asian American Studies in the South interrupt "Californic-paradigm" or "Pacific-dominated" paradigm within Asian American Studies. These projects make us attentive to the literal presence of Asian Americans in places outside of California, Hawai'i, and the Pacific Coast of the US, where large concentrations of Asian Americans reside. However, they also challenge the categories of analysis that hinge on majoritarian politics. They make us rethink the terms in which we seek to be included or visible. The political project then, as Uno asserts, is to acknowledge and create the community where you are and resist reifying "centers" of community formation. This differentiated relationship to Asian America emerges from a political practice of coalition and an understanding of racial formation (and its representation) as relational. In other words, the process by which Asian American subjects and communities become racialized is in direct relation to other racialized communities.

In my consideration of the politics of the archive and archiving through the Uno Collection, the notion of performance as ephemeral provides another possibility for re-thinking community, specifically in regards to the link between belonging and time. The presumption is that a community forms over time and hence deserves recognition and acceptance. Performance and the university setting urge a re-thinking of longevity and fixity as hegemonic values guiding our principles of what constitutes community and the politics of community. Student contributors to the establishment of the Uno Collection accurately demonstrate my point. Those of us who worked with Uno were students temporarily making our home in a largely unfamiliar western Massachusetts.[20] My involvement with the archive and the theater taught me to acknowledge and engage with the local community that supported the existence and operations of the University. Our contributions in helping to establish the Uno Collection were small but significant to the project of Asian American theater. My current research in Filipino migrant labor and performance studies grew out of these early understandings of access and institutionalization and informs my insistence on the acknowledgement of how temporary work contributes and ultimately transforms our notions of labor (regarding production and product) as well as social relations.[21]

From object to archive: a sampling of the works in the Uno Collection

> That I am specifically archived in the Asian American Woman Playwrights Uno Collection points towards a community that the dominant culture defines and expects certain issues and points of views to be procured. Because I write from the edgier side of my voice, I'm glad to be seen in this context and, hopefully, can contribute an unexpected view to the AAWP [Asian American Women Playwrights] canon.
>
> (Alice Tuan)[22]

> I remember UM-A [University of Massachusetts-Amherst] folks reminding me via many letters and phone calls that I should submit any updates or ephemera relating to my plays. And I remember hauling out, from my own haphazard filing system, boxes of scripts and agonizing whether or not to "rewrite" this one, or maybe that one, before sending it to any archives. . . . Once production is achieved, a stage play performed—in a moment—stamps a memory, instant, affecting, impressionable. Without further documentation, that moment would be difficult to re-create. Archiving all these amazing works by fellow Asian American women playwrights has, with this collection, moved us all into an uncarved niche of theater history.
>
> (Jeannie Barroga)[23]

Although it is beyond the scope of this chapter to provide an account of each archival entry, this following discussion is a glimpse of the richness of the materials collected in the Uno Collection.[24] Playwrights whose works are housed in the Uno Collection include some of those who have published and often produced plays, including as Velina Hasu Houston (*Tea*; editor of *The Politics of Life: Four Plays by Asian American Women* and *But Still, Like Air, I'll Rise*), Jeannie Barroga (*Walls, Bubblegum Killers)*, Diana Son (*R.A.W. 'Cause I'm a Woman*; *Stop Kiss*), Bina Sharif (*Ancestor's House*), and Brenda Wong Aoki (*The Queen's Garden*). Contents archived are records of scripts in varying stages—early drafts, versions that are finalized for production, and published plays. Because the archive is attached to a theater company, it also contains records of Asian American women artists who have developed works at NWT. For example, Leilani Chan's[25] *E Nana I'ke Kumu/Look to the Source*, thúy lê's *the bodies between us*, and Chitra Divakaruni's *Clothes* (adapted by Divakaruni from her short story with the same title, choreographed by Aparna Sindhoor and performed with Purva Bedi) found support in their early forms at NWT. These are examples of the direct imbrications of archival practice and the politics of production. In other words, the process of archiving is already implicated within the struggle for the limited resources for actual staging of plays, a material concern that continually plagues the genre of theater by people of color.

In its archiving of plays by early Asian American women playwrights such as Gladys Ling-Ai Li, Betsy Inoue, and Wai Chi Chun, the Uno Collection performs the task of what Josephine Lee, Imogene Lee, and Yuko Matsukawa call "re/collecting early Asian America."[26] Its commitment to "re/collecting" is not simply one that any archival project undertakes. Specifically for Asian Americans, whose "presence" in the US is often relegated as "contemporary" or "recent" phenomenon, the project of "re/collecting" becomes a political project that challenges the very ownership of and belonging to history. To "re/collect" the works of early Asian American women playwrights is not just to amass minoritized voices; rather such a process of "re/collection" mandates the very rethinking of forces of temporality, authorship, and community formation within histories of archives and documentation.

"Asian American woman playwright" as archival object already signals a deviation from conventional notions of a "playwright." The inclusion of pieces by Asian American theater artists who work in performance collectives or ensembles, for example, further expands the conventional definition of a "playwright" as a single author writing plays. These performance collectives include a wide range of community collaborations, such as the Vietnamese American theater ensemble Club O'Noodles, spoken word pan-Asian American collectives I Was Born with Two Tongues and Mango Tribe, and the multi-racial dance theater ensemble Maura Nguyen Donohue's In Mixed Company. One of the prized materials in the Uno Collection is the work of early women of color performance collaborations among Jessica Hagedorn, Ntozake Shange, and Thulani Davis (*Where the Mississippi Meets the Amazon*, 1971), and those among Hagedorn, Robbie McAuley, and Laurie Carlos, also known as Class Thought (*teenytown*, 1988). With the inclusion of these ensemble pieces, the Uno Collection acknowledges multiple forms of authorship and diverse modes of creative process. The playwrights sought out and invited to submit their works to the Uno Collection do not strictly nor necessarily develop or produce their plays with Asian American, multiracial, or women's, theaters. NWT's commitment to its profile as a multiracial theater company is attentive to the possibilities and the limits of strict cultural nationalism that may operate within the logic of ethnic-specific cultural projects. Uno, as well Velina Hasu Houston, for instance, has openly pointed to the ethnocentrism within Asian American cultural communities and in Asian American theaters in particular.[27]

The practice of collective creation and multi-racial collaboration takes a different form and significance in the work of Sining Bayan, one of the many unique archival materials in the Uno Collection. The scripts of the activist-theater group Sining Bayan made their way into the archive through Ermena Vinluan, a Filipina American political activist and multi-media artist. From 1972 to 1981, Sining Bayan staged plays about the struggle of Filipino people in the Philippines and in the US and was relentless in its criticisms of martial law and imperialism. Sining Bayan was the cultural arm to the radical political organization Katipunan ng mga Demokratikong Pilipino/KDP.[28] This group's original productions dramatized the pressing political concerns of Filipinos in the US. These concerns included the history of Filipino labor and labor organizing in the US, the U.S. military's and Philippine central government's joint intervention in the Southern Philippines's search for land-rights, and the fight for the acquittal of two Filipina nurses of murder charges in Chicago. The inclusion of the Sining Bayan materials alongside more recognizable dramatic productions makes the Uno Collection not just an archive for and about Asian American women. Its reach extends to include larger questions of imperialism and nation-formation, as exemplified by Sining Bayan's materials in the archives. I close this chapter with some thoughts that return us to the relationship of archiving and performance to rearticulate what I see as the Uno Collection's interventions.

Coda

> While I believe that the Asian American feminist voice is and must be a vital part of the overall American Theater voice as well as the global Theater voice, sociopolitical challenges remain that complicate the recognition of that voice. Special archives that focus on that voice aid in keeping those voices from being lost in history.
>
> (Velina Hasu Houston)[29]

I return now to the crucial question of the politics of archival formation as debated within feminist performance theory. The Uno Collection was instituted at the height of these debates, and any engagement with its history must thus necessarily trace its engagement (or lack thereof) with contemporary discussions of gender, performance, and archival formation. In the 1990s, stimulating conversations among feminist performance theorists centered on the impossibility of archiving performance. Peggy Phelan provocatively argued for an understanding of performance as that which is unrepeatable and thus cannot be archived. In Phelan's *Unmarked*, she challenges the dominance of a text-based Theater and Performance Studies, arguing for a shift towards the body-in-performance. The body-in-performance interprets performance as a "representation without reproduction."[30] Theater scholar Elin Diamond situates Phelan's body-over-text within the genealogy of poststructuralism's declaration of the death of the author.[31]

The turn to the body-in-performance raises questions of authenticity and the "real," as well as where the true interpretation of performance may lie. Phelan's "representation without reproduction" is informed by radical queer studies' critique that imagines an alternative to the normative notions of reproduction, lineage, and generation naturalized in the project of visibility and representation. Taylor's *The Archive and the Repertoire*, as previously noted, builds upon these conversations in the 1990s and argues for "repertoire" as a practice of memory-keeping and remembering that exceeds the materiality of the written text.

Phelan's theory of the body-in-performance provokes us to ask, "What are we archiving when we archive performance?" Within the context of the Uno Collection, I am wary of the oversimplification of the turn to the body-in-performance, where performance and embodied expressions displace conventional archival objects such as written materials. A polemical distinction between archive and embodiment advocates for a privileging of performance without accounting for the process of selection of what gets performed. An approach to performance that makes primary the body-in-performance must also account for the inescapable fact that what gets performed is necessarily what becomes the basis of what gets archived (through scholarly work, reviews, publication, etc.). Rather, one could ask more productively how Phelan's anti-representational theory informs the politics and poetics of ethnic theaters, including NWT and the Uno Collection, which focus on representing stories that have been deliberately silenced. Is the Uno Collection a recuperative project that maintains its unreconstructed attachment to materials and objects as well as to the project of preservation? Or is it merely reproducing the repressive categories of representation that produced its conditions of possibility in the first place?

This chapter has been an attempt to address these questions and suggest that the Uno Collection and its artist-centered process of archiving propose alternatives beyond recuperation and a disavowal of subjectivity. Even as we generatively critique the desire for fixed subjectivity offered through the recovery of lost archives, equally we must be attentive to a more complicated theorization, not abandonment, of agency, representation, and alternative social formation. A project such as the Uno Collection can only remind us that the struggle for agency, representation, and alternative social formation remains a powerful political project, a "new WORLD" archive of possibility and collaboration.

Acknowledgments

The initial idea for this chapter was presented at New WORLD Theater's 2005 Intersections IV conference (under the leadership of artistic director Andrea Assaf). I wish to thank Priscilla Page, who invited me to participate in a panel on the Uno Collection. This chapter also benefited from comments shared by Cindy Garcia, Priya Srinivasan, and Sansan Kwan. Lastly, I want to recognize Roberta Uno for her tireless envisioning of a new world. A version of this chapter first appeared in Monica Chiu, ed., *Asian Americans in New England: Culture and Community* (Durham, NC: University of New Hampshire Press, 2009).

Notes

1 For the rest of this chapter, I will refer to New WORLD Theater as NWT and the Uno Collection of Plays by Asian American Women as the Uno Collection.

2 For more on Gladys Ling-ai Li, see Roberta Uno, "Ling-ai Li: Remember the Voice of Your People's Gods," *Dramatist's Guild Quarterly* (1995): 18–23, and Sucheng S. Huang's bio-bibliography entry in *Asian American Playwrights: A Bio-Bibliographical Critical Sourcebook*, ed. Miles Xian Liu (Westport, CT: Greenwood Press, 2002). For Li's play *The Submission of Rose Moy,* see *Paké: Writings by Chinese in Hawaii*, ed. Erick Chock and Darrell H. Y. Lum (Honolulu: Bamboo Ridge, 1989), 50–64.

3 For a nuanced understanding of archival hermeneutics, see Anjali Arondekar, "Without a Trace: Sexuality and the Colonial Archive," *Journal of the History of Sexuality* 14 no. 1/2 (Winter 2005): 10–27; and *For the Record: On Sexuality and the Colonial Archive* (Durham, NC: Duke University Press, 2009).

4 Worth mentioning here is the Native American Women Playwrights Archive (NAWPA) at the King Library, Miami University in Ohio. For more information about NAWPA, see http://staff.lib.muohio.edu/nawpa/index.php. Of course, a playwright's work could be archived in several different places. For instance, Velina Hasu Houston, a hapa Afro-Asian American playwright, has her own collection, The Velina Hasu Houston Collection, archived at the Huntington Library's Art Collections and Botanical Gardens in San Marino, California, in addition to having a smaller number of pieces housed in the Uno Collection.

5 Although New WORLD Theater has been closed, ending its operations in 2009 (other chapters in this collection speak to the history of the theater's closing), the AAWPA remains open, administered by the W.E.B. Du Bois special collections department.

6 Objects in the archives include scripts, playbills, artistic notes from the director and designers, and production reviews, as well as budget reports and official company meeting minutes. Scripts and other materials that have been submitted for production consideration in these theaters, but were rejected, are not included in the official archival roster.

7 Diana Taylor, *The Archive and Repertoire: Performing Cultural Memory in the Americas* (Durham, NC: Duke University Press, 2005), 19, my emphasis.

8 Lisa Lowe, "Heterogeneity, Hybridity, Multiplicity," *Diaspora* 1 no. 1 (Spring 1991): 24–42. See Viet Nguyen, *Race and Resistance: Literature and Politics in Asian America* (New York: Oxford University Press, 2002), and Kandice Chuh, *Imagine Otherwise: On Asian Americanist Critique* (Durham, NC: Duke University Press, 2003) for works that take to task uncritical invocations of the notion of community. These works question the celebratory uses of community, as well as the presumed progressive politics it is made to connote.

9 Stephen Sumida, "East of California: Points of Origin in Asian American Studies," *Journal of Asian American Studies* 1 no. 1 (1998): 86.

10 I say "partial" control, as any archiving process already involves shared operation. Having (partial) control of the means of production, or more accurately the right to self-determination, was an abiding principle in NWT's projects.

11 Email interview, June 10, 2008.

12 Email interview, June 4, 2008.

13 For more about NWT's history, see Roberta Uno and Kathy Perkins' "Introduction" to *Contemporary Plays by Women of Color* (New York: Routledge, 1996); Uno's "Being Present: Theater and Social Change"; Uno's "Introduction: Asian American Theater Awake at the Millennium," in *Bold Words: A Century of Asian American Writing*, ed. Rajini Srikanth and Esther Y. Iwanaga (New Brunswick, NJ: Rutgers University Press, 2001), 323–332; and her introduction to *Unbroken Thread: An Anthology of Plays by Asian American* Women (Amherst: University of Massachusetts Press, 1993), 1–10.

See also Shauneille Perry, "Celebrating the Tenth Anniversary of New WORLD Theater," in a special "Ethnic Theater" issue of *MELUS*, 16 no. 3, ed. and with an introduction by Uno (Autumn 1989–Autumn 1990). Dissertations and master theses about New WORLD Theater include Donna Beth Aronson's "Access and Equity: Performing Diversity at the New WORLD Theater" (Florida State University, 2003); and Nona E. Chiang's "Speaking Up, Speaking Out: Negotiating an Asian American Cultural Identity at New WORLD Theater" (University of California, Los Angeles, 2001).

14 Roberta Uno, "Being Present: Theater and Social Change," part of "How Do You Make Social Change?" *Theater* 31 no. 3 (Fall 2001): 71.

15 Many of these videos are in the process of being digitally archived by the NYU Hemispheric Institute for Performance and Politics.

16 Arts administrator Sansan Wong observes that NWT often was, significantly, the first touring invitation for many Asian American artists (especially solo performers) in the 1980s and 1990s.

17 Other scholars who have found research support from the Uno Collection include theater historian Esther Kim, dance studies scholar Yutian Wong, and Japan-based literary scholar Iwao Yamamoto.

18 Before the 1990s, various faculty members had been teaching courses about Asian immigration to the US and Asian American communities at the University of Massachusetts-Amherst. There had been early efforts to increase the presence of Asian American Studies in the curriculum through the labor of professors such as Sally Habana-Hafner (International Education), James Hafner (Geography), Bob Suzuki (School of Education), and Lucy Nguyen (Southeast Asian Studies and the director of the United Asian Learning Resource Center), and through the support of Dean of Humanities Lee Edwards. Mitzi Sawada, professor of History at Hampshire College, and Peter Kiang, professor of Sociology at the University of Massachusetts at Boston, assisted in galvanizing efforts towards more formalized and sustained curriculum-building of Asian American Studies in the early 1990s. Graduate and undergraduate students and staff actively collaborated with faculty in these efforts. The University of Massachusetts-Amherst now offers a certificate program in Asian American Studies and the Five Colleges (Amherst College, Hampshire College, Mount Holyoke College, Smith College, and the University of Massachusetts-Amherst) have been granting dissertations and postdoctoral fellowships. A significant number of faculty with expertise in Asian American Studies have been steadily hired in the Five Colleges since the early 1990s; in addition, a joint, multi-campus faculty position has been filled.

19 Uno, "Introduction," *Unbroken Thread*, 3

20 Students who worked on the Uno Collection in its early years included Maya Gillingham, Hillary Edwards, Sangeeta Rao, Megan Smith, Patti Chang, Esther Kim, and many others.

21 Dance Studies and Asian American Studies scholar Priya Srinivasan draws out further interesting tensions between corporeal influences and kinesthetic traces among and between classical India dancers and modern dance choreographers in the early-twentieth-century US. Through her discussion of these early dancers as contract and temporary laborers, she argues for a transformation of our notions of labor, especially in Asian American Studies. See "The Bodies Beneath the Smoke, or What's Behind the Cigarette Poster: Unearthing Kinesthetic Connections in American Dance History," *Discourses in Dance* 4 no. 1 (2007): 7–48.

22 Email interview, June 10, 2008.

23 Email interview, May 31, 2008.

24 A complete list of the Uno Collection contents may be accessed through http://scua.library.umass.edu/ead/mums345.html. The website listing of the archive contents is a new phase of the collection that is now managed by former NWT literary associate

Priscilla Page. Page builds upon the notion of the Uno Collection as a "living archive" through her theater courses and her proposed graduate concentration on "Multicultural Theater" in the University of Massachusetts Boston's Theater department. NWT's project to transform theater and academic institutions continues.

25 It is beyond the scope of this chapter to analyze the role publication plays within the archival process. Some questions worth considering, however, include: Is there a difference between a performance text and dramatic literature? What is the role of publication in transforming a play script into dramatic literature?

26 *Re/Collecting Early Asian America: Essays in Cultural History* (Philadelphia, PA: Temple University Press, 2002).

27 See Velina Hasu Houston's introduction to *The Politics of Life: Four Plays* (Philadelphia, PA: Temple University Press, 1993), and Uno's foreword to *But Still, Like Air, I'll Rise: New Asian American Plays*, ed. Hasu Houston (Philadelphia, PA: Temple University Press, 1997).

28 *Katipunan ng mga Demokratikong Pilipino* translates as the Union of Democratic Filipinos.

29 Email interview, July 7, 2008.

30 Peggy Phelan, *Unmarked: The Politics of Performance* (New York: Routledge, 1993), 148. Also see Phelan's "Reciting the Citation of Others; or, A Second Introduction," in *Acting Out: Feminist Performances*, ed. Lynda Hart and Peggy Phelan (Ann Arbor, MI: University of Michigan Press, 1993) , 13–31.

31 Elin Diamond, *Unmaking Mimesis: Essays on Feminism and Theater* (New York: Routledge, 1997).

Part II

New world futures

Changing demographics, polyculturalism, and Future Aesthetics

Chapter 8

Beyond demographics

Cornerstone, New WORLD, INTAR and the Theater of the Possible

Michael John Garcés

A story . . .

In the summer of 2013, Cornerstone Theater Company is making a play, *Plumas Negras*, by Juliette Carrillo, in the Alisal neighborhood of Salinas, California. In the scene we are rehearsing, two cast members, playing Concha, the ghost of a migrant farm worker who died in an accident, and Perla, her now-adult daughter, enact a scene in which Perla confronts Concha with her anger and anguish at being abandoned—abandoned first when Concha left her behind in Mexico to find work, and again when she died far away from home. Concha responds, trying to justify the choices she made, confronted with the terrible challenges of poverty and misogyny. Perla migrated to the United Stages herself when she was very young, and is torn between two cultures, two languages, feeling a part of neither one nor the other.

There is a chorus of parents and children accompanying the scene, which we are only beginning to stage. The actors are mostly members of the community; most have never acted before. Some have arrived at rehearsal after a long day laboring in the strawberry and lettuce fields. Focus is difficult to achieve, particularly as we are having difficulty figuring out how the chorus is integrated into the scene. The lines spoken by the chorus feel like interruptions, and so it is difficult to unearth the dynamic between mother and daughter, and impossible to establish why the chorus is there and what space they should occupy. Finally they are asked to sit out for the time being, so that we can focus on scenework.

Gloria Calderón, who plays Concha, is a member of the Alisal community, and has not been on stage since high school. Zilah Mendoza, who plays Perla, is a professional actor from Los Angeles with an impressive résumé. We begin the scene again. They are asked to just feel it through, not push too hard. Just a first attempt to sketch it out. About halfway through the work, Zilah—Perla—begins to cry, and there is a great deal of emotive force in her addressing of Concha. Gloria is startled, unsure how to respond, but the scene continues. After the scene is over, the actors discuss the scene, though Gloria is mostly silent. They are encouraged to take it slowly, to build to what it might be later, to focus on the basic staging and laying the ground for their emotional work.

When we begin again, Perla suddenly begins weeping and the emotional stakes are immediately high. Gloria takes a step backwards, and pauses. Everyone in the room is watching intently, which is somewhat unusual. Usually, if they are not in the scene, community actors read, rest, or go outside to chat. There is some question as to whether the scene will go forward. Then Gloria—Concha—unleashes a torrent of emotion, and the actors match each other and rise to the occasion of what is less a scene and more a deeply felt ritual of sacrifice and reconciliation. Both women are weeping, and anger and love are pouring out of them, but at the same time they are in control of the words, of the story. It's remarkable. When the scene ends, quite a few of the people in the room are red-eyed, and all are serious. There is a quiet, and we take a break.

When we come back into rehearsal, there is a seriousness of intent that was absent before—not only tonight, but in prior rehearsals. The cast, young and old, are focused. There is a sense of having broken through, of understanding what the play is, of recognizing that the story being told is mythic and personal, is fundamental to the lives of the community, that the enactment of this story has tremendous importance. It becomes easy to understand how the chorus—the community—fits into the scene. We stage their participation, repeating key lines of the scene. And then we play it. It is extraordinary, and heart-wrenching. Subsequent rehearsals are quite different; not that there is not fooling around and general fun, but there is a distinct sense of purpose instilled in the people working on the play. When the play is finally performed for a public audience, the scene, truly a climatic moment in the play, has a deep and palpable resonance in the audience; it is clear the experience of the conflict is a communal one. In this sharing, the aesthetic interaction between audience and performer is rooted both in the origins of the story and in empathy, and is also full of possibility for transformation. It is one example of what theater should be, and, at its best, is.

Cornerstone: discovering the unknown

This is my understanding of what we strive to achieve at Cornerstone, to greater and lesser degrees of success. I write from the perspective of an ensemble member, one of many, each with a very particular and individual perspective on our work, committed to the mission of the company. We employ a practice of community engagement, by which we mean that we collaborate with non-professionals in a given context to create a piece of vivid living theater that is a result of the energy created by singular, strong, life-practice artists with distinct voices working together with equally powerful, idiosyncratic non-professional art-makers. The work created has a point of view. It is not a celebration nor a simple reflection of the community, some kind of pageant or hagiographical masque. It is, rather, an enactment, through the problematics of drama, of the vital questions of how and why community is, where it is, and perhaps most important, if it should be. It is a process of finding the questions that a community is asking itself, and activating them through creative processes of dramatic art-making and civic dialogue.

It is a collaboration, and a complicated one. By "collaboration," I mean specifically two or more people coming together to create something which neither would have been able do on their own, and which has a result that is impossible to predict. In fact, we believe it is only a collaboration if the outcome is unforeseeable. Anything else is, on some level, simple top-down manipulation. Leaving aside the moral quandaries of power dynamics, this can be a perfectly legitimate way to reach aesthetic ends, but it is not our method. Our goal is to produce a final, unexpected product that is born from the interaction.

In our process we engage in story circles and other activities over a period of several months. Story circles—which are hardly unique to Cornerstone and came to us through the practice of artists working at theaters such as Junebug Productions and Roadside Theater, among others—are just what they sound like: events in which people gather in a circle and tell stories. We've developed and borrowed a menu of exercises and activities to elicit narrative and concrete detail about a given community; creating a safe space for vulnerable story-sharing, and an opportunity for artists from outside the community to learn specific, concrete details about its emotional and physical life and history, out of which to fashion a fiction, a play. We also participate in community celebrations, conduct one-on-one interviews, and hold workshops in playwriting, and so forth.

After this process, our writer, inspired, informed, and challenged by what she has experienced, begins her writing process, while we continue to interact with and learn from the community. Once a draft play is written there are several readings, much response, and often heated discourse. We cast people from the community alongside professional actors, and this is central to the aesthetic of how we manifest the work in performance. The work challenges received notions of command and virtuosity as being necessary, or even important, attributes of excellence. That said, the work comes out of a disciplined and rigorous approach, and does not eschew craft. We simply do not value craft over passion and raw, direct connection to the material—or to the audience. The process is a radical embrace of democratic inclusiveness and multiplicity of voices; the product is a result of the process, and is varied, sometimes quite aesthetically challenging and politically questioning, and other times fairly conventional in form and content. Our method values social context and geographic place as central to the meaning of the performance event. Generally, and in the mold of many theatrical traditions, the plays are not documentary in nature but rather creative fictions that help us perceive and critique the truth of the constructs which shape our society and our lives for what they are, and also begin to imagine what might be possible.

This is what I love about Cornerstone: it is truly a theater of possibility; an aesthetic of potential. The connection between audience and performer is activated by the charged sense of possibility in what is being performed on stage; and what this possibility implies in terms of how story can transform culture. What I love about Cornerstone is that it is about fear, and overcoming that fear. Fear of failure, fear of the "other," fear of being found inauthentic, fear of vulnerability. It is a methodology that demands the practitioner making the choice, over and over again, a new and singular choice every time, to go down paths to the unknown, accompanied by strangers, towards a discovery. A "dis-covery" in the sense of uncovering what was always there but is only revealed by the particular and unique mix of voices and perspectives, passions and prejudices, agendas and hopes of any given process. What I love about Cornerstone is that the process is huge, messy, sprawling, democratic in the sense that everyone, anyone, can be part of the process, and yet also in the sense that we face the danger of the tyranny of the majority voice, and have to guard against the suppression of that minority perspective; we have to respect received notions of history and morality, and yet must interrogate them. At the same time, the process is deeply individual, painfully personal. The unknown element in the process is both the deeply individual loneliness of personal search, the writer confronting the empty page, and quite literally making art that is a result of a multiplicity of conversation, of genuine mutual inquiry into the other; both of these aspects impact the evolution of the play equally. At the beginning of any project we have a guiding question, one that may likely evolve, and that's about all. We have no idea where the many answers might take us. I find this to be a very pure expression of artistic exploration. The process guides the aesthetic choices, form and function, syntax and structure.

A story . . .

Lynette Alfaro is playing Chabela, who is speaking to a group of peers in group therapy. It's the spring of 2012. Homeboy Industries has partnered with Cornerstone to create a play, Lisa Loomer's *Café Vida.* It is focused on former gang members in Los Angeles, in this case primarily women, who are working to get out of "the life," get a job, stay out of jail, stay alive. Lynette came into the first day of rehearsal off-book for a significant part of her various monologues. It was impressive. She smiled and said that, given how much meth she had done in her life, she needed to start memorizing early.

So now, a few weeks later, we're in the midst of our first run-through of the play. This is the second act, and the text is a difficult monologue in which Chabela, for the first time, opens up about her life—a life of abuse as a child, of getting jumped into a gang, of killing another girl, of giving birth to a daughter who was already addicted to alcohol and cocaine. This is not Lynette's story, in fact, she was emphatic that her life, however violent, had been very different. At first she had been quite resistant to it, had wanted to change it. "I never did that. That's weak." She never talked much about what she had done. "I would never do that. That's not me." But, slowly she was starting to feel it, to embody it. She was serious about her role. And now, in the context of a run-through of the entire play, it is starting to come to life.

As she performs, the face of another cast member, whom we'll call Lucia, is very still. There is very little expression on her face as she intently watches Lynette play out the story—a story that Lucia had shared with the playwright several months ago. Lucia has come to rehearsal sporadically, usually with her two-year-old son in tow, often leaving abruptly without letting anyone know. We doubted she would last through performances and were making plans to work around her absence, figuring out who could cover for her, what scenes we needed to have someone ready to do, what scenes could just be done without her. She has a relatively small role, mostly chorus, though she has lines in some scenes.

After the run, Lucia is asked how she is feeling. "About what?" Well, the monologue. She replies that she thought that Lynette did a good job. Then she walks over to Lynette and says, "You were good. Lynette nods. "Thanks." Lucia nods back, picks up her son, and walks out of rehearsal. But she comes back after break. And she never misses a performance.

Lynette is remarkable in the play, makes the role of Chabela come alive—often says, after the show, that she was Chabela—and the audience responds strongly to her performance. Lucia, though, is a powerful, quiet presence, very centered, dignified. She plays a supporting role, a part of the community, has no featured moments. But when she is on the stage, she owns it. And some of that applause, more than the audience knows, is for her.

New WORLD: defining choice

New WORLD Theater was at the forefront of a movement that has profoundly shaped me and I think has sketched out a direction for the evolution of our company. What I think was central to the work of New WORLD, certainly as it has directly impacted and continues to influence me, was agency—artists inquiring, defining, problematizing, provoking, redefining, and then questioning the very notion of the possibility of definition. As art and practice are defined, that very definition becomes a limitation which any active, living practice seeks to subvert. Challenging socially constructed hierarchy not only in theme, but also in process and structure, in how the work was manifest, it was—and is, because "world" is still new—a kinetic theater of hybridity, of searching, upending, and overturning whatever is understood, stable, accepted as true.

I don't mean to riff on this for the sake of riffing, but it is hard to define what, for me, was all about a resistance to definition. Resisting not only definitions from above, or even outside—we are defined as a certain "kind" of artist as we are a "kind" of people—but even our own attempts at self-definition, which can be as limiting—and, so, destructive—as any other, perhaps more so. It was about movement and evolution. Quantum art that could not be contained, that eluded measurement. It was not about creating a sense of identity in relationship to power or majority, nor a bulwark against it. It was about forging a powerful sense of self in spite of an overarching structure of power and privilege, and in spite of an (almost) overwhelming history of oppression, of denigration, of appropriation. It was the radical nature of possibility.

New WORLD Theater drew from traditions of speaking truth to power that could be traced back to the Civil Rights era. Of necessarily being in opposition.

Of creating space for specific groups. But New WORLD, for me, was about the next step, or several steps: what happened after forward-searching artists deepened their inquiry into the nature and complexity of the groups they had been born into, placed into by the history of America, the assumptions of society and the sociology of their heritage, what it meant to be part of something at all, and of their own individuality both in relation to the group and to self.

Artists in the context of New WORLD made that inquiry not only the theme but the very structure of their art. Much as the generations before them, these artists made work with a powerful moral center and critical voice—of that there is little doubt. But this work was not circumscribed by the demands of speaking truth to power. It found inspiration in the radical individualism and self-dissecting subversion of artists such as Maria Irene Fornes and Adrienne Kennedy—speaking truth, period. Performing the queering of the private and public histories of the nation, rescuing hip-hop from reactionary commoditization through radical and defiantly complex practice, committing deeply and without prejudice to youth culture and respectful—and mutual—mentorship, valuing the high art of failure, embodying a feminist engagement with body and voice through generational change, and, most important, celebrating the impossible complexity of joy.

This was a seismic shift. Artists who once were on the margins of mainstream culture were taking center stage, not through revolution or negotiation, but by redefining where the center was. By making the center everywhere and nowhere. By decentralizing the structure. By celebrating the marginal as integral and implicit in the main American, or, better, human, narrative. It is this sense of anything, literally anything, not only being possible but necessary, that theater and performance need to encompass any and everything in the face of the nature of power—which is to impose limits, borders, laws, and walls—that is the living legacy of New WORLD, and is a legacy I strive every day to bring to my own practice and to the work of my company.

Cornerstone is currently at a crossroads in terms of its process, methodology of engagement, and art-making. It is a crossroads at which we are looking at what has defined us for a quarter century, and what we want our ongoing journey to be. We are a 25-year-old company that has focused on the aesthetics of community and collaboration between professional and non-professional artists. This encounter is at the center of our work. For years we worked with communities that, I would argue, could be characterized as "communities of circumstance": neighborhoods, towns, church groups, who were approached and engaged because of what we as an ensemble, in our conversations, imagined to be the circumstances through which their community was created, defined, and maintained. We might work with a small town in California's Central valley, a neighborhood in South Los Angeles, or perhaps the community around a mosque or synagogue.

The basic impulse of the company, I think, is the desire of its artists to make theater that has a vital connection to its audience, beyond entertainment, value as commodity on the art market, or achievement as defined by culture brokers. And I think we have come to realize that our work is not only engaging with community, but constantly challenging our own and others' notion of what community is, of questioning if it can even be defined or delineated, and, if not, what our practice should be. This has led us to entering our collaborations with a different question, one that asks whether there is community in a given situation, and, if so, what defines it. What I call "communities of choice": people brought together because they are activated to come together, who have found common cause: a shared aspiration, a shared sense of being under threat. Communities of people engaged in issues such as environmental preservation, or gang members who have decided to get out of the life. It's important to note that they may be the very same communities with which we might have otherwise engaged, but our inquiry is different—not assuming commonality, but asking if there is one that people have created. An inquiry that assumes agency. I choose to be part of this community, to create it, because I have moved here, or because I care about a given issue, or because I am passionate about this cause, not simply because I live here, or was born into a family of a certain religion, or because my skin is a certain shade of brown. Agency.

Our work has always been experimental theater at its core: each time out testing the hypothesis of whether, in this world of mass media and technology which offers portals of infinite access to information and endless content, the primal act of performance matters, can possibly matter, in the discourse of our lives. And in this, I think, ultimately there exists a personal search, for each one of us at Cornerstone, a sifting through of this anxiety. This desire for meaning, for the true voice, the singular language, the story that rings true for the players and the auditors, that some kind of connection, a real connection, will be made, and the whole will be greater than the parts, if only for the moment. And that this connection will effect some kind of transformation. And that it will matter.

A story . . .

We're sitting in his car, it's hot, and I'm frustrated. Pablo Alvarado, who runs the National Day Laborer's Organizing Network, and I have just left an anti-immigrant demonstration. We had stood across the street with a smaller group of immigrants and activists, holding some signs, protesting against the protestors. I'm not sure why I'm frustrated, exactly. Except that I'm not sure what I am doing here. I'm supposed to be writing a play, one that speaks somehow to the day-laborer experience. Which in Los Angeles County in 2006 is primarily Mexican and Central American. Which I'm not. Which is primarily an immigrant experience. Which I am not. An experience of being under- or undocumented. Again, which I'm not. I think I'm writing this play because I speak the language, though not every day laborer speaks Spanish, or English for that matter. Because I'm Latino. Which means exactly what here? Not much. I seem to be asking the wrong questions, or somehow not understanding the answers. I don't feel any closer to some fundamental understanding of the situation, the people I am to write about, than I did three or four months ago when I began to meet people, to stand on street corners and in the parking lots of Home Depots, to speak and listen.

Pablo asks me what I'm writing, what the play is about. I shrug. I don't know. He nods, smiles. "You should tell these stories." "I don't know how." "What kind of play are you going to write?" "What kind?" "Yes. A comedy?" I think about this. "Maybe, I don't know. It might be a comedy." "I hope it will be a play about justice," he says. "Are there any plays about justice?" "Sure," I say. "Like what?" And I find myself telling him the half-remembered story of Fuenteovejuna, which I have not read in a long time, but had liked in high school, telling him about the unjust and evil *comendador*, how he is killed, how the whole town takes collective responsibility, how the king, in the end, forgives them. How this was radical at the time. Pablo smiles again. "That's our play." I shake my head. "No, it's just an example." "No," he says, "it's our play. Write that play. For us." So I do. And six months later a group of day laborers take collective responsibility, and the audience cheers and I feel like we may have something in common after all.

INTAR: the lure of authenticity

As a young, culturally indeterminate person and artist in New York City in the nineties, Latino, white, Cuban, straight, Colombian, bicultural, American, and none of the above, the search for authenticity—of voice, of culture, of expression, of place—was of primary importance for me. I had the good fortune of working with INTAR Hispanic American Arts Center, which had been founded by Max Ferrá in New York in 1966, participating in projects as a director, writer, actor, and curator for over ten years, while also freelancing. In many ways I had the privilege of being there while the organization was in crisis, as were many culturally specific organizations across the country, organizations such as the New Federal Theater, the Puerto Rican Travelling Theater, and Pan Asian Repertory Theater.

Formed in the sixties out of a specific, if not militant, politics of identity, and laying claim to an expression and aesthetics of *Latinidad*, INTAR was foundering as the notions upon which it had built its reputation, and the framework within it had presented and produced plays, fractured. We were trying to evolve our understanding of what the circumstances were that defined *Latinidad* so that they made sense in the present. We were assuming there was a definition to be found. We were assuming there was a piece of the artistic pie that was ours as a Latino organization to both make and to consume. A piece that was only ours. But many of the artists, myself included, were troubled by these foundational concepts, did not accept these assumptions, and, profoundly, didn't care about them or the organization's investment in these notions. It wasn't generational, either—it was about where artists of all ages were at, in terms of how they wanted to work, who they wanted to work with, and what they wanted to work on.

INTAR's leadership had great difficulty changing with the times. It was a time of anxiety and tremendous grassroots creativity, a deep divide between what was officially produced on the so-called "main" stage and what was being done around that work, in the labs and workshops, in off hours and underground. What did it mean to be Latino? Who should be produced—what voice needed, deserved, demanded primacy. What was the context? Who had authenticity? At first I had plunged deeply into this query on authenticity, seeking a kind of enlightenment that would help me find my true voice, but I came to realize that, as a tool to shape a voice and identity, authenticity is dangerous, a sharp blade with no handle. The process of constant reinvention that is theater requires artifice, cunning, probing curiosity, subversion of whatever you happen to hold dear on any given day—all of that, but not, I'd argue, authenticity. In fact, theater at its core is about finding truth through deception, lies, pretending: inauthenticity, to be sure. Authenticity is another word for purity, which is deeply problematic and, if nothing else, implies arrival, which is the antithesis of any artistic process. Or rather, for an artist, arrival implies an ending of a process, which really means the beginning of a new one. I would go further and say that any artistic process that arrives at an end, and answer, has either failed on its own terms or been a facile, and not terribly deep one to begin with.

I believe the question came into focus for me at INTAR as it struggled with its place as an organization, was processed through collaboration with artists who were and are at the heart of what I'd call the New WORLD movement. It opened the way for me to find a manner in which to celebrate the constant searching around identity and, in my case, *Latinidad.* To make that search the spark and fire of my art-making, as opposed to losing myself in a fruitless and pointless attempt to prove myself (to whom?) as a "real" man or as authentic Latino. And I think it is that freedom, liberated to search, to fail, to attempt a process with no end in sight—to create in the most essential meaning of the word—that brought me to Cornerstone, a place and a process that makes a great deal of sense in today's—and tomorrow's—new world.

So again, what I think the challenge is, what I think is of the essence, is agency. Not allowing but demanding that artists have choice and possibility at the center of their practice. That risk be assumed by both producing entity and practitioner. That it be valued. That it be central.

That is where I see Cornerstone, and other allied sister organizations and artists of shared sensibility, going. Assuming the notion of race is racist while still acknowledging the point that we are not in a post-racial moment in terms of general social perception and, more important, the distribution of resources and opportunity. Assuming that borders are products of human imagination, and not necessarily descriptive of any natural or inherent categories. Assuming the value of a diversity of perspective, voice and passion. Assuming a constant critique of those very beliefs, of anything one holds as true. And then questioning all of these assumptions. Less interested in changing the conversation than having entirely new engagements. When I refer to "shared sensibility," I am referring specifically to these shared perspectives, to a shared commitment to deep exploration, to a desire to create theater that activates audiences, that seeks to awaken new ways of looking at the world, as opposed to theater that pacifies them, that reinforces their sense that the current structures as we perceive them have permanency and should be taken as given. I think these ideals reach across style, idiom, syntax and label.

At Cornerstone, we call ourselves "community-based" or "community-engaged" artists. I think we are interested in and challenged by communities of agency rather than of circumstance. It's less about what the groups may or may not be and more about our approach to conversation. Assuming that people make choices to join and leave and associate. Hip-hop culture, for example, is a community of agency. And more and more we understand communities that are created out of notions of gender, culture, and heritage to be about choice, to be fungible and flexible. The main inquiry of any community-engaged practice is the constant questioning of what the given community is, and this questioning should evolve throughout the process and grow and change. This method for producing art is tremendously exciting, and part of a greater picture of artists making work that matters in a time of catastrophic economic revolutions, of incessant technological evolution, of war and migration. I have no idea where we are going, and I think that is a good indication that we are doing what we need to be doing.

Chapter 9

Who tells your story?

Hamilton, Future Aesthetics, and Haiti

Chinua Thelwell

Picture Thomas Jefferson debating Alexander Hamilton in rap battle format. After delivering a particularly caustic strings of insults, Jefferson says "hey, and if ya don't know, now ya know." This reference to Biggie Small's "Juicy" flies over the heads of the traditional Broadway demographic and is encoded with a hidden message to hip-hop fans: "I speak your language." There are many moments like this in the *Hamilton* hip-hop musical, an awe-inspiring portrayal of the life of Alexander Hamilton and the founding of the United States. Lin-Manuel Miranda, the creator, lyricist, and star of *Hamilton* consciously includes points of reference that speak to the aesthetic sensibilities of a new generation of theater audiences. *Hamilton* employs a multi-racial cast with people of color portraying the founding fathers of the United States. The play deftly trapezes the space-time continuum—collapsing the boundaries between performance genres and generations, in a manner that delights and forwards our cultural imaginary.

A commercial and critical success, *Hamilton* has broken box office records as cast and crew members have collected an impressive tally of awards and nominations, including a Grammy for best Musical Theater Album, Pulitzer Prize in Drama and MacArthur "genius" award for Miranda, and more Tony Award nominations (16) than any other show in the history of Broadway. Miranda graced the cover of *Time Magazine*, a sign that he has arrived as a popular culture icon. His cultural impact cannot be overstated: recently a *New York Times* article suggested that his play may have kept Alexander Hamilton on the $10 bill, despite the many people who believe that a woman should take his place.[1] *Hamilton* proves how culturally significant, commercially viable, and critically successful a Future Aesthetic production can be.

The phrase "Future Aesthetics" was coined by New WORLD Theater founder, Roberta Uno, as a strategy for the theater world to engage the changing demographics of the United States. Every day, our country grows by about eight-thousand people, almost 90 percent of whom are people of color.[2] As the American population becomes younger and browner, theater producers will need to find new aesthetic strategies to remain relevant to future audiences, and achieve the bottom line of getting bodies into seats. At its worst, conventional audience outreach presumes that young audiences are culturally underprivileged and must be groomed to bend their tastes around the western canon. By contrast, a Future Aesthetics approach draws from rapping, DJing, breakdancing (b-boys and b-girls), spoken word poetry, step dance, and other polycultural forms of artistic expression to create new theater works. These forms have permeated the popular culture landscape of the United States. By using Future Aesthetics, artists are attracting younger and more racially diverse audiences into American theaters. Recently, Seth Andrew, the founder of Democracy Prep Public Schools, took 120 students to see *Hamilton*. He says "[i]t was unquestionably the most profound impact I've ever seen on a student body."[3]

Hamilton's rap lyrics are purposefully encoded with messages that speak directly to the hip-hop generation.[4] The lyrics are peppered with references to well-known rappers like Mobb Deep, DMX, and Busta Rhymes. The lyrical allusions reach back as far as Grand Master Flash and the Furious Five, and pay homage to a DJ who is often acknowledged as one of the "founding fathers" of hip-hop. In 1982, Grand Master Flash and the Furious Five released "The Message." This song portrays the destabilizing effects of neoliberial austerity measures and deindustrialization in the South Bronx, and was one of the first overtly political rap songs. In it, lead rapper Melle Mel says: "Sometimes it makes me wonder how I keep from going under." This line is reinterpreted in *Hamilton* when Jefferson says "[s]uch a blunder sometimes it makes me wonder why I even bring the thunder." *Hamilton* is filled with these "hidden transcripts" to use James Scott's terminology. A "hidden transcript" is an encoded message designed to fly over the heads of the dominant group and communicate messages, often subversive, to the subordinates.[5] The traditional broadway patrons in the audience of the *Hamilton* show who were clapping along to the song "Ten Duel Commandments" probably had no idea it was referencing Biggie Smalls "Ten Crack Commandments." Many of them voted for Ronald Reagan, the anti-drug crusader whose administration started a "war on drugs" and popularized the phrase "crack epidemic."[6] Hip-hoppers in the audience can laugh at the inside joke and the tables Miranda has cleverly turned.

Miranda uses rhyme scheme and rhythmic complexity to convey different levels of intellectual ability. In an early scene, Hamilton meets John Laurens, Hercules Mulligan, and Marquis de Lafayette in a bar. Laurens introduces himself with a single syllable rhyme scheme: "be," "three," "me," "free." Miranda intentionally wrote "eighties raps, great raps, but super beginners raps" for these three characters. By contrast, Hamilton introduces himself to the trio with a fast-paced, rhythmically complex rap with many internal rhymes in the song "My Shot." The single-syllable rhyme scheme is replaced by a multi-syllabic one. For example: "ahead of me" is rhymed with "let it be," "honest land" with "promised land," and "independence" with "our descendants." The character, Hamilton, employs a modern rhyme scheme in the vein of rappers like Rakim, Nas, or Big Pun, and in doing so, appears to be the smartest guy in the room. Miranda relates, "[Hamilton] needed to be like from the future. Just this world beating intellect. So every couplet had to be unimpeachable."[7]

Music is another barometer of intellect. Laurens, Mulligan, and Lafayette's verses are accompanied by relatively simple percussive break beats created by a single drum set, some beat-boxing, and a fist pounding a wooden table. Meanwhile, Hamilton's verse is backed by an entire orchestra, with percussive and melodic instruments, multiple layers of sound, and many musical transitions. Hamilton's brilliance is reinforced through sound.

Discursive meanings are embedded in the music genres that appear in the play. Two songs are performed in distinctly European styles: a Minuet variation in Waltz time for "Farmer Refuted" and a 1960s British pop song called "You'll be Back." Both songs feature characters who are loyal to the English metropole, most notably, the latter is sung by King George himself. Both songs are delivered by white actors ("You'll be Back" also features vocals from Miranda). This European sonic landscape is juxtaposed against the songs of the anti-imperial American revolutionaries: beat-boxing, polycultural sequences that blend record scratching over a string orchestra, dancehall reggae rhythms, blues piano walking baselines, and hip-hop break beats.[8] The message is clear: Afro-diasporic music represents anti-imperial democracy while European music represents the imperialism of the English monarchy.

In recent interviews, Miranda explains the reasoning behind the decision to use rap music in *Hamilton*: "You could do a [*Les Misérables*] type musical about Hamilton, but it would have to be 12 hours long, because the amount of words on the bars when you're writing a typical song—that's maybe got 10 words per line."[9] Rap is "uniquely suited [for telling Hamilton's story] cause we get more language per measure than any other musical form."[10] By using the rap format, Miranda was able to include more details than would otherwise be possible. In an article for a news journalism website that specializes on statistical analysis, Leah Libresco counted the amount of words in *Hamilton*'s cast recording and compared the tally with seven other musicals. *Hamilton* clocked in at 20,520 total words while the runner-up was *Phantom of the Opera* with only 6,789 words.[11]

Hamilton offers an effective aesthetic approach to musical theater storytelling.[12] If you have a complex story with a large amount of material to unpack, then rap music might be the best choice. The Future Aesthetics of rap music allows playwrights to create complex stories with richly detailed plot lines that develop multiple characters. This is an ironic development given the fact that some people still believe rap to be a low form of musical communication. One particularly notable cast member is Daveed Diggs, the actor who originated the roles of Jefferson and Lafayette and has the fastest rap in the show in "Guns and Ships."[13] Diggs was artistically nurtured by the San Francisco-based Youth Speaks, an organization that pioneered youth writing workshops in spoken word poetry and has built a mentorship network across America grounded in nearly 100 chapters in cities, suburbs, First Nations reservations, and rural towns. Youth Speaks and its counterparts are the training ground and pipeline towards tomorrow's Future Aesthetics productions (see Chapter 10 of this volume). Traditional BA programs in drama,

MFA Programs, and conservatories would be well-advised to make space in their curriculum and on their faculties for Future Aesthetics if they have not already.

Miranda writes plays that prominently feature actors of color, in a conscious attempt to create roles for performers who have few opportunities on Broadway. Miranda co-wrote with Quiara Alegría Hudes, his first Pulitzer Prize nominated Broadway show, *In the Heights* (2008), as a response to this structural problem:

> *In The Heights* very much came out of me wanting a career in musical theater. But there's only about three great rolls for Latino men in musical theater . . . So I wrote something that had so many parts for Latinos because I knew there was a void there. I knew it because I was going into that world and I was scared.

Furthermore, Miranda wanted to create "a Latino musical where we are not knife wielding murderers."[14] His plays are designed to create roles for people of color, challenge structural inequities, and counter the tendency to criminalize Latinos on Broadway. Here is a kind of desegregation project that boldly claims exclusionary spaces. Those of us who are committed to such projects are deeply indebted to Miranda. His commitment to write sophisticated and complex roles for actors of color is especially welcome, given the documented persistence of marginalization.[15]

Case in point, years ago I went to see *Les Misérables* on Broadway, and left the theater with some catchy songs in my head, and a bad taste in my mouth. The casting tasted bitter. I only noticed three black actors/actresses in the entire cast, and each played villains who injured the protagonists in one way or another. The message from the casting director was clear: black skin signifies evil. The contrast with *Hamilton* cannot be more vivid. In *Hamilton*, black skin represents new world freedom and democracy while white skin represents European monarchy, and English imperialism.

Many commentators have mistakenly attached the label of "color-blind" casting to the *Hamilton* production. Instead, Miranda has opted for a "color-conscious" approach that has raised the ire of some. In March of 2016, the *Hamilton* producers were criticized for posting a call for "non-white" actors.[16] The insinuations of "reverse racism" screams out a kind of privilege: the privilege to expect leading roles in every single Broadway show. White actors have enjoyed decades of preferential treatment from the casting gods of Broadway. Theater historian Warren Hoffman asserts: "[t]he history of the American musical is the history of white identity in the United States."[17] Now that *Hamilton* has established an innovative and commercially lucrative formula, some white people want access. The goal, of course, is not to erase the white presence from American theater. The goal is to diversify and desegregate American theater so that people of all races can claim space on American stages.

Hamilton is a self-aware response to the changing demographics of the United States. On the decision to reimagine the founding fathers as black and Latino, Miranda recently offered:

> I think one of our overarching goals with this show, with any show, is you wanna eliminate any distance between your audience and your story. So let's not pretend this is a textbook. Let's make the founders of our country look like what our country looks like now . . . We are every shade every color.

Ron Chernow, author of the biography on which *Hamilton* is based, views the show as a reflection of "Obama's America."[18]

Social demographers predict that people of color in aggregate will become the racial majority in the United States in 2042. These projections accelerate to 2020 for children under 18, the future of a multi-racial, polycultural America.[19] *Hamilton* is a nation-building story that tries to provide entry points for audiences who are often excluded from the story of the nation's founding. The final song of the play asks the crucial question: who tells your story?

In his writings and public appearances, Miranda contributes to a national discussion on immigration that has been going on since the nineteenth century. The Chinese Exclusion Act of 1882 banned Chinese workers from entering the country and ushered in a new era of "gate keeping" legislation.[20] Later in 1924, nativists scored another victory with the passing of an immigration act that created a "national origins quota system" favoring Western European countries and greatly restricting the amount of people who could immigrate from Asia, and Africa.[21] The Johnson–Reed Act of 1924 was a major victory for the advocates of eugenics science: the same pseudo-science on which Hitler's racial ideology was based. In the years that followed the Johnson–Reed Act, Mexican Americans became associated with "illegal" immigration.[22] All of which is to say that the demographic shift of 2042 would not be possible without hard won legislative victories. Miranda's home town of Washington Heights would look very different if it were not for the 1965 Immigration Act: one of the major legislative achievements of the Civil Rights Movement. This act removed the national origins quota system, opened the country to legal Latino, Asian, and African immigration, and paved the way for the changing demographics.

Now in 2016, the presumptive nominee of the Republican Party has promised to build a wall at the US–Mexico border.[23] Miranda directly responded to Donald Trump in a public forum:

> My reaction to his comments about Mexicans isn't important. What matters is that the world reacted, and he saw that speech has consequences. You can say the most hateful shit you want, and you can be boisterous and loud and get attention, and that has worked very well, but it's going to have consequences.[24]

Miranda is suggesting that Trump's demagoguery will drive Latinos/as away from the Republican Party. Miranda's musicals also offer rejoinders to nativist rhetoric. A couple of seconds into "Yorktown," the music drops out as Lafayette and Hamilton holler in unison: "Immigrants, we get the job done."[25]

The *Hamilton* soundtrack is the first Broadway score to reach number one on the Billboard rap album charts and because of the prohibitive cost of Broadway tickets and the democratizing access of high-speed internet, will reach exponentially more people than the live stage version. As a life-long hip-hop head, I celebrate *Hamilton* as a remarkably innovative example of hip-hop storytelling. It is a masterful concept album, lyrically on par with groundbreaking concept albums from years past: Prince Paul and Breeze Brewin's *Prince Among Thieves*, Aesop Rock's *Labor Days*, The Roots' *Undun*, and Kendrick Lamar's *Good Kid, M.A.A.D. City*. Using the hip-hop convention of the remix, *Hamilton* creates an aesthetic remix of the story of our national founding. But what about a demographic remix?

As an Africana Studies professor whose job is to redress racial imbalances in our national memory, I would be remiss not to mention *Hamilton*'s missed opportunity. *Hamilton* is a work of public history that could have done more to change an outdated narrative about the democratic revolutions of the eighteenth century: a narrative that erases the contributions of people of color. The play skillfully presents an aesthetic paradigm shift, but we also desperately need a shift in our historical memory. *Hamilton* could have diversified the pantheon of democratic icons, and achieved a demographic remix by acknowledging the role that Haiti played in the Age of Revolutions.

Historians use the phrase Age of Revolutions to describe the three democratic revolts that began in the late eighteenth century: The American Revolution (1776–1783), French Revolution (1789–1799), and Haitian Revolution (1791–1804). Each took place within Alexander Hamilton's lifetime (January 11, 1755 or 1757–July 12, 1804) and contributed to the advancement of democratic ideals. *Hamilton* skillfully draws connections between the American and French Revolutions, etching out a transatlantic conversation between the United States and Europe, but if we are serious about telling the story of multi-racial new world democracy, then Haiti must be included.

In August of 1791, the enslaved Africans on the island of Saint-Domingue revolted in a coordinated strike against their owners. Thirteen years later, the country of Haiti was born, the first independent black nation in the new world. Haiti quickly became a beacon of hope for enslaved people in the new world, and a frightening specter of insurrection for slave holders everywhere. The Haitian Revolution sent shock waves across the Atlantic world. One of the more progressive moments of the French Revolution was a direct response to the uprising. In a desperate attempt to regain control over Saint-Domingue, the National Assembly ended slavery in all French Colonies in 1794. Haitian rebels helped the United States almost double in size through the Louisiana Purchase of 1803. After Napoleon's military forces suffered huge casualties trying to end the rebellion, he scaled back his presence in the new world, sold away the major colonies, and retreated to Europe. Hamilton thanked the Saint-Domingue rebels in the *Evening Post* newspaper: "To the . . . obstinate resistance made by [Saint-Domingue's] black inhabitants are we indebted."[26] Later in 1815–1816, Haiti offered refuge, economic aid, and military support to Simón Bolívar, the general who is often described as the "George Washington of South America."

Thomas Jefferson, worried about a free black republic that had outlawed slavery in its constitution, "thanked" Haiti with a trade embargo in 1806.[27] Earlier, in 1801, Jefferson argued that the United States, England and France should work together to "confine this *disease* to its island. As long as we don't allow the blacks to possess a ship we can allow them to exist and even maintain very lucrative commercial contacts with them" (my emphasis). Jefferson's comment reflects a trend in western thought in which African culture and people are treated as pathogens.[28] Today, although Jefferson's call for confinement is unknown to most, it's still observed in history curriculum that discursively contains Haiti.

Hamilton could have broken the trend of silencing Haiti by including one line about the revolution. This line never comes, and the silence continues. From a public history perspective, we need new works that break the silence. *Les Misérables* portrays the French Revolution, *Hamilton* the American Revolution: Why not an entire Broadway show dedicated to Toussaint Louveture, Boukman, and the heroes of the Haitian Revolution? *Hamilton* inspires new possibilities that were previously "unthinkable."[29] Now in 2016, we might begin picturing what a full length Broadway production about the Haitian Revolution could look like.

Crispus Attucks offers a more readily achievable opportunity. Attucks, a mixed-race man, was the first casualty of the American Revolution and has been celebrated in song by Nas and LL Cool J. Surely there is space for him in a hip-hop musical about the American Revolution? By not acknowledging the roles that people of color played in the Age of Revolutions, space is conceded to the "take back our country" crowd who continue peddling the narrative that white people are the only builders of this nation. At times, *Hamilton* astutely disrupts this false narrative. For example, the song "Yorktown" acknowledges the fact that black Americans fought in the last major land battle of the American Revolution. After the British army surrenders, Laurens says: "black and white soldiers wonder alike if this is really freedom." Later in the story, Hamilton gives Jefferson a hard truth about the eighteenth-century Virginia economy: "We know who's really doing the planting." But more could have been done to recognize people of color as historical actors with agency and voice.

Lyra Monteiro has written an astute criticism of *Hamilton* examining how the show contributes to the whitewashing of American history. An historian who specializes on race in the Revolutionary era, Monteiro is uniquely suited to speak on this subject. Over the course of the essay, she lists the many contributions that black people made to the American Revolution. Her main argument:

> With a cast dominated by actors of color, the play is nonetheless yet another rendition of the "exclusive past," with its focus on the deeds of "great white men" and its silencing of the presence and contributions of people of color in the Revolutionary era.[30]

The Gilder Lehman Institute has received a generous grant from the Rockefeller Foundation so that 20,000 New York City public school students can receive subsidized tickets. The institute is creating a curriculum that will accompany the show. A majority of students will be of color. Monteiro asks a necessary question: "Is this the history that we most want black and brown youth to connect with—one in which black lives so clearly do not matter?"[31] Hopefully the institute will create a curriculum that includes people of color.[32]

All of this is not to minimize the aesthetic achievements of *Hamilton*, a play that greatly expands the realm of possibilities for hip-hop. Lest we forget, in 1980, the year of Miranda's birth, *Hamilton* was not possible. A young hip-hop culture was not ready to claim space on Broadway. The first recorded rap song to receive national attention, "Rappers Delight," was only one year old. Rakim, and Kool G Rap had not pioneered the multi-syllabic rhyme scheme that Miranda expertly wrote into his musical. The White House was entrenching an exclusionary agenda set on stamping out such imaginaries. By contrast, President Barack Obama inspires this kind of imaginary. He invited it into his home in 2009 for a "White House Poetry Jam." In turn, Miranda unveiled a song called "The Hamilton Mix Tape" in a jaw-dropping performance for First Family and guests.[33]

President Obama represents the changing demographics, and as such, has become a lightning rod for racist vitriol, and birther conspiracy theories. As the so-called silent majority becomes a new minority, many will dig in their heels, crying out to "Make America Great Again," and have to be dragged kicking and screaming into a twenty-first century multiracial democracy. Trump's presidential campaign is the most xenophobic and racist in recent memory. It is in this climate that the real contributions of people of color to the Age of Revolutions become ever more important.

Miranda should not be blamed for a systemic curricular gap. Educators need to do a better job acknowledging Haiti. Chernow's book mentions the Haitian Revolution once, only to suggest that a yellow fever outbreak in Philadelphia may have originated on Saint-Domingue. More than two-hundred years after Jefferson called Haiti a "disease," Chernow continues the tendency to pathologize the island.[34] Thankfully, for inquiring minds who want a more uplifting account of Haiti, resources are available. You could go to the New York Historical Society and look at archival materials from an exhibit that ran in 2011 called *Revolution! The Atlantic World Reborn*. This public history project offers the increasingly orthodox perspective that you have to study the Haitian, French, and American Revolutions in conjunction with one another to get the full story.[35] You might read some of the scholarship on the Haitian Revolution.[36] And if your research starts sounding like music you could grab a pen. Who tells your story? When the official textbooks forget us, we narrate ourselves. That's what rappers do. That's a hip-hop story.

The next question: is Broadway ready for such a play? The recent example of *Holler if You Hear Me* (2014) offers an entry way into answering this question. *Holler if You Hear Me* is a hip-hop musical featuring the songs of Tupac Shakur and starring the inimitable Saul Williams. This Future Aesthetics production closed after a month on Broadway. In a recent interview, Williams explained why he believes it failed. He gives a number of reasons but one story in particular is especially instructive. Williams remembers being approached by Harry Belafonte after the play. Belafonte said: "you took an [A]frocentric themed play and placed it on a [E]urocentric stage. The problems you'll face are larger than you think." Case in point, one of the negative reviewers described the show as "the generic tale of a thug named John." As sociologist Michael Jefferies has pointed out, "the word *thug* has come to stand in for *nigger* as an epithet for criminally inclined black men." I would add the observation that both words are often used to devalue black life. This traditional theater critic does not have the language or cultural literacy to arbitrate the new Future Aesthetics. Institutional space will need to be made for theater critics who understand the new forms (the reviewer said "the lyrics are almost unintelligible") and can speak about people of color without leaning on code words for racial epithets.[37]

A portrayal of the Haitian Revolution would be "Afrocentric" in that its protagonists would be black and brown historical figures played by black and brown actors. It's up for debate whether this country's current mix of neoliberal racial stratification, demographics, and curricular silencing allows for such a play to thrive on Broadway.[38] *Hamilton* has managed to draw audiences from both sides of the political aisle in a country that is extremely polarized. According to Monteiro, *Hamilton* received universal acclaim from conservative critics, and this was probably because of the draw of "founder's chic" and a pull yourself up by the bootstraps meritocracy narrative.[39] Haiti is a bootstraps narrative of enslaved people earning their freedom and attempting to create democracy which also includes moments when brown and black people slay white power holders: a kind of racialized nightmare in the conservative imaginary.

But even after acknowledging this potential hurdle, one cannot help but imagine Haiti within the realm of the possible. These are the intangible effects of *Hamilton*, the emboldened imaginings that will likely reverberate for decades. Think of the many creative minds who will produce *Hamilton*-inspired works in the coming years. Clearly Broadway is ready for Future Aesthetics, but is Broadway ready for the stories of the black and brown people who founded those aesthetics? Future Aesthetics is not only about a paradigm shift in form. A true Future Aesthetics must reflect the stories of all races, all genders, all classes, all sexual orientations. A true Future Aesthetics must flip the script of history, invent the new from the discarded, and create a wider social cypher.[40]

Maybe, in 2016, the American cultural imaginary is ready for Haiti. Perhaps we are ready for a more complete portrayal of the Age of Revolutions. Maybe not. Maybe we'll have to wait until 2042.

Notes

1 Michael Paulson, "Hamilton May Stay on the $10 Bill, Thanks to Help From Broadway," *The New York Times*, March 16, 2016, http://www.nytimes.com/2016/03/17/theater/hamilton-may-stay-on-the-10-bill-thanks-to-help-from-broadway.html, accessed June 2016.

2 Steve Phillips, *Brown Is the New White: How the Demographic Revolution Has Created a New American Majority* (New York: The New Press, 2016), 5.

3 Michael Paulson, "'Hamilton' Heads to Broadway in a Hip-Hop Retelling," *The New York Times*, July 12, 2015, http://www.nytimes.com/2015/07/13/theater/hamilton-heads-to-broadway-in-a-hip-hop-retelling.html, accessed June 2016. For an extended discussion on Future Aesthetics, see Roberta Uno, "Theatres Crossing the Divide: A Baby Boomer's Defense of Hip-Hop Aesthetics," in *Total Chaos: The Art and Aesthetics of Hip-Hop*, Ed. Jeff Chang (New York: Base Civistas, 2006), 300–305.

4 Jeff Chang defines the hip-hop generation by answering a set of questions: "So, you ask, when does the Hip-Hop Generation begin? After DJ Kool Herc and Afrika Bambaataa. Whom does it include? Anyone who is down. When does it end? When the next generation tells us it's over." Jeff Chang, *Can't Stop Won't Stop: A History of the Hip-Hop Generation* (New York: Picador, 2005), 2.

5 James Scott, *Domination and the Arts of Resistance: Hidden Transcripts* (New Haven: Yale University Press, 1990). Many Reaganites will go see *Hamilton*. Conservative critics have embraced the show. Lyra Monteiro, "Race-Conscious Casting and the Erasure of the Black Past in Lin-Manuel Miranda's Hamilton," *The Public Historian* (vol. 38 No. 1 February 2016), 96.

6 Michelle Alexander, *The New Jim Crow: Mass Incarceration in the Age of Colorblindness* (New York: The New Press, 2012), 52. Michelle Alexander persuasively argues that the so-called "war on drugs" is really a war on urban black and brown communities. I would add that even if the intentions of the "war on drugs" are still disputable, the outcome surely appears to be a form of warfare as the United States has the largest population of incarcerated people in the entire world.

7 Charlie Rose, "Charlie Rose interviews Lin Manuel Miranda," *Bloomberg*, (48:51 long), https://www.youtube.com/watch?v=IT5s1M9qJUE, accessed August 2016.

8 Grand Master Flash defines a breakbeat as the part of a song where "[t]he band breaks down, the rhythm section is isolated, basically where the bass guitar and drummer take solos." Quoted in Tricia Rose, *Black Noise: Rap Music and Black Culture in Contemporary America* (Middletown: Wesleyan University Press, 1994), 73.

9 Rembert Browne, "Genius: A Conversation With 'Hamilton' Maestro Lin-Manuel Miranda," *Grantland*, September 29, 2015, http://grantland.com/hollywood-prospectus/genius-a-conversation-with-hamilton-maestro-lin-manuel-miranda/, accessed June 2016.

10 "Hip-hop and history blend for Broadway hit 'Hamilton,'" *PBS News Hour*, November 20, 2015, https://www.youtube.com/watch?v=HAiEVjW-GNA, accessed June 2016.

11 Leah Libresco, "'Hamilton' Is the Very Model of a Modern Fast-Paced Musical," *Fivethirtyeight*, October 5, 2015, http://fivethirtyeight.com/datalab/hamilton-is-the-very-model-of-a-modern-fast-paced-musical/, accessed June 2016.

12 Of course, *Hamilton* is not the first work of hip-hop theater. The pioneering hip-hop theater artist, Danny Hoch, has a noteworthy perspective: "Lamentably, however, much of the acclaim that has and will accrue to *Hamilton* brands it as one of the first pieces of theatre to successfully incorporate hip-hop elements and sensibilities. That's like someone thinking they've discovered rap music after hearing Eminem's song 'Stan' (coincidentally, and arguably, another white narrative). This is unfortunate; it not only ignores the 20-plus year legacy of hip-hop theatre in the US—Idris Goodwin, Eisa Davis, Psalmeyene 24, Hip-Hop Theatre Junction, Teo Castellanos, Will Power, Universes, Marc Bamuthi Joseph, etc. It also, more disturbingly, ignores [Lin-Maneul Miranda's] own *In The Heights*, a hip-hop-infused musical with a contemporary story about Latinos in a changing neighborhood that ran on Broadway for 3 years, won 4 Tonys and recouped its money after just 10 months. Yet we're still in a cultural landscape where *In The Heights* and other hip-hop generation stories will never be celebrated to the extent that *Hamilton* will be, simply by virtue of who the show is about." Danny Hoch, "Sure, 'Hamilton' Is a Game-Changer, but Whose Game?" *American Theatre*, April 23, 2015, http://www.americantheatre.org/2015/04/23/sure-hamilton-is-a-game-changer-but-whose-game/, accessed June 2016. For an anthology of works of hip-hop theater see Daniel Banks Ed. *Say Word! Voices from Hip Hop Theater* (Ann Arbor: University of Michigan Press, 2011).

13 On *The Late Show with Stephen Colbert*, Miranda describes Lafayette's transformation from simple rapper to complex rapper: "The fun thing we do with Lafayette is: He's kinda struggling with the language at the beginning of act one and at the end of act one he's a commander and he has the fastest raps in the show. I call it the *Police Academy* rule. Which is, you remember the little lady in the *Police Academy* movies who would be like "please can you please go" and then she'd be like "hey freeze sucka!" So that's kinda what we did with Lafayette." "Lin-Manuel Miranda Talks 'Hamilton,' New York And His Influences," *The Late Show with Stephen Colbert*, December 12, 2015, https://www.youtube.com/watch?v=h7YTPuEMgaE, accessed June 2016.
14 Jeffrey Brown, "'Hamilton' the musical tells the immigrant story of a Founding Father," *PBS News Hour*, November 23, 2015, http://www.pbs.org/newshour/extra/daily_videos/hamilton-the-musical-not-your-fathers-founding-father/, accessed June 2016. Charlie Rose, "Charlie Rose Interviews Lin Manuel Miranda."
15 A recently released quantitative study makes it clear that people of color are underrepresented on Broadway. Randy Gener, "Asian Americans Push Back: An Actor's Coalition Confronts Broadway and Nonprofit Theater Leaders on the Lack of Minorities on NY Stages," *American Theater*, May 3, 2016, https://cultureofoneworld.org/2016/05/03/asian-americans-push-back/, accessed June 2016.
16 Michael Paulson, "'Hamilton' Producers Will Change Job Posting, but not Commitment to Diverse Casting," *New York Times*, March 30, 2016, http://www.nytimes.com/2016/03/31/arts/union-criticizes-hamilton-casting-call-seeking-nonwhite-actors.html, accessed June 2016. Joi-Marie McKenzie, "'Hamilton' Changes Casting Call Wording After Backlash over 'Non-white Casting Call,' *ABC News*, March 31, 2016, http://abcnews.go.com/Entertainment/hamilton-casting-call-wording-backlash-white-casting-call/story?id=38053630, accessed June 2016.
17 Warren Hoffman, *The Great White Way: Race and the Broadway Musical* (New Brunswick: Rutgers University Press, 2014), 3.
18 Jeffrey Brown, "'Hamilton' the musical," Jennifer Schuessler, "Starring on Broadway, Obama and Alexander Hamilton," *New York Times*, July 18, 2015, http://artsbeat.blogs.nytimes.com/2015/07/18/starring-on-broadway-obama-and-alexander-hamilton/?_r=0, accessed June 2016.
19 Bill Chappell, "For U.S. Children, Minorities Will Be The Majority By 2020, Census Says," *National Public Radio*, March 4, 2015, http://www.npr.org/sections/thetwo-way/2015/03/04/390672196/for-u-s-children-minorities-will-be-the-majority-by-2020-census-says, accessed June 2016.
20 Erika Lee, *At America's Gates: Chinese Immigration During the Exclusion Era 1992–1943* (Chapel Hill: North Carolina Press, 2003).
21 Mae Ngai, *Impossible Subjects: Illegal Aliens and the Making of Modern America* (Princeton: Princeton University Press: 2004), 3.
22 Leo Chavez, *The Latino Threat: Constructing Immigrants, Citizens, and the Nation* (Redwood City: Stanford University Press, 2008), 26.
23 Today's nativism is very similar to that of the 1920s with at least one major difference: Trump's rhetoric does not have the backing of scientists who study race as eugenics has been scientifically discredited and the argument of biological superiority is unavailable to nativists. See Daniel Fairbanks, *Everyone Is African: How Science Explodes the Myth of Race* (Prometheus Book: New York, 2015). Stephen Jay Gould, *The Mismeasure of Man* (New York: WW Norton & Company, 1981).
24 Frank DiGiacomo, "'Hamilton's' Lin-Manuel Miranda on Finding Originality, Racial Politics (and Why Trump Should See His Show)," *The Hollywood Reporter*, August 30, 2016, http://www.hollywoodreporter.com/features/hamiltons-lin-manuel-miranda-finding-814657, accessed August 2016.
25 Bold statements like this have the potential to unsettle nativists. While waiting in the lobby during the intermission of Hamilton, I overheard a white woman tell her kids "when they said immigrants get the job done I almost walked out."

26 Alexander Hamilton, "Purchase of Louisiana," *New York Evening Post*, July 5, 1903. Quoted in *The Papers of Alexander Hamilton, Volume 26*, Ed. Harold Syrett (New York: Columbia University Press, 1979), 130.
27 Pressure from France was another factor that fueled the decision to embargo. Laurent Dubois, *Haiti: The Aftershocks of History* (New York: Metropolitan Books, 2013), 138.
28 Laurent Dubois, *Avengers of the New World* (Cambridge: Harvard University Press, 2004), 225. Barbara Browning, *Infectious Rhythm: Metaphors of Contagion and the Spread of African Culture* (London: Routledge 1998), 57. For a work of theater that uses Future Aesthetics approaches to engage this topic, see Marc Bamuthi Joseph's *Scourge.* This play addresses the historical factors that contributed to Haiti's current day situation. Most importantly for our purposes, Joseph suggests that the Haitian "scourge" is often portrayed as a pathogen, http://livingwordproject.org/core/2009/03/20/scourge/, accessed June 2016.
29 Michel-Rolph Trouillot argues the Haitian Revolution was so paradigm shifting that it was "unthinkable" to many. As such, the revolution was silenced in the archives. Michel-Rolph Trouillot, *Silencing the Past: Power and the Production of History* (Boston: Beacon Press Revised edition, 1995).
30 Monteiro, "Race-Conscious Casting," 90.
31 Monteiro, "Race-Conscious Casting," 98, For an insightful review of Monteiro's essay, see Annette Gordon-Reed, "Hamilton: The Musical: Blacks and the founding fathers" *History@Work*. April 6, 2016, http://ncph.org/history-at-work/hamilton-the-musical-blacks-and-the-founding-fathers/, accessed June 2016. For an interview with Monteiro see Rebecca Onion, "A Hamilton Skeptic on Why the Show Isn't As Revolutionary As It Seems," *Slate*, April 5, 2016, http://www.slate.com/articles/arts/culturebox/2016/04/a_hamilton_critic_on_why_the_musical_isn_t_so_revolutionary.html, accessed June 2016.
32 In 2015, the Theatre Development Fund brought high-school students to see *Hamilton* when the show was at the Public Theater. One teacher used the pedagogical approach that I am proposing: "Bill Coulter, who teaches a sophomore English class at . . . Fort Hamilton High School in southwestern Brooklyn, had his class read the Declaration of Independence, the Universal Declaration of Human Rights, *even the Haitian Declaration of Independence*" (emphasis added). Lin-Manuel Miranda and Jeremy McCarter, *Hamilton: The Revolution* (New York: Grand Central Publishing, 2016), 156.
33 Lin-Manuel Miranda's performance can be watched at: https://www.youtube.com/watch?v=WNFf7nMIGnE, accessed June 2016.
34 Ron Chernow, *Alexander Hamilton* (London: Penguin Books, 2005), 448.
35 http://www.nyhistory.org/exhibitions/revolution-the-atlantic-world-reborn, accessed June 2016.
36 Of particular interest to people in the theater world is a play about the Haitian Revolution that ran in 1936 in London's Westminster Theatre starring the great Paul Robeson. See CLR James with Christian Høgbsjerg, *Toussaint Louverture: The Story of the Only Successful Slave Revolt in History* (Durham, NC: Duke University Press, 2012). Here are some of the major scholarly works on the Haitian Revolution: Dubois, *Haiti: The Aftershocks of History*. Dubois, *Avengers of the New World.* Robin Blackburn, "Haiti, Slavery, and the Age of Democratic Revolution. (*The William and Mary Quarterly*. Third Series, Vol 63, No 4. Oct., 2006, 643–674). David Geggus (ed), *The Impact of the Haitian Revolution in the Atlantic World* (Columbia: The University of South Carolina Press, 2001). Trouillot, *Silencing the Past*. Carol E. Fick, *The Making of Haiti: The Saint-Domingue Revolution from Below* (Knoxville: The University of Tennessee Press, 1990). C.L.R. James, *The Black Jacobins: Toussaint l'Ouverture & The San Domingo Revolution* (London: Secker and Warburg, 1938).
37 Jason Newman, "Saul Williams: Why Broadway's Tupac Musical Closed Early," *Rolling Stones*, July 21, 2014, http://www.rollingstone.com/music/news/saul-williams-details-why-the-tupac-musical-closed-20140721, accessed June 2016. Michael Jeffries,

Thug Life: Race, Gender and the Meaning of Hip-Hop (Chicago: University of Chicago Press, 2011), 86. Jeffries is paraphrasing a Todd Boyd interview: "Thug Life and the Effect of Hip-Hop on Language," *National Pubic Radio*, February 5, 2007, http://www.npr.org/templates/story/story.php?storyId=7179289, accessed June 2016. Marilyn Stasio, "Broadway Review: 'Holler if Ya Hear Me' With Songs by Tupac Shakur, "*Variety*, July 19, 2014, http://variety.com/2014/legit/reviews/review-holler-if-ya-hear-me-tupac-shakur-broadway-1201224122/, accessed June 2016.

38 Sociologists Omi and Winant argue that neoliberal economics is a "colorblind" racial project intended to distribute resources along racial lines. Michael Omi and Howard Winant, *Racial Formation in the United States* (New York: Routledge, 2015), 211–238. As the gap between the wealthy and the rest continues to grow in the United States it will likely become more difficult to bring racially progressive shows to Broadway. This is because of the issue of access and who has the money to afford such expensive tickets. As sociologist Douglass Massey points out, the two groups who are most vulnerable in moments of extreme economic inequality are "women and minorities." Douglass Massey, *Categorically Unequal: The American Stratification System* (New York: Russell Sage Foundation, 2007), 49. For a discussion of neoliberal ideology in *Hamilton* see Donatello Galella, "'I Want to Be in the Room Where It Happens': Neoliberal Multicultural Inclusion in Hamilton." Paper presented at the The Association for Theatre in Higher Education, Chicago, August 10th–14, 2016.

39 Monteiro, "Race-Conscious Casting," 96. Henry William Brands suggests that "Founders-Chic" is a recent trend in the historical imaginary that foregrounds the accomplishments of the founding fathers while downplaying the failures. He argues: "The Founders' revival is in part a reflection of the anti-liberal reaction that began with Ronald Reagan and continues today." Henry William Brands, "Founders Chic: Our Reverence for the Fathers has Gotten Out of Hand," *The Atlantic*, September 2003, http://www.theatlantic.com/magazine/archive/2003/09/founders-chic/302773/, accessed June 2016. In addition to the aforementioned frameworks contextualizing the conservative love affair with *Hamilton*, I suggest Jon Cruz's notion of "disengaged engagement": a mode of reception that celebrates the aesthetics of black music while disengaging from the politics of black people. Many conservatives appreciate Hamilton's celebration of the founding fathers because it offers ample opportunities for "disengaged engagement" with hip-hop aesthetics. Jon Cruz, *Culture on the Margins: The Black Spiritual and the Rise of American Cultural Interpretation* (Princeton: Princeton University Press, 1999). Relatedly, some conservative pundits have written rebuttals to Monteiro and Gordon-Reed's critiques of Hamilton. We may be witnessing the beginnings of a new kind of "model minority" logic where right wing pundits celebrate Lin-Manuel Miranda as a patriotic "good minority" and try to discipline "bad minorities" who demand a more inclusive cultural imaginary that includes the stories of people of color. For a discussion of the "model minority" logic as a rhetorical strategy for disciplining the Civil Rights Movement see, Robert Lee, *Orientals: Asian Americans in Popular Culture* (Philadelphia: Temple University Press, 1999).

40 By this metric, *In The Heights*' portrayal of a working class, polycultural, Latina/o community, is more reflective of Future Aesthetics than *Hamilton*.

Chapter 10

Life as primary text

Youth Speaks through the new world

James Kass

In 1996, I choose to start something. To put some ideas down on paper and tell people about it. To act on what I told people. To stick to it.

This is the story.

> *How to start a nonprofit and sustain it for 20 years in the San Francisco Bay Area during the height of the dot.com boom and bust and re-boom and re-bust and whatever it is called now. When you're twenty-six. With no money. And the nonprofit is about kids and poetry. Brown kids. And poetry. Which everyone assures you there is no money for. And wait, they ask, what is it that you do exactly? You do that full time? Really?*

1.
First, believe that entropy rules.
This is often referred to
as the 2nd law of thermodynamics but
think of it more as your bi-weekly staff meetings.

Believe in a counter-narrative.
Believe in the voice of 21st century America.
Believe in art that captures the changing
demographic of the country.
Of the need to say that I live here.

Believe in the moral imperative to speak.
The movement from silence to voice.
Believe in love, in mentoring, in possibility. Believe
that the voices of young people matter.

2.
Be proud of the tradition
and investment in public education
that you symbolize

Be able to read statistics and know that while US students
barely crack 20th in the developed world
in math and science proficiency
they remain number one in confidence.

So know that you do not need to tell kids
how great they are and that everything will be ok.

Just tell them it does not need to be this way
and they can't be afraid to speak or be responsible
to the work those words demand.

3.
Know that the number one fear
in this country is public speaking.
More than death, than war,
exploding airplanes or racist demagogues as president.
Public speaking.
Which means, as my Uncle Herbie might have said,
that at a funeral, most of us would rather be in the casket
than giving the eulogy.

5.
Work with thousands of young people
from all parts of the country for 15 years
and ask them to write and share their stories
with you.

6.
Walt Whitman is often credited with inventing free verse
to break the boxes that held him back from telling his story
honestly, from being able to capture what he thought
was the true American voice.

When I teach writing, I talk about place.
Not place as location,
but place as history,
as in what has happened here,
what is happening here now,
and what will happen here some day.

I want young people to believe
that they are not bound by
anything that has come before.
They are liberated by it.

History is a gift, not a curse.
And we make statements
through which gifts we decide to give.

Youth are neither responsible for
nor responsible to what people older
than them did, what they've been given,
although they come from it.
They are only responsible for the histories they make
for future generations to live in.

When I was a teenager I taught myself to beatbox
I had fat laces, tight jeans, a Members Only jacket. Ridiculous.
You move through things.
I went to school.
Grew a beard. Produced multiple-hour long concerts where the
Smoking of marijuana was common.
These things come and go. I was young.

Twenty years later I help produce a White House Poetry Jam, the first,

Edit the poems the first family hears. Get mocked
on national television by Jon Stewart.
Have my soul patch made fun of by a president I was
excited to vote for and who is not that much older than I am.

I'm a 3rd generation American. My great-grandparents
escaped from Tzarist Russia in a haystack on the
back of a truck and when they finally got to New York,
they spoke no English.

One hundred years later,
their great-grandson beatboxes in the White House
and gets James Earl Jones to say
Luke, I am your father pretty much on beat.
It's on youtube so you know it's true.

And when I speak, I carry with me
the sounds my great-grandparents must have made
when they stuck their head out of that haystack
and for the first time breathed free.

7.
Know that the American dream is real, the story of it. Know too
that in almost every poem you've heard by these kids

they talk about the constant barriers put in front of them
that keep them from dreaming.

8.
My father once joked he thinks I started the organization
because I'm the third son of three in a loud NY Jewish family
so I learned early on that to be heard, I needed to speak up.
But to make my voice matter, I needed to learn to speak me.

Because this is what being human is: we have evolved
over millions of years to be here, with voice,
and to understand that power. To revel. To celebrate
To hurl sticks and stones.

9.
Learn to ask for money.

But still trip out about it. Often and always. What it means to have it, to not have it, to want it, to give it, to get it, to lose it, to never having enough. Watch how this continues to be the pattern. Always underestimate the cost of everything and always expect more money than you're going to get. Then get righteously angry about how all of the money goes to the wrong places, and what's wrong with this country's priorities, and why do bills seem to not disappear when you pretend to ignore them?

10.
Try harder at ignoring them.

11.
Create a TV show with Russell Simmons. In the first meeting he will call you the n-word seven times in forty-five minutes and then get up to excuse himself briefly. When he returns two minutes later, he will stick out his hand and say, *Hi, nice to meet you, I'm Russell.*

Get the show onto HBO. Eight episodes. Five total hours. Robert Redford will speak at the premier and briefly confuse you with his son. People will henceforth refer to you as Jamie. The show will be nominated for a Peabody and an NAACP image award. Right along with Li'l Wayne. This is awesome.

Strangers will come up to you and compliment you for your hard work, others will come up to you and say that no one from your office ever called them back.

This too is awesome.

Balance all of that in your head and try to eat well and exercise.
Put on twenty pounds in fifteen years.
Keep pretending any day you will lose it.
Get your first grant. Then your second.
Eventually people will give you six figure checks.
And you will be working on seven.

But you will still forget your business cards when you read a poem at Facebook.

12.
Believe in democracy.
Believe in the impossible.
Believe in social change.
Believe that history moves forward always.
Believe in life. Believe in love. Believe in excellence.
Believe in loving young people enough that you're not
afraid to challenge them to be excellent.

Believe that our job as adults is
to create spaces in which people
younger than we are can thrive.

and

of course

believe that the creativity,
intelligence, imagination,
voice, identity, and power
of young people can change the world.

. . .

Youth Speaks is a child of New WORLD Theater. An adopted child maybe, but still a child. Let me explain. At this very moment, young people all across the United States are picking up pens, filling blank pages, grabbing microphones, and stepping proudly onto stages to declare themselves "poets."

These young writers come from all over the nation: from big cities and border towns, from Native American reservations, suburbs, the Northeast, the Deep South, the mountains, the plains, the desert—the entire panorama. It is—quite literally—a reflection of the voice of twenty-first century America. It's a voice written and spoken with a passion and intelligence that transcends boundaries of race, class, ethnicity, gender, orientation, language, geography, politics, and history. It's a voice that reflects what is possible. At Youth Speaks, we believe those voices matter.

Twenty years ago I started a poetry organization. Or more accurately, I set up a few free opportunities for young people to engage with poetry, writing and performance in San Francisco. I figured it would be a part-time thing while I finished up my Masters in Fine Arts in writing, and worked as a teacher and a low-level PR position at the local PBS affiliate; something that would keep me busy before I moved on to my real career. Little did I know that twenty years later, not only would it be an organization—and a five million dollar a year one at that—but that we'd have launched a global movement. And it would most certainly be a career.

Youth Speaks has become a landing place for thousands of hungry young poets, writers, performers, and MCs. It's a place where young people come to speak about what is most urgent to them, the stuff they need to figure out and speak to.

The organization has also created countless opportunities for teenagers to share and develop their stories with many of our national literary, entertainment, political, and educational luminaries. The young people claim that it has helped to inspire a new generation to embrace and redefine poetry as a written *and* performative activity that speaks to them, and speaks through them. Some talk about the ways in which Youth Speaks has made visible the voices of thousands of youth who had heretofore been invisible. Others love how we reflect the true demographics of the country, and the counter-narratives that accompany them. However you want to describe Youth Speaks, one thing is certain: young writers today are evolving the aesthetic. Audiences are swelling. The art form of performance poetry—or spoken word—is helping to create structure around provocative discussions and via innovations of form. Spoken word events are unveiling deeper levels of civic and cultural participation among young people while increasing literacy and providing stunning, memorable, and profound cultural moments. And it's perhaps the only place in which an incredibly diverse population of young people can come together to tell their own stories in a way that is true to them, to where they are in their lives.

But before all of this, it was 1996 and I was in grad school. I was running a lot of things around in my head. I'd wanted to be a writer my whole life. I come from a family of educators and social do-gooders. I'm a politically engaged person who is not satisfied with the state of the world and while I thought—and still think—that in my writing I can incorporate that aspect of myself, I knew I had to do something. That I had to be active in the world.

I began to ask myself —why do I write? Who am I writing for? Who are my readers? What does my writing mean to me and what do I want to do with it? Ultimately, what it kept coming down to was: I'm pretty well educated from a solidly middle class family; focusing solely on my own writing felt selfish.

I grew up a hip-hop kid in New York in the 1980s, and was always part of a diverse group of young people who were actively engaging in arts programs of our own doing. Not formal arts classes or staged events, but writing together, dj'ing, rhyming or dancing or writing graffiti or whatever it was individuals in our crew were interested in and thrived at. For us, as long as someone loved it, it was hype.

From the beginning, Youth Speaks was about creating free and public spaces for young people to find, develop and publicly present their voices outside of traditional academic settings in a way that spoke to them. Previously, I'd worked in an after-school arts center. I'd done a little behind-the-scenes jazz production work, a little concert promotion in college, some low-level public relations work at the local PBS/NPR station in the education department, little classroom teaching, and I was interning at a literary magazine. So I knew enough about how to write a press release, put together a cheap brochure, and even scour the city for donated computers which we'd give out to the first twenty kids who took at least forty hours of writing workshops.

I'd always liked the idea of a comprehensive literary arts program for teenagers, though I had no idea what the day-to-day management of one would look like. I really wanted to make sure that the workshops Youth Speaks would offer were free and open to kids who didn't have exposure to arts in their schools, and weren't attendees of private arts classes. Which meant, essentially, that we'd have to volunteer to do the work and get all of the spaces and materials donated to keep it all free—at least in the beginning. And we had to keep it fun.

To me, this has been key to our success. We celebrate. We celebrate the voices of young people in everything we do. We celebrate the cultural impact young people have. We celebrate the first time a young person writes something that is honest and authentic and real. As a group of folks who came up in the hip-hop world prior to launching Youth Speaks, we've always believed in the power of the party. For us, exploring the complexities of identity and language was as good a thing as any to start a party off right. There are a series of questions I always ask young writers. Why do you write? What are you writing about? And what about the way you're writing?

We believe the world needs the writing of these kids, and we know that a lot of these young people need what writing and performance has given to them (some talk about how writing has saved their lives, often literally). And maybe that's our most important job—creating spaces in which young people can thrive.

Importantly, at Youth Speaks we stress the use of *oral* poetry specifically, recognizing that it's also an *aural* art form. The work lives in the reciprocal relationship between the mouth and the ear: the poets, each other, and the audience. While we respect the need to write things that will and must remain private, we also challenge young people to the moral imperative of sharing what it is they feel is most urgent to share in that moment, to that audience, on that given day. We also recognize that the act of writing and reading poetry in this way does not stop with the poet. Each poem can inspire hundreds of new young people to pick up the pen for the first time. Each young writer enters into the stream, and hopefully opens up a pathway for dozens—if not hundreds—more to follow. It's truly a generative process.

When I started Youth Speaks, I was going to school in a strong poetry program in a city with a fantastic poetry tradition. But the thing was, my graduate writing program, like so many across the country, lacked real diversity and did not care about the generative. It was about you, the individual, and the language that you used. To me, that approach is important. But communication is about bringing people together to drive a narrative forward. Though I think language is a true gift, it's not a precious little thing that needs to be held onto with kid gloves.

I was seeing—at least through the narrow prism of my MFA program—just who was being groomed to have a voice in this world. Those of us in those graduate-level workshops were all trying to be professional writers, in one manifestation or the other. But we were not representative of the demographics of late-twentieth-century Bay Area. So part of launching Youth Speaks was about creating a free and safe space where young people outside of the sphere of writing and arts programs could meet the opportunities to be nurtured and supported in the development of their artistic voices that embraced their full selves—the good and the bad. And it was spoken word that pulled this idea together.

Because I grew up in a large public school system with all kinds of kids writing on their own, I knew that kids in the Bay Area were writing but they just weren't finding their way into structured, nurturing yet challenging environments. I had left New York, gone to college in the Midwest, and been excited to get back to an educational environment that embraced the demographics of our nation's future. But instead, I found a graduate program that was largely white. I figured that if a graduate writing program on San Francisco State's campus lacked diversity—the school which gave birth to Ethnic Studies and incorporated writing throughout its diverse undergrad body—then the pathway to *having voice* in this nation was extraordinarily limited. I wanted some disruption.

After a year of writing and going to many poetry readings, I went to my first poetry slam (June 1996). I had already learned how much I loved to hear poetry out loud, but I had grown increasingly frustrated by just how poorly some poets read their work. I had been to dozens upon dozens of boring poetry readings (San Francisco was then a terrific place to go hear poetry read, boring and otherwise), and they were driving me crazy. I loved the words, but some of these poets were so insular in their sharing of their poems that I preferred reading them on my own, rather than hearing them ruin it for me. Remember, I was a hip-hop kid. I liked parties. I liked the swagger that came with wanting people to recognize that you are *fresh*. And being open to knowing the next person is pretty damn *fresh* too.

At my first poetry slam, I saw something different. Some of the work was fantastic, others—like at any reading—not so much. But it was certainly the most diverse group of poets sharing a stage I'd ever seen. And it was not boring. The poets were youngish, very engaging, passionate about their work, and unafraid to share themselves with the crowd, opening themselves up to both positive and negative critique.

The poetry slam was the first place outside of a music venue where I saw an unadulterated celebration of language and writing and poetry that was raucous and fun and diverse. I'd been to plenty of book festivals and writing workshops, but this was different. This was alive (the Nuyorican Poets Café hadn't re-opened until 1989, and by then I was already in college and out of New York).

One of the things I should mention is that when I started Youth Speaks, I figured that maybe over the years, fifty or so young teenagers would participate, and when I got my degree, it would be a way for me to remain connected to arts and to education. But fifty young people showed up in the first two months. So I changed my thinking. I started reading books. I started taking free courses on how to start a nonprofit organization.

The population of young people coming out to the workshops continued to grow. At the same time, I began talking to the people who ran the small theater hosting the adult poetry slam and we began moving on the idea of holding a poetry slam for teenagers during National Poetry Month in 1997.

The poetry slams I was attending were exciting and while outrightly competitive in a silly way (I mean, we "judge" the quality of a poem with a number and have about 2 seconds to do so), challenged the writers to reach new heights in their writing and performance. Saul Williams and others had entered into the poetry slam scene, so there were videos and tapes of poets the kids could relate to and since they were responding positively to the tapes I brought in of poets reading their work. Why not give them an opportunity to be celebrated in public?

Again, I thought it would be great if ten kids participated . . . but for that inaugural Youth Speaks Teen Poetry Slam, we had more than fifty poets in the first event, and close to five hundred audience members over three weeks, selling out the small Mission District theater and getting a front page article in the arts section of the *SF Chronicle*. And, it turned out, this was the first real teen poetry slam in the country.

So then we had more events, and more kids starting showing up. And they kept showing up, saying incredibly provocative, thoughtful, and creative things in the workshops and from the stages. And schools started calling me, instead of me calling them. Other theaters wanted the young poets on their stages, and the SF Bay Area Book Festival wanted the poets to read with legendary beat poet Lawrence Ferlinghetti. Then people wanted to publish the poems and hear the poems again. Some even wanted to start giving us money.

Fortunately, I had read those books on starting a nonprofit, and had written our articles of incorporation, so about six months after I came up with the idea, I set up a nonprofit, 501(C)(3) organization (though still fiscally sponsored for a few years) that worked with young people to write poetry, to read poetry, and to share poetry. To expand poetry. To be active in the world while doing so.

The success has been tremendous. But in many ways, I measure our successes by looking back at the very first public Youth Speaks program. In October 1996, I took three poets with me to George Washington High School in San Francisco, a large public school with a diverse population.

One of the teachers had set us up in a small auditorium with about a hundred public high school students. We were there to perform a few poems, to do a quick writing workshop, and to let the kids know about the opportunities we were offering. I introduced Youth Speaks—we were a diverse group of poets in our mid-twenties. I asked if anyone in the room wrote poetry. Two hands crept up slowly. The rest of the room just stared at us. Our performance and workshop went well and we recruited three to four new participants. After which, the teachers told of how they hated when the poetry section came up because they didn't really know how to teach it and the kids had no interest at all. They were glad to see the spark we'd ignited in the room, and hoped we could keep it up.

Recently I went to Washington to observe how our school-visit program is doing. In a similar room, almost twenty years after the first George Washington High School visit, our Poet Mentor asked how many of students in the room wrote. There were about one hundred students present, and half of them raised their hand. The teacher had been trying to get us to their school for months, but we were all booked up, because now poetry is a hot thing on high-school campuses.

I'm not going to say that this is only because of Youth Speaks, but I will certainly say that Youth Speaks has helped inspire young people and teachers to think about poetry in a whole new way. *Spoken Word* is no longer Hillary Clinton reading a children's book; it's the children of twenty-first century America telling their stories.

This July, Youth Speaks will hold our nineteenth annual Brave New Voices Youth Poetry Festival, an event that takes place in a different city each year. The 2016 festival will be in Washington, DC three months before a presidential election. There will be more than six hundred young writers from close to sixty cities deeply engaged with the power of poetry and performance. These six hundred young poets will be selected from more than ten thousand young people participating in poetry slams in their local cities, all of whom are part of a generation hungry for the experience that only spoken word can offer.

This is what I take away every year when I'm witnessing new writers come out to workshops, storm the stages at open mics, and take part in this amazing Brave New Voices Festival: the poetry of young people is helping to define the new American voice. This incredibly diverse population of young writers are talking about critical issues in their lives, and they are doing so from every corner of the country. They are writing in the styles and sounds that make sense to them; they are tapping into the continuum of poetry but do not feel bound by it. Poetry has become a liberating force in their lives that is allowing them to proudly put their identities, voices, power, and imaginations center stage.

These young writers are embracing the opportunity to have their voices heard, to have their ideas validated, and to have their intellects celebrated. They are open to critique. They love to be challenged and asked what they mean when they write a particular line, stanza, or poem. And mostly, they love each other. We adults might be blown away by the wordplay or the excitement of a performance, the profoundly personal and critical statements some of these young poets make in their work. But the young writers focus on the honesty and effort each writer puts into each piece. Ultimately, they may like the poem, but love the poet.

I've heard more cheers and support for the new young poet who is reading something really important to them for the first time, the page shaking, their voice cracking, than I've heard for the super polished poet who is technically proficient but isn't really saying anything significant.

The way that young people approach the word is a thing of real consequence to them, and this is what inspires me and I imagine the thousands of adults who keep coming out to support these emerging writers. The teens who are putting pen to paper and stepping onto stages are benefiting from an opportunity to be heard seriously. They are telling real stories, sharing real joy, exposing real pain. To them, poetry is not a luxury.[1] It's as necessary to them as breathing.

I'm a product of creative writing programs. I have undergraduate and graduate degrees in writing, and have been a student in dozens of writing workshops at two major universities. Through the years, I developed my own thoughts on how workshops should happen, who should be in them, and what they should be for. But it wasn't until the Youth Speaks workshops started filling up that I really began to see the poem-building space as sacred.

Where else can young people define themselves, using the most simple of technologies: pen, paper and ink? Where else are young people given a platform from which they can be heard? And this is where New WORLD Theater comes in. If Youth Speaks staff had never gone to the Intersections Conference at New WORLD Theater, we would have thought we were the only ones doing what we were doing.

A quick digression: Back in the early days of Youth Speaks, it was a much more free-flowing kind of thing. I had DJ'd a bit in high school, so I approached the curated live Youth Speaks events from the view of a DJ. I invited certain kids to do certain poems, but there was no pre-set order. It kind of was like the kids were the records in the crate, and I pulled out the next record based on the flow of the night, the stage, and the crowd. Now that we're in much larger union houses, we can't do it like that, but in the early days, there was a certain elegance to it. And it left some space open for new poets to drop in or teachers to bring them.

On the night of our 2nd annual Bringing the Noise for Dr. Martin Luther King Jr event in January 1999, a guy came down from the crowd in the middle of the show said something like, "Hey, this is kind of dope. I have a student with me who is a great poet. Can he get on the mic?" I said something to the effect of sure, let's see how the night plays out. He's good? "Yes," the teacher said. "He's good." So at the end of the night, I called him down. His name was Biko Eisen-Martin, and the teacher was Marc Bamuthi Joseph and that was the first time we met.

Six months later, Bamuthi had left his teaching job and we began the journey of working together for the next 15 years. Bamuthi has since gone on to become one of the world's respected theater artists, curators, and arts educators.

But back in the day, we were two pretty young guys, both from New York, both lovers of hip-hop, and both believers in the next generation. An incredible writer, Marc helped shape our pedagogy and practice, and—as in all great collaborations—expanded my original vision for Youth Speaks by adding his own to create something neither of us could have done by ourselves. He, along with other key people from the early days of the organization—Paul Flores (one of the poets on the first school visits) and Melinda Corazon Foley—were invited to the Intersections Conference at New WORLD Theater near the end of Roberta Uno's tenure there.

After many successful events, we knew we were onto something special here in the Bay Area. From the kids and audiences flocking to the space, to the incredibly profound moments unfolding, to the opportunities that kept coming Youth Speaks' way—and the funding that started showing up—we felt we were ahead of a rising wave that was bigger then us.

When we went to Intersections and saw all of the other young artists and performers of color from across the country who in their own communities were ahead of the waves too, we got a sense of just how big our movement was. We realized we weren't alone. No one was doing it just like us, but others were doing it in their own way and in their own cities, but with the same kind of excitement and possibilities unfolding.

The hip-hop generation, as it were, was entering into the field of nonprofit performing arts and theater in a way that was powerful and would go on to be so until today. And I know dozens of artists and arts leaders still in the field who point to that conference—and the leadership of Roberta Uno—as a catalyst for a generational shift. Not only were we recognized for our work, but we also met other incredible people from across the county who we continue to work with today.

Just as I knew that young people were out there writing, there was no place for them to be supported and nurtured unless they already had access, Roberta knew we were out there doing what she'd done when she was younger. We just didn't have access.

One of the core tenants of our pedagogy is that in order to engage young people who may be marginalized, alienated and silenced by traditional teaching practices, we start with the purpose of writing before moving into the mechanics of writing. Roberta has always talked about the purpose of performing arts programming as the key thing. Yes, the mechanics are important so that we can be sustainable if not robust, but there are plenty of "mechanically sound" organizations whose work is not really necessary. She saw in us organizations that ultimately would need to get our mechanics in place, but the first thing was to recognize our value and to help nurture and guide that. Which is the exact same idea we take when we work with young writers. I don't care how polished your writing is; I care about where it comes from and what its trying to do.

Multiple studies show that teenagers—particularly marginalized teenagers—are attracted to arts programs that combine the best of arts education and youth development practices. This means it's not about the art work created, it's about the process of making art. What that does for an individual, and what that does for the community of individuals engaged in arts practices. This doesn't mean we don't celebrate the writing and performance, it just means we celebrate even more the picking up the pen and stepping to the mic in the first place. It's in this way that we think the best of arts education is a radical practice at work to re-democratize the future.

Young people tell me time and again that it was in these poetry workshops and performances that, for the first time, they got to write and speak about themselves. Not always in reaction to any particular prompt, just in a space where they could say who they are and what matters to them. How they see the world. How the world sees them. How they'd like to live their lives. How they think they are living their lives. How they think the world they are living in should be. What they love and what they want to change. It's a space that simply asks them to tell their stories. To write. Not to write well or write poorly. Just to write. And to take it seriously.

Our approach to this is pretty simple. We offer a lot of programs to take advantage of if you're a teenager. Teenagers just need to show up, and they have been, and do, and they keep showing up. It is now typical for us to expect to sell out three thousand seat venues for a poetry reading by teenagers on a Saturday night in downtown San Francisco or Oakland. At an unprecedented moment in human history when we have more technology competing for our attention than ever, many people are choosing to come together to celebrate young poets. This kind of thing is happening all across the country. Come hear them. They are pretty incredible.

Note

1 "Poetry Is Not a Luxury" is the name of a remarkable Audre Lorde essay. Check it out. Audre Lorde. *Sister Outsider: Essays and Speeches* (New York: Quality Paper Book, 1984).

Chapter 11

Hip Hop as pedagogy

The Hip Hop Theatre Initiative[1]

Daniel Banks

> When you go into any culture, I don't care what the culture is, you have to go with some humility. You have to understand the language, and by that I do not mean what we speak, you've got to understand the language, the interior language of the people. You've got to be able to enter their philosophy, their worldview. You've got to speak both the spoken language and the metalanguage of the people.
>
> (Wole Soyinka)[2]

> Have you had a substantive conversation with someone under twenty, not your son or daughter or their friend, in the past month?
>
> (Roberta Uno)[3]

New WORLD Theater was a creative crossroads for an extended community of artists working at the intersection of a contemporary, intercultural aesthetic and a commitment to social justice. Project 2050 was one of NWT's great innovations. Developed in 2000 by Roberta Uno, this visionary, 10-day summer program for teens was born out of demographic research indicating that people of color would be in the majority in the year 2050.[4] Project 2050 brought together established artists and scholars working in politically progressive fields with a broad sector of youth from the Pioneer Valley area of Western Massachusetts. Many of the artists were part of the nascent Hip Hop theater movement in the US. On any given day, a visitor to the Amherst College campus could see: students practicing the polyrhythms of the "stepping" dance form outside the dining hall; every participant with a notebook furiously scrawling lyrics, verses, or scenes; posters, white boards, and flip charts full of tags, lists, diagrams, and outlines; and the Open Mic nights turn into giant jam sessions—constant creative rehearsing and self-expression. It was, in essence, a 10-day cipher.[5]

The curriculum paired performance-based skill-building sessions such as DJ'ing, Hip Hop dance, drumming, singing, verse writing, Beatboxing, and visual arts with "Knowledge for Power" sessions led by the scholars. Then, in teams with a director and a playwright, the youth would craft a short performance piece around a societal issue that impassioned them. The participants presented these compositions in a full-length piece performed for the community at the end of the summer session. The pieces were often reprised in various ways throughout the year—in performance at UMass-Amherst as part of the NWT season, as well as on tour to other schools and cities.

The devised and well-researched performance work addressed such topics as incarceration, immigration, COINTELPRO and the "war on drugs," cultural appropriation, racism, sexism, classism, and homophobia. The youth participants' commitment to social justice and their ability to integrate critical historical and sociological data into their Hip Hop theater work created a new paradigm for the role of Hip Hop in a creative learning environment. By encouraging youth to explore this intersection of aesthetics and activism, Project 2050 was an incubator for the next generation of artists and critical thinkers.[6]

This unique approach to arts education encouraged the participants to explore what NWT founder Roberta Uno termed "Future Aesthetics."[7] By combining art-making with critical thinking, the youth participants developed an understanding of the history, economics, and politics that impacted them. As described by Chris Rohmann in his case study about Project 2050:

> Creative approaches to pedagogy inspired artists and youth alike to inscribe their creative work with themes that engage in an exploration of their world, deter a position of "victim," and grant agency towards making change for the future.[8]

What resulted was an inspiring blueprint for cross-generational engagement while creating social justice-driven performance work at the cutting edge of contemporary performance strategies and methods. 2050's process embodied the essence of a culturally driven pedagogy—in this case, Hip Hop pedagogy.

HHED, HHPED, and multiple intelligences

One of the fundamental reasons for Project 2050's success, I submit, is that it accessed the "ways of knowing" of both its participants and leadership. In my thinking, this process embodies the difference between what is often named either Hip Hop Education (HHED) or Hip Hop Pedagogy (HHPED).[9] HHED tends to focus on the content of the class or lesson by introducing some aspect of Hip Hop production into a lesson to teach a requisite skill, for example, introducing a rap song to learn about textual analysis, rhyming, history, and/or the intersection of all these areas. The potential of HHPED is that it is a total re-imagining of the classroom experience and speaks to the cultural intelligences of the students, which includes the language, history, rituals and mores of the forty-year-old global, youth-oriented social justice movement known as Hip

Hop. Accordingly, I use the term "generations" to reference the fact that, since the 1970s, several generations and millions of youth have been born under the sign of Hip Hop and influenced by a culture of art and activism. HHPED engages both the structure of the learning environment as well as the cultural ethos of Hip Hop in addition to, and sometimes more significantly than, the content. Although the terms HHED and HHPED are often used interchangeably, I suggest that each practice is unique.

This foundation of cultural ethos is what makes Hip Hop a model for pedagogy in and of itself. HHPED asks, "How do educators learn about and engage the cultural intelligences of their students?" As demonstrated by Project 2050, Hip Hop as pedagogy presents an effective way of engaging today's youth learners while simultaneously modeling participant-centered approaches to leadership and community engagement.

HHED and HHPED each owe a debt to critical pedagogy and Paulo Freire's work of "education as the practice of freedom—as opposed to education as the practice of domination." Reconsidering the relationship between classroom content and structure has direct application to teaching and leading in any environment. Innovations in the field of education already point toward Freire's notion of *praxis*, "reflection and action upon the world in order to change it."[10] I have found that this generation of students has similar goals for their education.

In 2004, responding to my New York University students' desires to make work that had cultural, social, and political meaning for them, together we founded the Hip Hop Theatre Initiative (HHTI). Project 2050 greatly inspired HHTI, both in terms of approach and the opportunity to collaborate with artists who would become HHTI faculty. HHTI was built on this model of integrating Hip Hop intelligences with critical pedagogy and has worked in cities around the US and ten countries around the world. In almost every venue we have visited in the United States and abroad, participants and community members formed a project or organization after our departure.

We collaborate with artists, students, community leaders, and activists to model this same methodological shift—the classroom and rehearsal room as cipher with shared responsibility, relying on the group mind and spirit. In developing a curriculum rooted in the values of Hip Hop culture, I was struck by the ways that the pedagogy intersected with the intelligences described by developmental psychologist Howard Gardner in his theory of multiple intelligences (MI). The theory has gained popularity in education, the arts, grassroots organizing, and social justice fields over the last thirty years.[11] That same time frame corresponds to the increased number of students in the United States coming into contact with Hip Hop culture.

And so, in HHTI, I began to put the two theories in a kind of genealogical dialogue by exploring parallels between the intelligences of MI theory and the explicit performative elements of Hip Hop culture—DJing, MCing (rap, especially freestyle), B-boying/B-girling (dance), Writing/aerosol art/graf, and human beatboxing.[12] I believe that MI theory is a useful heuristic or window for understanding why it is important to consider the structure of the learning environment in addition to the content of the lessons. Therefore, in this chapter I trace the parallels between Gardner's theory and what I call "Hip Hop intelligences" and include suggestions for "remixing" the learning environment to play to the cultural strengths of Hip Hop-generations youth. Numerous critical pedagogy-based initiatives already accomplish excellent work of this nature with educators and community leaders; HHPED is a part of this movement. My hope is that this focus on a culturally based pedagogy will assist practitioners of all backgrounds in continuing to transform modes of classroom interactions, both in theater and non-theater settings.

The Hip Hop Theatre Initiative: Youth Voices First

> Young World, your work has the power to provoke movement from silence to empowerment based in liberatory pedagogy and youth development. It democratizes a civic population of youth by giving them a platform to speak. Your elders in rhyme challenge you to find your own voice, to work hard to apply it, and to do so responsibly. If you're not afraid of your own potential, we promise that we won't be. Hey Young World, the word is yours.
>
> (Mark Bamuthi Joseph)[13]

For the purposes of this chapter, I am discussing the global activist culture that self-identifies as Hip Hop and has its origins in a peace-building practice that dates back to the early 1970s in New York City.[14] Iconic of this ethos are Afrika Bambaataa's Universal Zulu Nation, founded in 1973, and the Hip Hop Declaration of Peace organized by the Temple of Hip Hop and signed at the United Nations in 2001, as well as many initiatives around the globe (in which Zulu Nation also figures prominently). The social and economic circumstances of first-generation Hip Hop youth in the South and West Bronx and other parts of the United States are reflected in the resistant aesthetics forged by these environments.[15]

Hip Hop culture is, paradoxically, not synonymous with the genre of music and commercial products marketed under its name, although at times there are areas of overlap as the two interact in a global marketplace. It is critical that the reader overwrite the influence of certain commercial industries that have more marketing dollars than Hip Hop culture, which, for many artists and activists, is the "real" Hip Hop. While these industries themselves put out very real images and messages that are often not at all progressive or positive, I ask readers to remember that misogyny and greed, for example, are not unique to Hip Hop; they are omnipresent in consumer culture and have appropriated Hip Hop's voice, beats, and rhymes to sell products.

HHTI strives in workshops to begin and end with youth participant voices rather than the facilitators'. At the start of a workshop this can take the form of a name game in which participants introduce themselves with a word and gesture and declare what they bring to a room when they are at their best; or it might be a round of the call-and-response rhyming song "Shabooya/Roll Call." Often, we also begin with a wall-write, which is the first thing that people are asked to do when they enter a room. Participants respond to a prompt written on a sheet of butcher-block paper hanging on the wall—such as "What Is Hip Hop to You?"—through writing, drawing, doodling, and/or co-signing and extending what others have written. After taking time to observe the community-generated documentation, we discuss what they observe about the collective offering, such as common themes, differences of opinion, and styles of self-expression. We also structure the workshops so that participants have the last word, introducing such activities as:

- going around the circle sharing something that they "liked or learned" during the gathering;
- offering something they are putting into the center of the community cipher and something they are taking away; and
- verbalizing a declaration to the ensemble that is spiritually sealed and actualized with the collective utterance of the Yoruba word "*ashé*!"[16]

The HHTI pedagogy, as it developed, was clearly impacted by cultural ethos. In working with the various performative elements of Hip Hop, we were inherently appealing to multiple ways of knowing the world—among them visual, musical, aural, physical, and philosophical. Students came to the work with different access points—firsthand, lived experiences of systemic cultural and/or economic marginalization, or empathic ally/observer status. The majority of these students sought an alternative to a traditional top-down, "banking" style of education as described by Freire in his landmark book *Pedagogy of the Oppressed*. In this system educators make "deposits" into students qua banks, only to be "withdrawn" at exam or evaluation time. As Freire writes, in this system "knowledge is a gift bestowed by those who consider themselves knowledgeable upon those whom they consider to know nothing." He advocates a model of partnership rather than "bank-clerk" teaching.[17] What became immediately clear is that, in order to excel, the students drawn to HHTI needed interactivity, a project-based/problem-solving learning approach, and to move frequently from one modality (seated/aural/literary) to another (physical/embodied/participatory). It was necessary to change rhythms as often and as seamlessly as a Hip Hop soundtrack changes beats.

Multiple intelligences, Hip Hop, and the "elements"

At about the time HHTI was getting started, Gardner's work in MI theory seemed to be omnipresent at conferences, in journals, and in live and online discussions about pedagogy. Gardner defines an intelligence as "a biopsychological potential to process information that can be activated in a cultural setting to solve problems or create products that are of value in a culture."[18] Given Hip Hop's status as a culture, I noticed with some curiosity that Gardner describes the intelligences in cultural terms, and that MI theory's listed intelligences mirrored my Hip Hop–generation students' pedagogical needs and ways of engaging with the world (also reflected in my own educational predispositions). Thus, I began an inquiry into the parallel historical geneses of Hip Hop culture and Gardner's research that led to MI theory.[19] Gardner began his research in the 1970s and published his first MI book in 1983. He proposed seven intelligences: linguistic, logical-mathematical, musical, bodily-kinesthetic, spatial, interpersonal, and intrapersonal.[20] Gardner stresses that these intelligences do not necessarily "operate in isolation," but rather are the intersecting strands of the ways in which people perceive and know the world. Each individual has a unique blend of intelligences, what he calls a "repertoire of skills for solving different kinds of problems."[21]

Taking both Hip Hop culture and MI theory as late-twentieth-century zeitgeists, Gardner's description of a problem-solving "repertoire" also aptly captures the spirit and origins of Hip Hop culture. Hip Hop was produced in a crucible that collided cultural richness with severe economic marginalization. In the Bronx it was the inevitable consequence of the systematic practices of redlining and planned shrinkage by the New York City government and other institutions, as well as mass insurance fraud by landlords that left many of the buildings in the area burned-out shells.[22] Even in the absence of financial capital, Hip Hop celebrated the cultural capital of the residents of its birthplaces, making something from something, flipping both the frequent description of Hip Hop as "something from nothing" and the dominant culture's notion of "nothing." The phrase "something from nothing" obscures the intermingling of cultural heritages already present in the areas where Hip Hop developed.

Returning to MI theory, Gardner suggests that some intelligences are a result of both nature and nurture while others are directly related to culture and environment.[23] Gardner also explored other possible intelligences since first introducing this theory: spiritual, humor, moral, naturalist, and existential. He added "naturalist" to his list as an eighth intelligence, and "existential," conservatively, as "8 ½."[24] I discuss below how these key points of MI theory reveal additional ways that Gardner's work and Hip Hop culture speak to each other.

In terms of the historical overlap between the two, Gardner's original intelligences parallel Hip Hop youth's creative responses to their environments. Each of Hip Hop's elements stages an act of resistance to an oppressive, marginalizing society. For example, writing/aerosol art is a way of asserting one's presence, creating an avatar-like mobility. In the early days of Hip Hop, writers would sit at a look-out point and watch subway trains as they left and then reentered the Bronx. Even youth who did not have the economic means to leave the Bronx found a way to "visit" all five boroughs virtually, through their public art. Today's writers around the globe similarly assert their presence on the world's stage through photography uploaded to the Internet.

KRS-One, the founder of the Temple of Hip Hop, remixed this notion of the five elements, calling them the "refinitions." These practices cannot be "defined" (as in definitions) because they are ever innovating, morphing, and evolving, and practitioners leave something of themselves while "refining" and "redefining" the form. KRS-One added street fashion, street entrepreneurialism, street knowledge, and street language to the five elements.[25] More recently, Hip Hop theater and HHED have joined this growing list.

None of the elements exist in a vacuum; they are interdependent, born and developed one in relation to the next. In the early days, at parties where there were DJ competitions, the DJs needed the MCs to help draw crowds to their side of the basketball court or rec room and win popularity; the DJs extended rhythmic sections of records known as "break-beats" so that the B-boys and B-girls could dance/battle to them. Even today, writers, as a kind of global Hip Hop PR machine, announce the presence of the culture to the world through their hypervisible public art. And Beatboxers imitate DJing techniques and draw on rap and cultural references to create their soundscapes. Many artists practice more than one element, demonstrating Hip Hop's interdisciplinary way of being in the world and echoing Gardner's theory about the intelligences working intersectionally.

Other connections between the two thought systems include the "intrapersonal" and "existential" intelligences that overlap in Hip Hop. As I have written elsewhere,[26] today's Hip Hop culture demonstrates a deep connection to multiple spiritual forms in its writings, music, and art—including, but not limited to, ancient Yoruban and Kemetic cosmologies, Buddhism, Hinduism, Taoism, Christianity, Judaism, Islam, and Indigenous thought systems. Some examples of this spiritual side of the culture include: the frequent utterances and references "*Ashé*," "Word!" "Say word!" "Word is bond," and "Word becomes flesh"; KRS-One's fascination with the *Bhagavad Gita* and flipping the nickname Krishna, originally used to taunt him, to KRS; the RZA's remix *The Tao of Wu*;[27] and Hip Hop theater pieces such as *Goddess City* and Chadwick Boseman's plays. These are only a few examples of how, in the United States, Hip Hop culture has embraced a spiritual way of knowing and being in the world. Hip Hoppers from around the globe, similarly, weave their own spiritual foundations into their music and cultural practices.

Gardner, by his own admission, shies away from declaring a spiritual intelligence. Yet, this deeply spiritual side of Hip Hop culture is reflected in "existential intelligence": knowing and understanding the world through, as he writes, "the human proclivity to ponder the most fundamental questions of existence."[28] The birth of Hip Hop itself could be explained as a function of existential intelligence, in that it was born out of a need to find possibility in an economic landscape of seeming impossibility—that is, something from something.

In addition, Gardner's definition of "naturalist intelligence"— "the capacities to make consequential discriminations in the natural world"[29]—might be reflected in what I propose is Hip Hop's "environmental intelligence," when thinking about the Hip Hop practice of writing and the ability of Hip Hop-generation youth to navigate an urban landscape. Naturalist intelligence privileges people with access to a nature environment; in the same way, "computational" abilities exist within urban settings, including Hip Hop's fundamental reliance on entrepreneurial survival, that is, hustling. The ways of knowing and interacting with the world described by MI theory approximate a manifesto of Hip Hop culture. Although MI theory is not written from a Hip Hop perspective, for the person from outside Hip Hop culture approaching this work, Gardner's theory may provide a useful access point.

A Hip Hop cultural intelligence

Hip Hop culture has the makings of its own form of intelligence. In addition to the elements, equally integral to Hip Hop is an understanding of what constitutes a Hip Hop cultural environment and how the ethos of the culture plays out in gathering spaces. This structural question is, in fact, one of the crucial dynamics that defines Hip Hop as a culture: it has its own discrete ceremonies and rituals.

Below is a preliminary list of practices and values found within the global Hip Hop and Hip Hop theater communities to which I belong. They are not a recipe, but rather speak to a cultural intelligence, a way that many people born under the sign of Hip Hop perceive the world and one another:

- *Hip Hop culture is essentially a democracy-building practice.* The cipher as a fundamental site of engagement demonstrates this ideal. Hip Hop-generation writer Adam Mansbach calls Hip Hop a "structural metaphor for democracy,"[30] which is one reason for the increased interest in Hip Hop by the peace-building field.[31]
- *Hip Hop has at its core a competition of skills.* This ethic is embodied by battling, ranging from friendly to fierce, and driven by virtuosity. Originally only of value within the culture, all these skills have since been appropriated in commercial markets. Paradoxically, these art forms are often also questioned, degraded, and criminalized outside of the culture (for example, writing/aerosol art classified in media and politics as "vandalism," rap music

as "noise," and the complex history and aesthetics of B-boying and B-girling reduced to "kids spinning on their heads").

- *Hip Hoppers live in a world of mixture*. These mixtures often result in something appearing contradictory to a non-Hip Hop or non-youth observer, but they are held and sustained by the members of the culture. This capacity for paradoxical thinking is in the DNA of these generations: increasingly, Hip Hop "gen-ers" come from mixed-heritage backgrounds or live at the intersections of ethnicity and appearance. These youth face a national language of demography that is out of date, inaccurate, and rooted in the pseudobiology of "race." What these prescribed identity locations do not address are the ways that colonization shaped, and continues to shape, contemporary identities. Many individuals of these generations choose not to select one identity, but claim them all, asserting their multiple heritages, backgrounds, and cultural influences.

Other seeming Hip Hop contradictions that will be useful in reconceptualizing a pedagogy for the Hip Hop generations include:

- Hip Hop is revolutionary, and it is also commercially entrepreneurial.
- Hip Hop draws from and acknowledges its past cultural connections and influences while also innovating.
- Hip Hop gen-ers have grown up in a music-video inflected world, which is non-linear, episodic, and marked by the fragmentation of quick takes. These aesthetics influence and reflect the attention span of a generation of expert multitaskers. Many of today's young people are pathologized as ADD and ADHD, while the information and stimuli they receive from the world around them, including mainstream media and advertising, promote a behavioral response that matches this energetic signature.

Understanding these and other fundamental aspects of Hip Hop youth's lived experiences—as Soyinka writes, the "metalanguage of the people"—is critical for developing a pedagogy that is organic to the culture.

Hip Hop as pedagogy: a jumping-off point

> Education as a process of freedom is not just about liberatory knowledge, it's about a liberatory practice in the classroom.
>
> (bell hooks)[32]

In 2009, a Google search for "Hip Hop" and "multiple intelligences" in the same source yielded 14,200 hits. In 2012, there were 217,000, but at that time, fewer than ten journal articles appeared under those search terms across multiple educational and humanities databases.[33] This disparity suggests to me that the notion of a Hip Hop cultural intelligence is widely understood in the community and at a grassroots level, but not yet at an academic or research level.

What is also more evident at the community level is that, for something to feel truly Hip Hop, the practice—the rituals of engagement—will reflect the culture. In other words, for the pedagogy to be remixed or flipped successfully, it is not enough to create a lesson plan that plays to the individual intelligences of Hip Hop-generation students; HHPED requires a restructuring of the learning environment to reflect the totality of young people's cultural intelligences and values.

Therefore, introducing rap, spoken word, Hip Hop dance, writing/aerosol art, and other Hip Hop elements into assignments while employing traditional methods of discipline and assessment and relying on old-school classroom hierarchies is merely a lure. This practice does not transform the learning environment and positions students as a kind of guinea pig—as if to suggest that an experimental spoonful of Hip Hop sugar will entice students to do their homework or pay attention. Form is as important as content. The learning environment needs to reflect and speak to the cultural values of the participant learners. By contrast, a classroom that does not take into account the cultural intelligences of its students reinscribes traditional relationships of power. Such an environment is a form of structural violence, which is clearly not optimal for learning or growth.

This last point explains why some experiments with Hip Hop in the classroom are more fruitful than others. HHPED at its best, like critical pedagogy, is concerned with catalyzing students to have a voice in their own education, thus learning how to take responsibility for their own futures. As Sam Seidel describes in *Hip Hop Genius*, HHPED values a learning environment in which "students are engaged not as consumers but as creators."[34] This approach encourages self-expression and leadership as a path to building and/or strengthening community.

I recommend that educators, activists, and artists attempting to weave Hip Hop into their work experiment with a few fundamental distinctions and practices. I acknowledge that many of these will be familiar to readers; yet, I consistently hear from educators that they wish they had access to new resources and ideas for structuring classroom culture and interactions. Therefore I offer these with the hope that they will introduce new approaches to some readers and serve as welcome reminders to others:

1 *Distinction:* Make the space look and feel like a Hip Hop space.

   Suggested practice: Meet in a circle, even if it means reorganizing the whole space every class—the effort will pay off. This formation breaks down traditional classroom or group hierarchies and makes it easier for all to connect on an equal plane. If using chairs, only have the number of chairs of participants that are present so the group feels whole and complete. More chairs can be added as people arrive.

2 *Distinction:* Community is the first priority.

Suggested practice: Start with a check-in (and set a time limit, if needed, such as one word, one sentence, or one minute). This process will help build community and a sense of trust, which result in an ability to focus more clearly on the work at hand. Also, see what happens if you wait to begin until all participants are accounted for (including a phone call or text message to those who are late or absent to ascertain their well-being or to find out if they need help). While there may be initial push-back ("It's not my fault if someone doesn't come to class"), this practice builds community-mindedness and deepens levels of caring. I have had students who did not come to class because they were in the hospital or in prison; in one case, we went as a class to visit a student pre-surgery in the hospital. This practice brings home to students how interdependent we are. It also contradicts the tendency for students to think that they do not matter and will not be missed, thereby modeling community accountability.

3 *Distinction:* The leader does not need to be an expert on the material, only a thoughtful moderator of a group-learning process.

Suggested practice: In the context of HHPED, as in critical pedagogy, the teacher's or leader's role is as a facilitator—to introduce the project or lesson and keep it moving while encouraging ongoing student critique and assessment. Allow for an organic process and for the group work to unfurl. If using Hip Hop–related content, the facilitator can engage the expertise of participant learners to analyze this subject matter, explain vernacular terms and intertextual samples, and suggest further study materials. Non–Hip Hop facilitators, as respectful tourists, need to be versed in the core values of the culture, but do not need to feel (nor should present themselves) as authorities. There are many Hip Hops—no one person "owns" its history. As stated above, this structural approach is as important as the specific lesson content.

4 *Distinction:* Hip Hop youth are the experts of their own experiences.

Suggested practice: Teachers from a traditional education background will want to notice tendencies to talk down to or aggressively discipline participant learners (the dominant educational experience of previous generations).[35] If the goal is to have a student-centered learning environment, the facilitator needs to build community together, as a team. The facilitator-teacher's interactions with students will, therefore, be different if contextualized as being in the presence of a cohort of experts, eschewing "adultism."

Repositioning the teacher's role in this manner—what HHTI calls "take yourself out of the middle"—connects with Freire's pedagogy and engages a fundamental paradigm shift from other models of education. Transforming the learning environment into one that reflects a liberatory pedagogy does not mean forsaking a respectful or ordered gathering space. Rather, this approach builds trust, mutual respect, and collaboration so that everyone has "buy-in" and is empowered to take responsibility for the collective experience. Practices to encourage this ownership might include: (1) asking the group at the beginning of the class/workshop/course to generate agreements about classroom decorum and the work environment; (2) introducing a conversation about time management and co-creating a group relationship to time; and (3) if an exercise or lesson is not working, taking suggestions from the participants how to flip or transform it, thereby inviting students to be partners in the educational process.

Another way to achieve this decentralizing approach is for the leader/teacher/facilitator to introduce a story-circle or a deep-listening exercise at the beginning, so as to privilege the students' or participants' voices. Both of these practices generate community support and a generosity of listening. Especially for teachers who are not fully comfortable moderating large group conversations about sensitive topics, it is a way for participant learners still to have an opportunity to express themselves and have someone listen to them.

Clearly, there are situations where these ideas are impracticable; they may also function differently at various institutions and levels of education and learning. Much of this restructuring of the learning environment will be trial and error, with an interweaving of personal style. It is essential to connect with colleagues who are attempting to carry out similar work for mutual support. Hopefully, these suggestions will reveal the productive potential in generating an environment that closely reflects the cultural intelligences of the Hip Hop generations.[36]

In and Out of the Classroom: a case study

I now return to HHTI as a case study in how Project 2050 inspired a practical application of working with Hip Hop intelligences. In 2004 I was working closely with the Hip Hop Theater Festival and on other similar projects. Students at NYU urged me to create an opportunity for them to combine their love of Hip Hop with professional acting training. One course led to another, and soon there was a core group of students deeply engaged—HHTI was born.[37]

As described earlier, the program was built on the model of integrating Hip Hop intelligences with critical pedagogy. Its mission, instigated by the students, is (1) to integrate the rigors of theater training with the performance elements and politics of the youth-driven, grassroots, activist culture of Hip Hop; and (2) to train participants to lead arts-based workshops and facilitate dialogue about the social issues pertaining to Hip Hop. The HHTI curriculum at NYU included courses on the history of Hip Hop and Hip Hop Theater, including research into African diasporic performance aesthetics and the philosophical underpinnings of Hip Hop culture; strategies for creating devised, ensemble Hip Hop theatre performance pieces; the history of world ritual theatre (linked with the creation of a new devised production with over fifty students involved across three departments); a double-credit, intensive lab practicum; and an applied theatre-based curriculum, "Hip Hop Theatre: In and Out of the Classroom." In this class, participants learned to facilitate creative workshops in self-expression and leadership-building in the various and intersecting communities with which they identified.

Faculty interest grew out of this student-generated curriculum and I was invited to offer pedagogical workshops. In the resulting "Hip Hop as Pedagogy: Reaching Today's Youth through Multiple Intelligences and Literacies," participants working in education and community organizing discuss student- and community-centered approaches to learning and their own roles in the classroom. In the workshop, we work with such questions as: What does it mean to teach this Hip Hop generation? How can educators best engage the significant strengths of young people in the classroom environment? What constitutes a safe and productive learning space for this generation? The intent is that this learning experience for teachers also structurally models a Hip Hop, culturally based environment.

HHTI was the first of several campus-wide Hip Hop-related initiatives at NYU with which I was affiliated. I was one of the conveners of a new HHPED work group and I co-founded the Hip Hop and Pedagogy Initiative with colleagues Marcella Runnel Hall and Martha Diaz.[38] Diaz was herself in the early stages of creating the Hip Hop Education Center (HHEC), on whose founding board I serve (currently connected to both NYU and Columbia University). Both of these initiatives brought together faculty from different disciplines throughout the university to connect with students in their shared, growing academic interest in Hip Hop history and cultural production. I relate all of this to demonstrate the breadth of activity and educational innovation in the field.

Conclusion

Returning to my initial point of fascination—the synergy between the early development of Hip Hop culture and the beginnings of MI theory—Gardner writes about assessment as "simple, natural, and occurring on a reliable schedule." He suggests that "after a while, much assessment would occur naturally on the part of student and teacher with little need for explicit recognition or labeling on anyone's part."[39] This point is at the core of critical pedagogy: ongoing, continuous (self-)reflection and examination. In terms of HHPED, it is important for the educator-facilitator to remember that Hip Hop is a self-critical culture and practice. From battles in which artists reference and version one another's performances to raps that critique political and social systems, Hip Hop developed among young people who created their own governance and mentorship systems in an environment where adults (often single parents) either worked long hours to support families, did not appear to understand or sympathize with the struggles of the young people in their lives, or were absent altogether. Therefore, a work or learning environment in which there is a pre-agreed structure for ongoing critique and assessment will activate the fullest use of Hip Hop intelligences.

As previously discussed, I recommend creating these assessment strategies in partnership with the communities being assessed so that it is not a top-down, imposed process, but rather an organic, grassroots approach. This practice is another example of how, at its best, Hip Hop proposes to dismantle certain traditional power structures.

Several practical implications regarding HHPED emerge, given that Gardner's description of MI closely resembles Hip Hop culture's ways of knowing and being. MI theory is useful when developing a pedagogy for today's Hip Hop generations. First, it is a lens for understanding how to engage young people effectively in the classroom. In addition, as a framework, MI theory helps describe the interdisciplinarity and intertextuality of the first generation of Hip Hop youth's self-expression. Finally, Gardner's theories elucidate the biopsychological drive behind the continued global development of Hip Hop culture's creative production and activism.

On the flip side, educators and community leaders practicing HHED and HHPED may be able to persuade more conservative institutions and gatekeepers of the validity of their work by invoking the ways in which MI theory is in close dialogue with these approaches. Those of us engaged in this work envision the day when Hip Hop and its canon will not need such vetting; but in the meantime it could be useful in environments where MI theory is respected and has currency to show its deep resonance with Hip Hop.[40] Applications of MI theory in the classroom often translate into using a Hip Hop skill or Hip Hop-related object of inquiry to stimulate learning. An attention to HHPED can help both Hip Hop and non-Hip Hop educators discover new ways of engaging youth that extend beyond content and to understand that it is not enough only to tap into intelligences that speak to practical skills. A specific context needs to be created to activate the *cultural* intelligences of Hip Hop-generation youth so that they can fully engage their inherent creativity and brilliance.

Project 2050 exemplified such an environment and demonstrated the efficacy of this type of integrated approach. As this volume attests, NWT and Project 2050 marked a critical moment in the development of Hip Hop pedagogy and theater, solidifying and uniting the two forms.

Notes

1 A previous version of this chapter appeared in *Theater Topics* 25 no. 3 (Sept. 2015): 243–259.
2 Quoted in Susan C. Haedicke and Tobin Nellhaus, eds., *Performing Democracy: International Perspectives on Urban Community-Based Performance* (Ann Arbor, MI: University of Michigan Press, 2001), 17.
3 Quoted in Jeff Chang, ed., *Total Chaos: The Art and Aesthetics of Hip Hop* (New York: Basic Civitas, 2006), 303.
4 That estimate has now shifted to 2042. Sam Roberts, "In a Generation, Minorities May Be the U.S. Majority," *The New York Times*, August 14, 2008.

5 The cipher is a circle formation in which members of Hip Hop culture gather, share, improvise, battle, and negotiate their relationships to both one another and the culture.
6 I served as the Resident Scholar for Project 2050 in 2001 and the Coordinating Scholar in 2002. Project 2050 held its last summer session in 2010. For more information about Project 2050's history, curriculum, and community involvement, see Donna Beth Aronson, *Access and Equity: Performing Diversity at the New World Theater*, doctoral dissertation, available at http://diginole.lib.fsu.edu/cgi/viewcontent.cgi?article=1032&context=etd, accessed January 2, 2016; and Chris Rohmann, "Project 2050 Case Study: New World Theater," for Animating Democracy, http://animatingdemocracy.org/sites/default/files/documents/labs/new_world_theater_case_study.pdf, accessed January 2, 2016.
7 Quoted in Chang, *Total Chaos*, 72.
8 Rohmann, "Project 2050 Case Study," 14.
9 HHED has been around almost as long as Hip Hop. It is a global practice that in the US alone has resulted in numerous national and international symposia. The Hip Hop Education Center (HHEC), for example, sponsored three years of international think tanks on the topic, attended by over 500 educators, activists, and community leaders. HHEC has also completed an international scan of organizations participating in Hip Hop education and pedagogy and is soon launching an online platform—"A 21st-century Communiversity"—to facilitate discussion and training of leaders and educators around the world. See www.hiphopeducation.org.
10 See Paolo Freire, *Pedagogy of the Oppressed*, trans. Myra B. Ramos (New York: Continuum, 1985), 36, 69.
11 As many readers will be aware, there is a substantial body of literature challenging the validity of MI theory, and an equal amount of responses to those challenges attempting to disprove their criticisms. While it is not the intent of this chapter either to validate or disprove MI theory, these arguments and conversations provide a fascinating window into the relationship between educational theory and in-classroom experience, what is valued in each, how education is currently discussed, and how success is measured. This chapter instead focuses on the intersection of a cultural movement and an education-based theory/practice/approach and the potential productive synergies that emerge by putting the two in dialogue.
12 Borrowing from Michel Foucault's notion of *genealogy* as "cultivat[ing] the details and the accidents that accompany every beginning." *Language, Counter-Memory, Practice: Selected Essays and Interviews*, ed. Donald F. Bouchard (Ithaca, NY: Cornell University Press, 1977), 144.
13 Quoted in Chang, *Total Chaos*, 17. Bamuthi was one of a core group of artists who worked closely with Hip Hop Theatre Initiative students.
14 See Daniel Banks, "Youth Leading Youth: Hip Hop and Hiplife Theater in Ghana and South Africa," in *Acting Together on the World Stage: Performance and the Creative Transformation of Conflict*, ed. Cynthia Cohen, Roberto Guttierez Varea, and Polly O. Walker, vol. 2 (Oakland, CA: New Village Press, 2011).
15 For more information on the birth of Hip Hop and its politics and aesthetics, see, among others, Jeff Chang, *Can't Stop, Won't Stop: A History of the Hip Hop Generation* (New York: St. Martin's Press, 2005), and Tricia Rose, *Black Noise: Rap Music and Black Culture in Contemporary America* (Middletown, CT: Wesleyan University Press, 1994).
16 In the interest of performance genealogy, the first exercise came to HHTI from DNAWORKS co-director Adam McKinney, the second one from the students at the MA in Applied Theater at CUNY, and the third from HHTI student Archie Ekong. For more about HHTI's work, see Banks, "How Hiplife Theater Was Born in Ghana," *American Theater*, November 2008, and Banks, "Youth Leading Youth."
17 Freire, *Pedagogy of the Oppressed*, 58, 62.

18 Howard Gardner, *Intelligence Reframed: Multiple Intelligences for the 21st Century* (New York: Basic Books, 1999), 33–34.
19 I corresponded with Gardner and several of his then researchers, as well as colleagues at Project Zero, to inquire about this relationship. No direct connection was offered.
20 For more specific information on each of these intelligences, see Gardner, *Frames of Mind: The Theory of Multiple Intelligences* (New York: Basic Books, 1983); *Changing Minds* (Boston, MA: Harvard Business School Press, 2006); and *Multiple Intelligences: New Horizons in Theory and Practice* (New York: Basic Books, 2006). Gardner's set of criteria for what constitutes an intelligence includes a neurological component. For the purposes of this chapter I am not going to address this part of his theory, and focus instead on the question of cultural context. This neurological area, however, merits further study.
21 Gardner, *Multiple Intelligences*, 8, 21.
22 See Chang, *Can't Stop, Won't Stop*.
23 Gardner, Multiple Intelligences, 45.
24 Gardner, *Multiple Intelligences*, 21, 45.
25 KRS-One, *Ruminations* (New York: Welcome Rain, 2003), 179.
26 Daniel Banks, ed., *Say Word! Voices from Hip Hop Theater* (Ann Arbor, MI: University of Michigan Press, 2011).
27 The RZA, *The Tao of Wu* (New York: Riverhead Books, 2009).
28 Gardner, *Multiple Intelligences*, 20.
29 Gardner, *Changing Minds*, 36.
30 Quoted in Chang, *Total Chaos*, 101.
31 For more information, see http://www.brandeis.edu/ethics/peacebuildingarts/acting together/casestudies/ and www.hiphopdiplomacy.org.
32 bell hooks, *Teaching to Transgress: Education as the Practice of Freedom* (New York: Routledge, 1994), 147.
33 In 2015 there were 299,000 web hits for both terms on the same page. It is hard to know if this reflects an increase in the terms being used, a change in Google's search algorithms, or a combination of both. Since many of the sites have both terms on them, although not in relationship to each other (for example, in the form of an advertisement), I would suggest that there has been a spike in usage, but not quite as large as the numbers suggest. There are still relatively few journal articles that discuss both topics; however, several dissertations have been written engaging the two subjects.
34 Sam Seidel, *Hip Hop Genius: Remixing High School Education* (Lanham, MD: Rowman & Littlefield, 2011), 3.
35 This point is critical not just to the philosophy of educational practice, but also in terms of its efficacy. See Therese Quinn and Joseph Kahn, "Wide Awake to the World: The Arts and Urban Schools—Conflicts and Contributions of an After-School Program," *Curriculum Inquiry* 31 no. 1 (2001): 11–32.
36 Freire's writings are an invaluable resource, as are bell hooks's and other excellent sources that address critical pedagogy and HHPED and culture. One of the most thoroughly documented examples to date of Hip Hop in the classroom is Marc Lamont Hill's *Beats, Rhymes, and Classroom Life: Hip Hop Pedagogy and the Politics of Identity* (New York: Teachers College Press, 2009).
37 For its first five years, HHTI was in residence in the Department of Undergraduate Drama in the Tisch School of the Arts, NYU, due in large part to the vision and support of then-Chair Kevin Kuhlke. It is now a project of DNAWORKS (www.dnaworks.org). For more information, see www.hhti.org.
38 The Hip Hop and Pedagogy Initiative was one of the funders of the Hip Hop Theater Lab. See Richard Chavolla and Marcella Runnel Hall, *NYU's Hip Hop and Pedagogy Initiative*, 2010, available at http://www.naspa.org/images/uploads/main/Gold624.pdf.

HHTI received funding widely from both within the university and outside partners and sponsors.

39 Gardner, *Multiple Intelligences*, 180–181.

40 Take, for example, Harvard professor Cornel West's much-publicized departure from the university in 2001, in large part due to the school's then-president, Lawrence Summers, criticizing West's recording a Hip Hop-inflected album including rap. See Jacques Steinberg, "At Odds with Harvard President, Black-Studies Stars Eye Princeton," *The New York Times*, December 29, 2001, available at http://www.nytimes.com/2001/12/29/us/at-odds-with-harvard-president-black-studies-stars-eye-princeton.html.

Chapter 12

An uncharted persistence

Alternative minoritarian theater in austere Chicago

Jasmine Mahmoud

Narratives obscure it. The political economy precludes it. This theater is not supposed to be here. In the attic of a public field house, neighborhood youth stage viscerally stunning ethnographic theater based on interviews with residents of Albany Park, a largely Latino/a Chicago neighborhood where over forty languages are spoken. This is *Home/Land*, a show which twice extended its sold-out run into April 2012.

On the first Monday of every month, dozens cram into an attic above a LGBTQ-friendly restaurant for cabaret-style performances that accentuate the diversity of queer black woman aesthetics. This is *Accept Variety*, a performance showcase staged in Andersonville, the arts-hip Northside Chicago neighborhood.

In a church basement in downtown Chicago, sold-out staged readings expose audiences to the humor, bias against, and polyculturalism practiced by Arab and Asian American communities. This is Silk Road Rising, the decade-old theater company that began soon after the attacks of September 11, 2011.

In an air-conditioned tent in his parents' backyard, Mexican-American cartoonist David Pintor stages *Southside Ignoramus Quartet* (SIQ), a sketch comedy show performed weekly in the summers since 2010. In the summer of 2011, all of SIQ's shows sold out. But as Pintor told me, "We are not supposed to have this. We are not supposed to be able to do this."

This theater, alternative minoritarian, and its persistence are not supposed to be here. The political economy ostensibly precludes it. This is the post-crash era, where high unemployment, increasing poverty, staggering student loan debt, and government fiscal crises cast the contemporary political economy as austere. This is Chicago, Illinois, America's "second city" of 2.7 million people, known as much for its hyper-segregated neighborhoods[1] as for its moniker "Theater capital of America"[2] due to its theater density, with myriad storefront theaters that produce hyper-realist and avant-garde works for largely white audiences. Dominant narratives also obscure this theater. This contemporary Chicago—austere and segregated—is not supposed to buttress non-white alternative performance. But somehow it does. Sold-out shows, regular runs, and critical acclaim carry much work by theater artists of color in Chicago. In this chapter, I investigate that uncharted persistence and ask, How does minoritarian alternative performance persist in post-crash, austere, segregated Chicago?

I argue that minoritarian alternative performances—although inextricably bound to neoliberal spatial, political, and economic conditions—are largely uncharted because their logics of operation produce affective experiences, and possibilities that go beyond austere capitalist logics. Those possibilities—which embed shared closeness in their audiences and activate an aesthetic consciousness of emancipative sharing—negotiate with and imagine alternatives to the neoliberal political economy. How those practices do so, persistently, focuses this query.

Tensions and concepts

Three concepts are central to this investigation: *austerity*; *minoritarian performance*; and *neighborhoods*. I define austerity, in the U.S. American postmillennial context, as government policies that ostensibly seek to reduce deficits, but also support neoliberalism through cuts to social services alongside increases to public funding of the private sector. [3] My definition of austerity differs from those found in most dictionaries, which do not emphasize neoliberalism, but rather the "difficult economic conditions created by government measures to reduce a budget deficit."[4] My definition also emphasizes austerity at the local rather than national level. In the United States, austerity budgets were enacted at city and state levels in the wake of the Great Recession of 2007–2009. Chicago as a contemporary austere city is made evident by two actions. One: the December 2010 dismantling of Chicago's Department of Cultural Affairs (DCA), when all 29 staff members were laid off,[5] and the department was incorporated into Chicago's Office of Tourism. The purported reason for DCA's dismantling: the recession-induced city fiscal crisis. And yet, two: from 2002 to 2010, the City of Chicago spent $1.7 billion in tax increment financing (TIF), to fund private and public projects.[6]

Austerity, then, is salient to this query because it frames the post-recession political economy as a schizophrenic one where overall economic growth accompanies wealth for a few and a pervasive economic depression for many. The Great Recession technically began in December 2007 and ended in June 2009, and was an outgrowth of the extreme conditions of financial collapse that ushered it in: Wall Street speculation and the bank crises of 2008, and a drastic increase in housing foreclosures.[7] Even though the Great Recession technically ended in June 2009 with an increase in economic growth, high unemployment and increases in poverty continued, in part, because of neoliberal austerity policies.[8] Austerity, then, has not been utilized as an economic tool to balance budgets. Rather, as David Harvey argues, austerity has been perpetuated at the local and state level to wage political battles that support neoliberalism and class and racial inequality, and to further recession-like conditions in a post-recession political economy.[9]

I follow José Muñoz's theorization of minoritarian as "identities-in-difference"[10] to detail the second concept, minoritarian performance. "I use the term *minoritarian*," Muñoz describes, "to index citizen-subjects who, due to antagonism within the social such as race, class, and sex, are debated within the majoritarian public sphere."[11]

Although minoritarian performance aesthetics are disparate, their antagonisms position their practices vis-à-vis what has been canonized[12] as alternative: the avant-garde. Coined in the nineteenth century, avant-garde came to label boundary-breaking aesthetics and innovative, risky, and often non-mimetic works. Today, the "avant-garde" often eschews artists of color who produce intimate, boundary-breaking performance that could be, but is not labeled as, avant-garde in newspaper and academic reviews. In Chicago, theater reviews often attend to physical avant-garde works for largely white audiences. Mike Sell argues, "The avant-garde possesses an uneasy . . . proximity to racism." I use the terms "experimental" and "alternative," then, to hint at the double bind[13] in which these alternative minoritarian performances find themselves. Minoritarian bodies represent identities-in-difference: on stage those bodies exceed[14] the narrative and aesthetics performed and also signify upon race, gender and sexuality. Katrina Sanford, executive director of Earth Pearl Collective, which produces feminist queer of color performance, told me, "It's only 'alternative' because we're gay. . . . People already see us as different."

Alternative minoritarian practices, I am arguing, reveal what are evaded when avant-garde theories frame alternative performance. I assert that for alternative minoritarian performance, marginality functions differently than it does for avant-garde performance framed through Eurocentric whiteness that is in tension with capitalism. I attend to Kimberly Benston, who contrasts white avant-gardes with black radical performance to assert that minoritarian marginal performance redeems, rather than denies, consciousness of the real. I also follow the black feminist Jazz Aesthetic which advances boundary-breaking aesthetics (presentness, immersion, and multiplicity) to reclaim "safer geographic and psychic spaces".[15] I thus consider how minoritarian performance makes spaces for justice and consciousness within the neighborhoods of Chicago which also evidence neoliberalism and displacement.

The persistence of alternative minoritarian performances during austerity reveals this intervention—into neighborhood space—in two ways; (1) these performances often eschew capitalism operationally, through a reliance on free or low-cost neighborhood space that exceeds the capitalist logic of paying rent; (2) each performance often produces vital closeness, not through exchange, but through sharing—through shared laughing, crying or re-feeling as an experiential epistemology, or a beyond-logical way of learning closeness. Those qualities instantiate alternative minoritarian theater with the operational persistence to imagine alternatives to normative political and aesthetic economies.

This query is by no means comprehensive, and does not include performance practices on the Southside, including David Pintor's Southside Ignoramus

Quartet and performance associated with Theaster Gates's Dorchester Projects, among others. This bias represents my own situatedness, as a Northside Chicagoan. But there is also a politics behind this representation. Narratives of Chicago often perpetuate the Northside as whites-only and the south and west sides as areas for neighborhoods of color. In my attention to performance practices that permeate Northside neighborhoods and Chicago's downtown Loop neighborhood, that attention to Chicago's urban geography and racialized neighborhood space threads what I am attempting to argue: minoritarian performance practices, although inextricably bounded to neoliberal spatial, political, and economic conditions, may still endeavor to produce a closeness and consciousness that exceeds neoliberalism.

An epistemology wept: Albany Park Theater Project and Northside Theater in Chicago

Endless suitcases overwhelmed a long and broad stage positioned in the middle of a cavernous theater space. On the stage's right and left ends, the suitcases stacked high to the tented, attic-like ceiling laced with thick wooden beams. Underneath that sloped ceiling, rows of audience members sat on either side of the stage, such that the audience—a packed house of eighty—faced each other as they looked across the stage. This stage—at the Eugene Field House in the Albany Park neighborhood of Chicago—is the Laura Wiley Theater, the space for *Home/Land*.[16]

Homeland—the word—evokes longing and belonging, a shared commonality among peoples, or at least a commonality generated by closeness among people who share. *Home/Land*, produced in 2012 by the Albany Park Theater Project, evoked all this, and surprisingly something beyond: an audacious commonality among the artists and audience to explore immigration, loss, and home through the sharing of stories that were at once so recognizable and so exceptional. Those stories? A queer Latino youth is proud as he is arrested after protesting on Capitol Hill in support of the DREAM Act, the proposed (but as of this writing, unpassed[17]) legislation to secure a pathway to citizenship for undocumented students. A woman born in Jordan and raised in the United States is offered a job by a Muslim American Community organization but is unable to take it because she lacks American citizenship. An immigrant father drills the narrative of a new identity into his young son to stave off immigration agents. Chicago-based Catholic nuns audaciously lobby their state representatives so that they can offer support to those people who are being deported from the United States.

These stories and more came from interviews with residents in and near Albany Park, a multiethnic and largely Latina/o Northside neighborhood (population 50,000) where over forty languages are spoken. The treatment of these stories rooted the audacity of this performance. They were collaboratively articulated and performed by the twenty-five mostly Latina/o neighborhood youth comprising the Albany Park Theater Project (APTP). According to their website (aptpchicago.org), APTP is "a multiethnic, youth theater ensemble that inspires people to envision a more just and beautiful world. APTP creates original theater that shares the real-life stories of urban teens, immigrants, and working-class Americans." In February 2016, APTP received the prestigious MacArthur Award for Creative and Effective Institutions, the organizational counterpart to the foundation's coveted "genius" awards.

The story-sharing went beyond the interviews the young actors performed and reimagined. Before *Home/Land* began, I met two of the performers, Noella and Carmel,[18] a junior in high school and a sophomore at Truman College, respectively. They asked about my interest in the company and told me how they were drawn to acting with APTP. Talking to the ebullient young actors before the show engendered an unexpected pre-show closeness.

The performance itself did not simply share the stories from the interviews, nor did it just stage these stories. Rather, through care and beautiful composition, *Home/Land* generated a profoundly emotional fabric that cohered those in the theater. The performance began and ended with the youth actors collaboratively performing live music: a song about a tree that grows among what is wicked and wonderful. The use of the song foreshadowed much of the emotion of the performance. From a scene where two young teenagers first meet at a dance in Mexico, to one where Latin American youths gleefully play soccer in immense fields before all but one are killed by the army, to the mother who plans for her daughter's *quinceañera* while battling the threat of deportation and working multiple jobs below a living wage—the performance aligned plural, ostensibly incompatible emotions of sadness, joy, wonder, defeat, and endurance.

Playfulness also carried the performance. One scene generated a game show, "Who wants to be an American?" Led by host "Bob Whiteman," who performed with a bombastic, elongated voice, the game show staged a competition between an undocumented worker and an audience member who was an American citizen and revealed the ridiculous notion of "fairness" in immigration policy. Other scenes made use of a sliding floorboard to convey travel: on a plane from Arizona where the anti-immigration law SB1070 shook a Jordan-born resident with chronic worry, and on perilous boat ride from Latin America to the United States. This theme of movement, however sad or necessary or joyful, continued in the bodies of the twenty-five actors who permutated into various characters, across different combinations. The cast inserted a lively near-impossibility in this performance, given that such a large cast is so rare in contemporary theater.

And yet with all of the composition and care, the most audacious component came from something the production gave to the audience: tears. On stage, the actors performed a wordless, choreographed scene about a family—stemmed from those teenagers who met at a dance in Mexico—growing up together in the United States. Music accompanied the movements as the five actors—as a father, a mother and three children—intertwined with one another. Playfully, two children climbed on top of their father, the mother lifted a child in the air, and the children crawled underneath each other. And then heartbreak came. An actor playing an ICE (Immigration and Customs Enforcement) agent took away the father. As this transpired, a teenage audience member sitting across from me began to cry uncontrollably. I could not help but watch her watching the scene. Then I felt my own tears, and I cried uncontrollably. Through tears, we shared the sadness of watching a family being torn apart. After the performance ended and the lights rose, I noticed most audience members had red and watery eyes. I have never before shared crying with so many others in a theater space. The tears recognized the uneasy knowledge: immigration in the United States is a fraught issue; non-citizen American residents, often indigenous to the American continent, often face inhumane, burdensome treatment while often providing below-minimum-wage labor to sustain American mythologies and standards of living.

Although not named, those shared tears—and their communitarian affect—were recognized by reviewers of *Home/Land*. "Truly astonishing," wrote Hedy Weiss, *Chicago Sun-Times* theater critic.[19] "*Home/Land* is a Gift to Chicago," declared the headline in *Chicago Theater Review*.[20] "Some Theater is timely, some striking—and some vital," wrote *Flavorpill Chicago* writer Katherine Zien. Her review continued,

> tackling the increasingly hostile anti-immigrant climate in the United States . . . *Home/Land* is a complex, meticulous tapestry crafted over two years by its talented student-actors. . . . The piece's layered emotional notes culminate neither in defeatism nor contentment but in an energy mirroring that of the youthful cast.[21]

After my experience of seeing *Home/Land*, its two-month, sold-out extension, and the overwhelmingly laudatory reviews, I became curious: how did *Home/Land* produce a shared anti-oppressive affective experience within austere Chicago, within an environment that ostensibly has no room for emancipatory closeness?

I therefore interviewed APTP's producing artistic director, David Feiner, who made it clear that although the recession had affected operations, it did not so do prohibitively.

> We have not curtailed programming or producing as a result of the recession and we haven't cut staff or salaries as a result of the recession. In fact, we continue to grow our staff and the way we compensate our staff. Even in a couple of years that we did reduce our budget, we found ways to do it that weren't hurting core programming. Most of our funders . . . kept us very high on their priority list. We did not lose funding as a result of the recession.

I was surprised when Feiner told me this. Founded in 1997 by Feiner and his wife Laura Wiley (now deceased), APTP has grown to have a staff of thirteen who work with scores of youth each year. The "how" of that persistence under austerity comes, mainly, from two structures. One is Arts Partners in Residence, a program whereby the Chicago Park District offers free underutilized park space to arts organizations. In exchange, those arts organizations provide free community services. Through that partnership, APTP is housed in Eugene Field Park and provides free performing arts workshops to neighborhood youth, including weekly Theater Thursdays and a week-long Theater Camp. The second sustaining structure strengthening APTP's persistence is a bequest from the late Dwight Conquergood, former chair of the Department of Performance Studies at Northwestern University. "We used that to help us survive the recession when funding raising fell short," Feiner told me,

> We remain one of the most truly diverse ensembles that you can see on stage in Chicago and one of the most consistently diverse audiences that you can see in Chicago. . . . Increasingly we think of our work in the context of Chicago. We have to make a very intentional effort to be sure to continue that as our work grows in popularly, to be sure our community doesn't get squeezed out.

Given its rich involvement with neighborhood youth and ethnographic performance practices, Albany Park Theater Project is community theater in the best and broadest sense. Thinking of APTP through the lens of austerity and as alternative minoritarian performance—that is, as ontologically antagonistic, aesthetically boundary-breaking, and "poor"—reveals how APTP does something different to theater categorizations. Feiner embeds community closeness in APTP's alternative aesthetics. "Certainly, I think the coming together, melding the very direct, accessible storytelling with a lot of abstract movement, is something that is still not common in a lot of places," he told me,

> When we see experimentation [in other theaters], it's more common that things get very abstract and become nonlinear and plot and story are subsumed by style and the work is intentionally more obscure and more rarified in some ways. I do think it's somewhat rare to see storytelling with the physicality.

Feiner also articulated that what is experimental may land differently on different audiences. "I think aesthetically our work is certainly experimental in the context of a lot of community-based work you might see," he said. "I think our work is aesthetically experimental . . . for audiences who come just to see us. Still, compared to a lot of what you see on mainstream stages, it's innovative as well, it's different, it's 'other.'" Feiner thus recognizes that for Albany Park Theater Project, the labels "avant-garde" and "experimental" may mean different things to different audiences. "Teenagers play all of the roles in our plays, and . . . we are casting cross-culturally, cross-ethnically all the time," Feiner told me,

> Where in a great many theaters in this country, non-traditional casting remains very much a debated topic, . . . it is second nature for us. It is second nature for our audiences. . . . I think we are at the forefront of something a lot of folks are trying to figure out.

This is an important observation in reference to avant-garde theories that frame a singular middle-class against which to "break in" new aesthetics. Instead, APTP makes aesthetic labels irrelevant as its work acknowledges various audiences and various boundaries.

Albany Park Theater Project, then, practices aesthetics—of shared closeness, of boundary-breaking casting, and of aligning ethnographic storytelling with movement-based theater—that produce new possibilities in a Chicago otherwise immobilized by segregation and austerity. *Home/Land* rethought Chicago as a place where meaningful aesthetics and operations wage against and imagine beyond racist political economies.

Placemaking the Northside: *Accept Variety*

Other Northside performance practices, too, embed shared closeness—and in doing so rethink their neighborhoods. But how? That question lands on Chicago's Northside, which is particularly known for its proximity to Lake Michigan and its mostly white neighborhoods. Although theater and performance take place across Chicago, much of the experimental and storefront theater scenes recognized by mainstream press are located on the Northside. How does the popular branding of Chicago's Northside as a theater district influence alternative minoritarian performance therein? And how does that performance rethink Chicago neighborhoods? A query into Earth Pearl Collective's *Accept Variety* approaches the question.

Dozens cram into a former laundromat-turned sleek coffee house, with brick and wood on the wall and pastries and espresso at the counter. A few doors down, the red and wood of mid-century modern furniture fills a well-designed storeroom. Across the street, made-to-order artisanal pizza fills a wood-burning oven. This is Clark Street, the main thoroughfare of Andersonville. Settled in part by nineteenth-century Swedish immigrants, Andersonville (population 16,000, about 50 percent white and 25 percent Hispanic)[22] is now a middle-class, gay-friendly neighborhood in far Northside Chicago. Residents in Andersonville have a median household income of $55,000, about $10,000 more than the Chicago average. The experience of walking down Clark Street, with its colorful storefronts, gyms, LGBTQ-friendly gastropubs, suggests Andersonville is an inviting and eclectic, largely white neighborhood.

Performance allows for different ways to make racial and aesthetic sense of Andersonville. At Mary's Attic—an airy space with a 75-person capacity above the popular, LGBTQ-friendly restaurant Hamburger Mary's—the windows face east; by dusk, that dewy light shades the audience—often at capacity. On the first Monday of every month since 2011, they have come to *Accept Variety*, a cabaret revue of spoken word, movement works, and storytelling, dedicated to performance by queer women of color. Po'Chop performs seductive burlesque dance that make "even vegetarians want to take a bite out of her."[23] Musician Cheryl Lynn leads PIPES, a collaborative, guitar-laced experimental music performance. Performance artist Nikki Patin addresses body image and sexual assault.

The idea for *Accept Variety* arose in April 2011 when artists Iman Crutcher and Natasha White produced *That's What She Said*, "an evening of art and performance that examine[d] the socially-constructed parameters of womanhood" performed by black feminist Chicago artists. Crutcher and White were then co-artistic directors of Minor Details, an organization "that embrace[d] . . . lives lived on the margins, particularly queer, black, female lives."

That's What She Said, intended to make space for feminist queer-of-color works, included *Dyke/Warrior-Prayers*, a short play by Sharon Bridgforth, whose work is rooted in the feminist Jazz Aesthetic. "There were so many people who had never heard of [Bridgforth's] work," Crutcher told me, "or didn't know who she was, and we thought she was doing amazing stuff." Rhaisa Williams, an audience member, remembers being "mesmerized by Bridgeforth's piercingly beautiful writing and the vocal deliveries of the actresses." She told me "The performers brought a life to the words that were both gritty and fragile, personal and universal. I was utterly in love with the piece."

That's What She Said set the format for subsequent *Accept Variety* shows, which typically begin with an open mic, followed by performances of three to five featured artists. Performers treat the monthly showcase, according to Crutcher, as "a place to try out new forms of experimental, avant-garde, traditional, whatever." Crutcher conceptualizes "avant-garde" performance at *Accept Variety* not in terms of aesthetic boundaries, but social boundaries, through performance by queer women of color that is accessible and, according to Crutcher that "anybody can relate to." She told me, "We are breaking boundaries . . . on a social, political viewpoint as opposed to an artistic viewpoint. I don't feel like we've done any work artistically that's just so out of the box. It's just the things that we are dealing with through the work that we are doing are so out of the box."

That's What She Said also influenced the mission and leadership of Earth Pearl Collective (EPC), the organization that produces *Accept Variety*. The mission, according to Crutcher, is "to produce and promote queer women of color and help them grow as artists, grow as people, make more communities where we are together." Katrina Sanford, a psychologist, attended *That's What She Said* and later became EPC's Executive Director. Sanford brought a focus on what Crutcher calls "artivism—art and activism" and added an attention to "art, feminis[m] and politics."

With that focus, Crutcher and Sanford have continued to produce *Accept Variety* every month, sustaining community for queer feminist artists of color and audiences against the expectations of where those bodies should be in Chicago. "We both live on the Northside," Sanford told me, "and we find that a lot of events for queer people of color in Chicago are supposed to be on the Southside. People expect them to be there." Crutcher added, "And many people on the Northside feel like there's not any black or of-color stuff on the Northside. Everyone is saying, 'We want to see queer people of color at an acceptable spot.'"

In 2012, Earth Pearl Collective produced an adaptation of *A Streetcar Named Desire*, an "all womyn of color, queer adaptation, to bring to light the serious issue of intimate partner violence in same-sex womyn-of-color couples." *Streetcar* was staged at the Athenaeum Theater in Lakeview, Chicago's largely white, theater-rich neighborhood. One intent of this performance was to bring attention to "those individuals who are not viewed as a part of the status quo (heterosexual, white men)" who "have had their issues severely ignored." The poster for *Streetcar* claimed,

> Earth Pearl Collective has chosen to use this play in conjunction with a panel discussion on same sex Intimate Partner Violence in womyn of color relationships to help this community heal wounds through open and honest portrayal and discussion on the consequences and struggles that these womyn are consistently enduring.

Streetcar also made space to play with how queer women of color are represented. Iman Crutcher, who directed the play, told me,

> Everybody has their certain view of how queer looks. . . . So when [the actors] were asking, "What's the costume?" I was like, "Lets play. Let's see what happens." Through that, the character Stanley, [a] very very macho character, became this . . . very feminine woman. . . . We don't need to make you masculine to make you powerful. . . . She could be so powerful in her femininity. That was what the community was about, the characters' different roles: "This is my kind of queer, this is my kind of lesbian, this is my kind of trans." . . . And people started thinking and asking questions and having conversations.

The economic downturn has acted as both foe and friend to the politics behind EPC's work. "The economy's not helping," Sanford told me. And yet, she also said, "that hasn't stopped us from doing work, and as a matter of fact it's actually built up what we were going to do anyway. But we collaborate more with other groups and bring our resources together so that we can still do these amazing events, but do it with other people." As an example, during each *Accept Variety* showcase, black female vendors sell handmade and artisanal goods like jewelry and soap.

In fact, this kind of performance persists as a medium for Earth Pearl Collective because of Crutcher's background in musical theater and because as Sanford told me, "it's one of the mediums where it costs the least to produce. . . . Being able to perform at Hamburger Mary's and bringing people in is a lot cheaper than doing a gallery show. Crutcher added that the space is "affordable, [with] the flexibility to be kind of like a lounge and bar. It gave us that freedom."

I asked Crutcher and Sanford how they see Earth Pearl Collective as part of Chicago. They told me that gaps in Chicago communities revealed a need for this work. "Women of color are . . . pushed to the back burner," Sanford said. "It's either you are pushed to the back burner in the gay community, or you are pushed in the back burner as women."

Iman Crutcher and Katrina Sanford have placed queer women of color at the front, and through performance, have made a space for feminist queer-of-color artists and audiences in a neighborhood otherwise celebrated for white LGBT cultural production. Audiences accept Andersonville not as an affective destination, but rather as a social imaginative space where black queer female labor that engages a variety of aesthetics and the quotidian may be received and not obscured.

A polycultural loop: Silk Road Rising and Downtown Chicago Theater

An elaborately staged reading of *The Mummy and the Revolution*, Yussef El Guindi's 2012 comical farce tethering the ancient to the new Middle East, sold out. Chris Jones, the *Chicago Tribune*'s chief theater critic, called Shishir Kurup's *Merchant on Venice*, an omnicultural take on the troubled Shakespearean classic, "a big, new, risky, rambunctious show . . . funny, smart and intellectually stimulating." The production was labeled "Best of Theater 2007" by the *Tribune* and "Ten Most Wanted" by *Time Out Chicago*.

Rory Leahy of *Centerstage* wrote that the creators of *Re-Spiced: A Silk Road Cabaret*

> gently mock the slightly dehumanizing 1980s pop songs "Walk Like An Egyptian" and "Turning Japanese" and the outright bloodlust of Toby Keith's "Courtesy of the Red, White and Blue." . . . They also give us a wonderful rendition of the antiracist classic "Carefully Taught" from "South Pacific" sung by a woman of color instead of a well meaning white man. . . . "Re-Spiced" is a rare and admirable production that perfectly combines thought provoking content with an overwhelming sensibility of lighthearted fun.

These acclaimed pieces were produced by Silk Road Rising, the decade-old theater company dedicated to sharing stories and aesthetics from Silk Road peoples, including Asian and Middle Eastern Americans. The performances were staged neither along Devon Avenue in West Rogers Park, a Chicago neighborhood known for South Asian eateries and communities, nor in Chinatown. Rather, they were performed in a church basement in the Loop, Chicago's downtown neighborhood full of skyscraping buildings, named for the "loop" of public transit trains circling overhead. The population of 29,000 residents in the Loop are demographically 62 percent white, 11 percent black, 7 percent Hispanic and 16 percent Asian.[24] For the last decade, Silk Road Rising has produced and sustained successful minoritarian theater in this neighborhood, Chicago's commercial center.

How Silk Road Rising persists in the epicenter of Chicago's downtown centered my conversation with co-founder and artistic director Jamil Khoury. A refrain throughout our conversation hinted that polyculturalism anchors Silk Road Rising's aesthetics and operations, and its persistence. Polyculturalism, as articulated by Vijay Prashad, "offers a dynamic view of history, mainly because it argues for cultural complexity." There is a refusal in Prashad's definition, a refusal of "the 'West' to arrogate these combined and uneven developments of so many sociocultural formations."[25] For Silk Road Rising, that refusal lands in staged theater that allows for an interrogation of cultural complexities beyond the neoliberal framework.

"I tend to be drawn to those stories where different communities are actually meeting," Khoury told me, "and sometimes colliding and trying to figure out how to live together."

This polyculturalism also frames the company's inception. Silk Road Rising (renamed in 2011 from Silk Road Theater Project) was co-founded in 2002 by Khoury and Malik Gillani. "We really were moved to create this company as a response to attacks of Sept. 11," Khory told me, "and particularly the climate of anti-Arab and anti-Muslim sentiment that had swept across the country." The original goal—to tell Arab and Muslim stories—quickly expanded, however, when the two founders continued to find polyculturalist references to the Silk Road. For Khoury, the Silk Road became "a really interesting metaphor for cross-cultural exchange, because the Silk Road was known for the storytelling tradition, and stories being translated from Mandarin to Hindi to Farsi to Arabic, Turkish, Greek, Italian . . . and also filtered through different cultural lenses and religious beliefs."

"We thought, 'Why don't we take both this geographic guide and this metaphor,'" Khoury told me,

> and apply it to a twenty-first-century Chicago diasporic theater company that would connect people to the Silk Road and focus on the authorial voice—so essentially, playwrights of what we call Silk Road background, Asian and Middle Eastern background. . . . We would build upon this age-old tradition of stories being potentially transformative and having a cathartic value and allowing people to empathize and to make connections and to understand, when there was previously not understanding.

The neighborhood further fostered Silk Road's polycultural vision and aesthetics. Although near the up-market Goodman Theater and touristy Broadway-in-Chicago venues, the company's venue in the Loop allowed for audience convergence among diverse minoritarian communities, and enabled a polycultural aesthetic and social space in a city as hyper-segregated as Chicago.

"Sometimes people have suggested, 'You should be in Indiatown or Greektown or Koreatown or Chinatown,'" Khoury told me.

> We've always felt that's kind of the last thing we should do because we're about all these communities. So for us the Loop actually makes a great deal of sense because it is that point of convergence for everyone in the city, with the idea that all roads lead to the Loop. It is also this space that is kind of seen as everyone's space. . . . Chicago has this history of segregation, and sometimes very rigid segregation. . . . So we see our work as helping break those barriers and that mindset.

Another mindset broken: the expense of operations in Chicago's downtown. Silk Road Rising skirted that cost—and the logics of capitalism—through an agreement with First United Methodist Church of Chicago, which occupies the historic Chicago Temple Building. For performances, Silk Road Rising utilizes, for no cost, the building's 85-seat basement venue, which First United renovated for Silk Road Rising near the beginning of their relationship. Khoury described the arrangement as "a bit of a miracle story," which grew out of conversations around a Silk Road production.

"It was our first production *Precious Stone*, which has an Israeli/Palestinan theme," Khoury said.

> We were going into religious communities. We struck up a conversation with a pastor at the Chicago temple. It eventually turned into an invitation to turn into a resident arts organization in the community. They were very keen on our mission and our vision and they were a very secure congregation. We created a framework of understanding, which was all documented, that we have full artistic freedom and it is a shared space and they host us.

That intimate space instantiates Silk Road Rising productions with alternative aesthetics of intimacy. "We are kind of an off-Loop theater in the Loop," Khoury said. "We are kind of this traditional theater-making and theater-consuming that you might associate with theaters on the Northside, yet we're two blocks from the Goodman and from the big Broadway touring houses. You are just few feet from the actors—that kind of experience." Thus Silk Road Rising's venue produces aesthetics that re-imagine the neighborhood, the Loop, away from large-scale productions and toward intimacy.

Polycultural consciousness, accessibility, and intimate and safe aesthetic spaces—these were the values initiated at Silk Road's inception. The company was founded in 2002 after the attacks of September 11, 2011. "Most people thought we were nuts to create a non-profit theater company at that time, because it probably wasn't the wisest time from an economic standpoint," Khoury told me.

> So many resources that would otherwise be allocated to arts funding had either disappeared and were being allocated elsewhere. The political climate, of course, was a very tense climate. It was the Bush years and the war years—a tremendous amount of suspicion . . . and profiling of Silk Road peoples. It was a political climate that in many respects screamed out for an organization like ours. We really saw ourselves as antidote to that climate.

Despite these difficulties, Silk Road's operational model has been instantiated in paying all artists—"That was a decision that we made from day one," Khoury said—and in accessibility for audience members. Even though productions cost an average of $68 per audience member, ticket prices usually range from $25 to $35, and Silk Road Rising offers discounted tickets for every show. "We take very seriously . . . the reality that a lot of people in the Silk Road communities and in other communities for whom, although $35 or $25 may not be a lot compared to the Goodman, . . . that it is a prohibitively high ticket cost," Khoury told me. "It has always been important to us to make ample opportunities for audiences to access our work."

Much like Albany Park Theater Project, Silk Road Rising has persisted with these aesthetics and operations and, I am arguing, has successfully resorted to non-traditional economic arrangements. Thus the Great Recession and continued economic downturn have not proven prohibitive. "It has slowed our growth," Khoury said, but he continued "we are surviving and we are producing. We are commissioning work and we are engaged in online work as well, and short-form video plays. . . . I would venture to say that we would be a larger organization in terms of budget if the climate were not what it is. We are slowly but surely getting out of it, but we are by no means out of it."

Conclusion

Chicago's hyper-segregated geography reveals much of the city's meaning, past and present. What's more, an austere political economy has made Chicago the city with the third-highest extreme poverty rate in the United States.[26]

But theater, as scholar Gay McAuley has argued, is a space for making meaning, where "fiction and reality come together." McAuley writes, "What is presented in performance is always both real and not real, and there is constantly interplay between the two potentials." Theater stages alternatives and negotiates the real of the present.

This theater—from Albany Park Theater Project to Earth Pearl Collective to Silk Road Rising—negotiates Chicago's present, Chicago's austerity, poverty, and racial segregation. Albany Park Theater Project barters space with the Parks Department; the company listens to the stories of nearby residents to produce ethnographic and physically evocative theater, and to engender an affective sense of togetherness. Earth Pearl Collective uses performance to promote works by queer women of color—works by those whose experiences are often excluded—and to emphasize accessibility, collaboration and the possibility of enacting shared, social space. Silk Road Rising negotiates the reality of its geography—the Loop, a neighborhood with skyscrapers evidencing immense wealth—by presenting polycultural performance on a stage shared with a church to produce intimate, safe, and culturally complex performative spaces. All of these theaters stage sharing and closeness, and reveal that performance stages alternatives by negotiating and imagining beyond the present.

Notes

1 Steve Bogira, "Separate, Unequal, and Ignored," *Chicago Reader*, February 10, 2011, http://www.chicagoreader.com/chicago/chicago-politics-segregation-african-american-black-white-hispanic-latino-population-census-community/Content?oid=3221712.

2 Michael Billington, "New York's Stages Are in a Slump: Now All America's Liveliest Theater Is in Chicago," *The Guardian*, June 23, 2004, http://www.theguardian.com/stage/2004/jun/23/theatre1.

3 Neoliberalism, as defined by David Harvey, is the economic theory and practice, ushered in during the 1970s to 1980s, in which the state creates institutional frameworks that support and encourage private property and free trade. See his *A Brief History of Neoliberalism* (New York: Oxford University Press, 2007).

4 "Austerity," *The New Oxford American Dictionary, Second Edition* (New York: Oxford University Press, 2005).
5 Jim DeRogatis, "What's Really Going on at Cultural Affairs, and What Happens to Art and Music Now," WBEZ, December 20, 2010, http://www.wbez.org/blog/jim-derogatis/what%E2%80%99s-really-going-cultural-affairs-and-what-happens-arts-and-music-now, accessed March 14, 2012.
6 http://www.chicagonewscoop.org/chicagos-1-7-billion-in-tif-spending-aided-public-and-private-projects-almost-evenly/.
7 David Harvey, *The Enigma of Capital: And the Crises of Capitalism* (London: Profile Books, 2010), 1.
8 The enactment of austerity counters proven economic theory that supports increased spending on social services during economic downturns; austerity policies have thus sustained many conditions of the Great Recession, such as high unemployment. "But one significant factor in our continuing economic weakness," Paul Krugman wrote in a March 2012 column, "is the fact that government in America is doing exactly what both theory and history say it shouldn't: slashing spending in the face of a depressed economy" "States of Depression," *The New York Times*, March 5, 2012, A19.
9 David Harvey, *Right to the City*. "On top of all this comes a class politics of austerity that is being pursued for political and not for economic reasons," Harvey writes. "Radical right wing Republican administrations at the state and local levels are using the so-called debt crisis to savage government programmes and reduce state and local government employment" (52). These conditions substantiate austerity as an economically illogical policy that furthers recession-like conditions in a post-recession political economy.
10 José Esteban Muñoz, *Disidentifications: Queers of Color and the Performance of Politics* (Minneapolis: University of Minnesota Press, 1999), 7.
11 José Esteban Muñoz, *Cruising Utopia: The Then and There of Queer Futurity* (New York: New York University Press, 2009), 56.
12 Grant Kester writes, "While the notion of an avant-garde tradition may seem oxymoronic, it is my contention that certain historically specific modes of artistic production have achieved a canonical status in contemporary theory and criticism." *The One and the Many: Contemporary Collaborative Art in a Global Context* (Durham: Duke University Press, 2011), 11.
13 Gayatri Chakravorty Spivak defines double bind as "how one speaks abroad at home." *An Aesthetic Education in the Era of Globalization* (Cambridge, MA: Harvard University Press, 2013).
14 Hortense J. Spillers writes about the excess signification attached to being a black woman "the names by which I am called in the public place render an example of signifying property plus." "Mama's Baby, Papa's Maybe: An American Grammar Book," *Diacritics* 17 no. 2 (Summer 1987): 65.
15 Omi Jones, Lisa Moore, Shared Bridgforth, eds. *Experiments in a Jazz Aesthetic: Art, Activism, Academia, and the Austin Project* (Austin: University of Texas Press, 2010).
16 The Laura Wiley Theater is named after Laura Wiley, co-founder of the Albany Park Theater Project. From APTP's website: "Laura Wiley, co-founder and co-director of Albany Park Theater Project, died on June 18, 2007. The cause of Laura's death was ovarian cancer, with which she was diagnosed in 2003. Laura was 41 years old. . . . The City of Chicago and the Chicago Park District will dedicate The Laura Wiley Theater at Eugene Field Park on January 11, 2008, in honor of Laura Wiley, co-founder and co-director of Albany Park Theater Project," http://www.aptpchicago.org/laura/.
17 In November 2014, President Obama "asserted the power of his office to provide work permits and protection from deportation for those immigrants," but in 2015, "his plan remain[ed] under assault by conservatives who have tied it up in legal limbo." Michael D. Shear, "Immigration Overhaul May Be in Limbo Until Late in Obama's Term," *The New York Times*, May 28, 2015, A13. In November 2015, a federal appeals court ruled

that President Obama "could not move forward with his plans to overhaul immigration." Michael D. Shear and Julia Preston, "Appeals Court Deals Blow to Obama's Immigration Plans," *The New York Times*, November 10, 2015, A18. As of 2016, the Obama administration was waiting to hear from the Supreme Court about his executive action on immigration.

The Development, Relief, and Education for Alien Minors Act or DREAM Act, S. 1291, was introduced in the Senate on August 1, 2001 by Senator Orrin G. Hatch (R-Utah). Among other things, the act amends the Illegal Immigration Reform and Immigrant Responsibility Act of 1996 to repeal the denial of an unlawful alien's eligibility for higher education benefits based on State residence unless a U.S. national is similarly eligible without regard to such State residence. Section 3 "Authorizes the Attorney General to cancel the removal of, and adjust to permanent resident status, an alien who: (1) has attained the age of 12 prior to enactment of this Act; (2) files an application before reaching the age of 21; (3) has earned a high school or equivalent diploma; (4) has been physically present in the United States for at least five years immediately preceding the date of enactment of this Act (with certain exceptions); (5) is a person of good moral character; and (6) is not inadmissible or deportable under specified criminal or security grounds of the Immigration and Nationality Act."

18 Names of performers changed.
19 Hedy Weiss, "Stories of Immigration, Cleverly Told by Teens," *Chicago Sun-Times*, February 26, 2012, http://www.suntimes.com/entertainment/weiss/10872394-452/stories-of-immigration-cleverly-told-by-teens.html, accessed March 10, 2012.
20 Darcy Rose Coussens, "APTP's 'Home/Land' is a Gift to Chicago/Extended Dates Announced Soon!" *Chicago Theater Review*, March 1, 2012, http://www.chicagoTheaterreview.com/2012/03/aptps-homeland-is-a-gift-to-chicago-extended-dates-announced-soon/, accessed March 10, 2012.
21 Katherine Zien, "Albany Park Theater Project: Home/Land," *Flavorpill Chicago*, January 20, 2012, http://flavorpill.com/chicago/events/2012/1/20/albany-park-Theater-project-home-land, accessed March 10, 2012.
22 http://www.city-data.com/neighborhood/Andersonville-Chicago-IL.html.
23 From "Start Your Week off with EPC!!!" an email invitation to an *Accept Variety* event, Desla Epison, November 4, 2011.
24 Rob Paral, "Chicago Demographics Data," accessed February 26, 2016.
25 Vijay Prashad, "Bruce Lee and the Anti-Imperalism of Kung Fu: A Polycultural Adventure," *Positions* 2.1 (2003): 51–90.
26 http://www.chicagonow.com/chicago-muckrakers/2013/03/chicago-has-third-highest-extreme-poverty-rate-in-the-nation/.

Chapter 13

Whose space is it anyway?

Will Power

December, 1996. I'm acting in a holiday show by popular local choreographer Robert Henry Johnson. The piece, if you can dig it, is an Afrocentric take on the Nutcracker and Johnson deftly incorporates African and modern dance to illuminate the spirit of Kwanza. Robert Henry is from our neighborhood; a primarily African-American, culturally rich-economically poor part of San Francisco called the Fillmore (recently because of Gentrification it's no longer a black neighborhood, but that's another essay). He and I both attended the local children's theater group in the local cultural center as kids, and though he recently has garnered stunning reviews and a whole new audience outside of the Fillmore community, he is still considered one of our own. It's opening night, and Robert Henry has decided to forgo Yerba Buena Center for the Arts, and open the show right in the cultural center where we got our start. I'm playing Brother Zawadi, a jolly old man who doles out gifts and too many stories at the drop of a hat (my kind of part to be sure).

Suddenly, we actors feel a tension in the audience. It seems that some of the folks from the community are beginning to vocalize their appreciation, in the way that black folks in the community do: laughing loudly, saying "uh huh" in approval to a lesson being taught on stage, even "Amening" here and there. The community makes up about half of the audience in this intimate 200-seat theater. The other half of the audience is composed of Johnson's newer fans, folks from Pacific Heights, Noe Valley, and recent gentrifiers from the Mission District. They are primarily white with means, and love Johnson and his work, and claim him as their own. When the community folks began vocalizing their approval like a congregation, these newer fans begin to take offense. First with the staring and eye rolling, next with the "shhh, would you pleeeease be quiet" in barely concealed hushed tones that says much more than "would you please be quiet." Usually, this would silence folks from our community if they were in a theater downtown, since the assumption would be that this is not their home and they are guests and should be thankful that they were even invited to the party. However the Western Addition Cultural Center is a flagship, dare I say iconic institution in the Fillmore, and outside of the church and a few other local places, the center is claimed by the community as home base. So community members push back,

"You be quiet!" "This is our center," and so forth. Now the performers on stage get nervous. Johnson is trying to speak to two communities, and values them both, and frankly needs them both to continue his work as an artist. The rumbling and verbal spats between members of the audience grows and intensifies—and begs the question—who does this artist belong to? And more to the point, whose theater is this anyway?

Eighteenth-century French philosopher Denis Diderot described theater as "the Secular Church."[1] It's fascinating to view theater in this regard, as a kind of church. In America today there are many churches that have primarily one culture represented in their congregation, as well as those that have dozens of cultures present in the pulpits. A preacher (who would be the actor in the secular church) gets to know his congregation over time and by doing so can develop a deep understanding of the community that he serves. However, for the artist trying to express his or her aesthetic in a secular space, things are more complicated. Though the artist and preacher share common roots, theater is not church after all. And it's commonplace for artists to perform and have plays produced at various theaters with many different kinds of communities.

Of course this is nothing new. Shakespeare and company, back in the Elizabethan days, held performances in London on the other side of the Thames for citizens of the city as well as the royalty. They would then "take the show on the road" and play an entire season in various small towns and provinces throughout England.[2] The great soul singer Sam Cooke recorded two different live albums—one in 1963 in a lively African-American nightclub in Miami,[3] the other the following year at the Copacabana in New York, where it's so quiet you can hear the glasses clink and the dinner served as Cooke works the crowd.[4] It is fascinating to hear and compare these performances. Cooke seems just as natural and at home with black folks as he is with whites. By utilizing different stylistic approaches, musical arrangements, and song selections, Cooke wins both groups over. The artist who can remain true to his vision while adjusting his artistry to please different audiences is a study in of itself. In more recent times however, as legal segregation has fallen (after all, many of Cooke's audiences in the 1950s and 1960s had to be composed of exclusively different communities—it was the law), the modern day performer can often face a trickier, harder to define complication when trying to engage an audience. In my travels as a performer in the 1990s and early 2000s, my contemporaries and I interacted with a variety of crowds at bars, clubs, concert halls, barns (in Munich, I played a barn), converted medieval castles, small theaters, lofts, and many, many colleges. And each venue might have a vastly different cultural makeup than the one before. An audience in an old warehouse space in Durban, South Africa may be primarily composed of East Indians. A performance in the rural areas of Iowa may be mostly white farmers and their families. After a while on the road, as a performance artist you become good at keying into who your audience is on any given night. But what if you have a mix of cultures and kinds of people at a performance, and what's more, how do you (you meaning the performer as well as the cultural institution in which the performance is taking place) ensure cultural equity at all levels; from keeping tickets prices low to making sure all members of the audience are culturally validated when they come into the theater and experience the performance?

A huge challenge for artists, as they jump from one community to another and speak to multiple communities on any given night, is how those shows are judged in the media? What is the criteria by which a show is reviewed and subsequently discussed? This can be problematic for artists coming from non-western cultures as their work will ultimately be judged by western critics. In some cases, the critiques have little impact if the artist is deeply entrenched in a community that doesn't care for reviews (think Tyler Perry). However, for most theater artists who combine communities and attempt to bend and reinterpret cultural identity through their artistry, a positive review from a newspaper or popular blogger can be critical to a show's success. Through my work in hip-hop theater and now in more traditional theatrical forms, I usually pull from both western and non-western lineages to create work. This has given reviewers a way into understanding my work, but sometimes that is not the case. Michael Feingold, lead critic for the *Village Voice*, praised *The Seven* (my adaptation of the Greek tragedy *The Seven Against Thebes*) while at the same time stating that Greek drama and the hip-hop aesthetic had no place in the same theater together:

> The problem, in a sense, is that Power and his collaborators have done their vernacularizing too well. Where Aeschylus was hieratic, ritualistic, and steeped in pubic concerns, hip-hop is colloquial, profane, individualistic, and satiric . . . Hip-hop, with its barrages of words on the beat and its constant shift of samplings, is tragedy's virtual opposite.[5]

Feingold's review wasn't a critique of the work's quality; it appeared to be a value judgment on the artistic validity of the attempt to meld the two genres. Feingold's final statement on the work, that *The Seven* was "brilliant and wrong headed," speaks to the access he had into the work through Greek tragedy, but the limited understanding he possessed of hip-hop culture and performance.

When it comes to building bridges between artists, audiences, and institutions, there's one central question that all parties are currently wrestling with: is the goal to have large, traditionally white and exclusionary LORT theatres (League of Resident Theatres) continue to expand and become more diverse and inclusive in programming, in staff and board leadership, as well as audiences. Or is the goal to develop large groups of thriving "culturally specific" theaters and together form the diversity and inclusion that the American theater so desperately wants to reflect? What is the goal? And if the answer is both—because of course it should be both—then where should the limited resources be placed? Should resources be used to entice the LORT theaters to diversity, or should major funding go to culturally specific institutions to survive and prosper? When one looks at the movement for integration that came about in the 1960s, the question at heart was never simply about living and working and using the bathroom with white people, it was about access to resources, better textbooks for the kids, living in housing with decent plumbing, and jobs that paid better and offered more security. In education for example, foundations put major resources into black colleges throughout the 1950s and early 1960s when mainstream universities weren't interested in pushing policies of diversity and inclusion. During this time, black colleges were greatly benefiting from these resources, and put them to good use. Once so-called "mainstream" (white) colleges began opening up to policies of inclusion (and opening up to the money they would receive), the Ford Foundation and others redirected their funds accordingly.[6] This move was great for "mainstream" institutions, not so good for black colleges, as resources at HBCUs (Historically Black Colleges) continued to dwindle. Theaters and funders of theater feel a similar tension today.[7]

But with tension comes great innovation. As an artist, I enjoy the challenges of bringing different communities together. Imagine what conversations can be had when different people from various cultural backgrounds come together to experience a theatrical work and discuss it afterwards. This is the heart of theater, the live interaction that no other narrative form can adequately match. Presently I'm on staff at the Dallas Theater Center as the Andrew W. Mellon Playwright in Residence. At the Theater Center we are attempting to push our theater into the twenty-first century, and have it reflect what present day Dallas looks like. There have been some successes—the staff is diversifying and expanding. As we diversify, the collective experiences of the staff are more varied and I've seen such expansion have a positive effect on the institution. The programming at the theater is fairly inclusive, and there are now various programs in place to make the theater more accessible to the whole city. There are still some problems. We recently premiered my musical *Stagger Lee*. The piece was very well received and broke various audience engagement and attendance records. However, the theater still utilizes the concept of dynamic pricing, which means that as the show grows in success and word of mouth spreads, the ticket prices go up. By the last week, tickets were selling for a whopping $130 and up. That's great for royalties to be sure, but it greatly limits certain communities from seeing and engaging in the piece. I witnessed this first hand. During the first week of the run, when tickets were from $20 to $30 on average, the audiences were incredibly diverse. As ticket prices went up and dynamic ticket pricing kicked in, those who weren't affluent became a rarity at the theater, and the audiences began to look more racially homogenous and began to conform to the traditional, the dare I say, stereotypical image of who attends and supports the American theater. Surely, running a theater is a tough financial undertaking; and, when a show is popular of course it's important to maximize on that popularity. But the critical question is how to do so while not leaving many communities out of the conversation? Cultural equity in the theater isn't just about the programming, it's about giving many communities access to the theater, so that they can influence the institution that is supposed to be serving and representing them.

Back to 1996 and Robert Henry Johnson. The crowd is getting restless, as several mini-arguments erupt and threaten to end the show. I was on stage wondering if Robert Henry was going to stop the show and make a speech, telling the two communities to pipe down. But no, he continued on with the play. And after a few moments, the audience followed suit. The tension was not resolved, but each community was holding their anger and resentment just enough to let the show continue. Johnson took the position that it is up to the artist to bring the people together and spark responses. And it's up to the audience to take that opportunity and engage or not engage, to decide as a newly formed community in the theater what to do. Looking back on that night, I'm not sure if allegiances were made across the segregated landscape of San Francisco. I don't know if people got into their cars and cursed the others, vowing never to return; or if conversations were sparked that led to more cross-cultural dialogue and engagement. Ultimately, the citizens are the audience who must decide what and how to engage artists and the artistry that emerges from the poet's labor. Johnson could have stopped the show and made a speech I suppose, telling folks to hold hands and get along. Instead he delivered the work and put the onus on the audience, to decide how to move and be moved by the art on stage.

Notes

1 Renee Troiano, *Diderot and the Theatre: Toward a Secular Church*, PhD dissertation, Rutgers University (UMI Dissertations Publishing, 2012).
2 Barbara A. Mowat and Paul Werstine, "Shakespeare's Theater," introduction to *The Tragedy of Hamlet, Prince of Denmark* (New York: Folger Shakespeare Library/ Washington Square Press, 1992).
3 *Live at the Harlem Square Club, 1963*, recorded January 12, 1963, Miami, released June 1985, RCA Records.
4 *Sam Cooke at the Copa*, recorded July 8, 1964, released October 1964, RCA Victor.
5 Michael Feingold, "Hip-hoplites: Remixing Aeschylus, The Seven Spills Classic Tragedy onto Today's Mean Streets," *Village Voice*, February 22–28, 2006.
6 Fabio Rojas, "The Ford Foundation's Mission in Black Studies," in *From Black Power to Black Studies: How a Radical Social Movement Became an Academic Discipline* (Baltimore, MD: Johns Hopkins University Press, 2007), chap. 8.
7 Janine Sobeck, "Do We Actually Want Diversity?" part 3 of "Defining Diversity," report on a convening of theater artists and leaders on the topic of diversity in the new play sector, *American Voices New Play Institute*, Arena Stage, Washington, DC, January 2010, https://www.arenastage.org/artistic-development/pdf/AVNPI%20Monograph%20 WEB.pdf.

Chapter 14

A future for American Indian theater?

Hanay Geiogamah

What does an indigenous theater movement do when it realizes that it is in the middle of an epochal identity and economic transition that's fast developing throughout the community of people it strives to depict and represent? And the movement itself is grappling with its own urgent needs for solid, visionary leadership, for funding and support to survive, and for new ideas and approaches to the many challenges at hand? That's what the artists of the American Indian theater are up against early in 2016 as they continue to seek acceptance, relevance, stability and a future for their work while life and the world bristle with changes all around.

An epochal identity transition? There is a discernible change occurring with American Indian identity and self-respect in America today. One senses a shifting in our collective understanding of who and what we are as people and of how we view ourselves and project our image. So many of the old worn stereotypes of us are fading out, losing relevance and recognition, in our minds and even, it seems, in the minds of many people in America, and an opening to take control of our identity is forming and gaining strength. Taking firm grasp of this opportunity will provide us with vital self-confidence, creative courage and freedom.

And an economic transition? There is talk that what could be called a post-casino economy in Indian Country is taking shape and will soon by a reality—and what will that reality be? One feature of it will be the bursting of the false hope and dependency bubble so many of us have floated in for way too long. As we move further into the twenty-first century, life is changing in ways that would have been incomprehensible even twenty years ago. The social and political problems of Indian people continue as heavy and demoralizing burdens, and we have not yet found solutions for many long-standing evils, especially alcohol and drugs and genuine and sustainable economic empowerment.

American Indian theater, as it has come to be viewed by its artists and Indian people, took shape in the 1960s, a time of enormous change, upheaval, hope, militancy and political and cultural activism. There was the famous American Indian Movement (AIM); the National Indian Youth Council (NIYC); a re-energized National Congress of American Indians (NCAI); and the National Tribal Chairmen's Association (NTCA), pounding the drums for the cause. Red Power, Indian self-determination, and an Indians Will Win mentality propelled hopes and dreams of nearly every American Indian, young and old, reservation and urban, traditional and contemporary. So many things seemed possible, so many programs were conceived and launched, and so much transformation would occur. The American public and its politicians, from Nixon to the Kennedys, began to pay attention, and the media, Hollywood and the counter-culture joined in the Indian celebration. Forty-plus years later, in 2016, the artistic-cultural movement that is American Indian theater needs a galvanizing blast of this 1960s to 1970s fervor to re-energize its work and potential.

Casinos and post-casinos

In the early 1990s, the phenomenon of tribal gaming and revenue-earning casinos took hold of the American Indian imagination, while notions of empowerment and tribal sovereignty as well as economic development and opportunity for all Indians seemed visible on the horizon. It was a big blast from the get-go. Federal, state, county and local governments jumped to identify gaming as an omni-competent solution to all problems and challenges. The billions in riches that would pour in would solve, heal, cure and strengthen everything. Everything will be A-OK! Many, many Indians accepted these predictions and began behaving accordingly. It was a heady fervor, alluring, fascinating.

A wave of hope, anticipation and expectation ensued, and many fastened their seatbelts and held on to the rails to wait out the period for the cash to flow their way. But the money did not come, and the waiting continued, right up to today. Meanwhile, a slowing down of effort and enterprise set in, and the action of waiting and hoping replaced working and creating, and dreaming and expecting took the place of inspiration and innovation.

So over the past twenty years, the institution of tribal gaming attached itself firmly to the American Indian national community, enriching many, not always in a good way, but excluding the majority of tribal citizens in Indian Country. Particularly for the arts and culture of Indian Country, it is my view that the benefits of Indian gaming has turned out to be a failed dream for the artists and has not helped foster their work, or arts education or experimentation, dissemination and sustainability in any significant degree. Most of the giving to the arts has come in small grants of several thousand dollars max, nothing near the millions that meaningful, adequate support for the arts would require. The results of this are that our writers have not been producing new, ground-breaking work. Many of our composers are not writing new operas, or musicals, or songs. Our playwrights wonder if they should invest their effort in writing a new play or any new work for theater, knowing that it might never get a production. Even our poets are not as enthused and productive as they were in the 1970s and 1980s, when volume after volume of works were being published and studied.

There are no new theaters being created or built, very few cultural programs for communities, very meager funding for arts education at all levels of the system, hardly any fellowships, and no meaningful prizes.

There is a lot of frustration and inertia, not simply because funding from tribal gaming did not materialize as it could and should have, but this failure is without question the most negative contributing factor to the current creative ennui. This assessment can be applied to the overall picture of American Indian affairs today and is visible in our lack of participation and representation in many areas of American life, in the continued gulf of misunderstanding and disrespect millions of Americans, have for us, in the clear lack of meaningful economic development, and in our lack of political clout. The gaming juggernaut has been a very mixed bag for American Indian tribes and has made a mockery of the hopeful slogan "Gambling is the new buffalo!"

And now, we arrive at the onset of the post-casino era in Indian life, the beginning of a fade for the neon lights and dinging slot machine bells that have provided a backdrop in many reservations and communities. Many factors have coalesced to bring about this decline in fortunes, and though the casinos will not disappear overnight, their allure is waning and their influence is slowly diminishing.

A refreshing, encouraging spirit of honest and true self-reliance based on individual and group respect and enterprise must now unite us and guide us forward.

Act two

It is February, 2016, and the curtain is rising on the second act of the saga of American Indian theater. What's in store over the next 5 years, the next 10 years, 25 years? Will the Indians win? Is it going to end in a good way? Are the artists of the Indian theater going to be able to dramatize the events and dramatic actions of a very challenging and even perilous period of tribal life?

I've given the survival question much consideration and declare my belief that Indian theater will survive and maybe even prosper in the coming years. No, it's not the fabled casino billions opening up and flowing our way that will be the major factor for a productive continuation, though I still hope, probably in vain, that some of that fortune will find its way to supporting our work. I am convinced that Indian theater can live a good life for at least 25 more years if its artists rally and rise to the challenges, calmly and courageously, and maintain the best possible attitude even though many have little money in hand to pay the bills at this moment. We have to focus our efforts in three major areas: technology, renewed and re-focused creativity, and an all new agenda for creating our own methods of sustainability. This includes developing new approaches to storytelling, production and training and educating younger performing artists. All of this will require the combined work of a leadership team of fully dedicated and committed artists to initiate and move forward, a group of four or five veterans who must be called forward and persuaded to lead the charge. They must be supported, backed up, and given full and complete cooperation.

I believe technology to be the force that will give us the mightiest lift; the dazzling, amazing and fantastically capable world of computers, the Internet, iPhones, tablets, and Skype, and all the iterations these tools are rapidly evolving and morphing into. These cool gadgets can help us to create theater for American Indians and all interested others and present it to them in ways none of us could have imagined when Native American theater came on the scene half a century ago. This is all totally possible, but we need to learn how to make it work for us, and that shouldn't be too difficult. Technology, computers and the Internet are changing everything in the world, and Indian theater can be a broad, open canvas for applying and experimenting with the benefits of these wondrous inventions. Furthermore, this will not cost loads of casino dollars.

Over the past thirty years, radio and television have filled the airwaves with around-the-clock programming, making it possible for Americans to come together easily in massive numbers for a public event, a hit sitcom, or major sports event. While the airwaves buzzed in the 1970s and 1980s, a band of techno geniuses were working away on creating the Internet and the cyberspace it requires to do its awesome things. Out of all the wonderments that have been created in the age of computers and cyberspace, the specific technology that I think can have a major impact on the future of the American Indian theater are the incredible cameras, wirings and accompanying inventions that make it possible to telecommunicate, to see entire films on a smart phone, to visit face-to-face with a person in New York and the other in Oklahoma or California.

Theater is already offered to audiences via this technology, and it is almost as good as being in the same space where the live production that is being broadcast is happening. Over the past couple of years I've made a determined effort to attend many techno performances of plays, operas and dance programs beamed into cinemas in the Westwood and Santa Monica areas of Los Angeles. I've seen the Royal Shakespeare Company perform, the Metropolitan Opera, some live Broadway productions, and others. And I've been trying to figure out if this technologically produced experience—seeing the Benedict Cumberbatch *Hamlet* being performed live on the stage of the Barbican Theater in London being channeled into the Laemmle Royal Cinema on Santa Monica Boulevard in West Los Angeles—is duplicable for Indian Country and the performances and productions of American Indian theater, dance, and live shows. I think we can make this happen for Indian theater and Indian Country if we firmly make the commitment.

An ideal scenario of what I'm imagining: the American Indian Dance Theater performs *Ceremony For Mother Earth: A Healing* live on the main stage of the Los Angeles Theater Center in downtown Los Angeles, and the telecom technology carries the performance to audiences at IAIA in Santa Fe, Columbia University in New York, the Penobscot Theater in Orono, Maine, and the community space at the Minneapolis American Indian Center, among many other venues. An audience of maybe 50,000 viewers could be in attendance. The very thought of this is highly encouraging!

A clear vision of this kind of technological approach to reaching audiences occurred at two national American Indian theater conferences held at UCLA and organized by Project HOOP (Honoring Our Origins and Peoples). Project HOOP is an initiative designed to advance Native Theater as an art form and educational tool. The aforementioned teleconferences connected Project HOOP constituents at various locations across the nation. Over 100 Native theater artists—writers, actors, designers, producers, directors—came together in a focused and intimate space. It took about fifteen minutes for a full nationwide comfort level to settle in.

The most successful feature on the agenda was the live performances and readings of excerpts of new plays and productions by performers at each of the conference sites. The feeling of being gathered around a national Indian theater stage combined strongly with the rewarding experience of hearing and seeing new work being performed by American Indian theater artists in each region of the country. The budget for both conferences was just over $6,000!

More recently, many of us have seen a zany and entertaining preview of the new options that technology affords in our viewing of the insanely funny vimeos posted on YouTube by the wonderful American Indian comic troupe known as the 1491s. The material, the script, the staging, the performances, the camera and sound equipment are all assembled, the action begins, the piece is filmed, edited and posted on the web, and we watch it and laugh our heads off. It's not much more complicated than that. This is Indian theater, Indian performance, Indian creativity, and it's very contemporary. I don't think the 1491s' YouTube sketches cost a lot of money to produce, and they are seen by thousands and thousands of viewers. A more developed webisode series with American Indian writers, actors and crew would not be much more complicated to produce, and producing a full-blown series is definitely possible at a place like the studios housing the San Manuel Tribe's FNX station on the campus of San Bernardino Community College in San Bernardino, California. All the creative elements are in hand to accomplish this, and somewhere down the line, hopefully soon, somebody or some tribe with the courage, the commitment and the money will invest in this and make it happen. To launch this in a grand way, American Indian performing artists can develop and present a series of American Indian Theater classics, including such gems as *Changer* by Gerald Bruce Sobiyax Miller; *Evening At The Warbonnet* by Bruce King; *Songcatcher* by Marcie Rendon; *What's An Indian Woman To Do*? by Mark Anthony Rolo; *The Education of Eddie Rose* by William YellowRobe Jr.; and *Na Haaz Zaan* by Robert Shorty and Gerry Keams, for audiences across Indian Country, across cyberspace, and on tour too if feasible.

More uses of techno

There are numerous subsidiary benefits that come with all of this technology, including:

- The challenges of Indian Country's coast-to-coast geographic expanse can be partially addressed with the live broadcasting of an Indian stage production from its premiere theater to many other venues in tribal communities.
- Social media can be employed to develop and sustain audience interest and participation.

- Audiences will benefit from the convenience of seeing a live performance of an American Indian play on their laptops, PCs, iPads and cell phones.

It is entirely possible that a full educational curriculum of American Indian theater courses and performance events can be produced online, a development which will give Indian theater a nice shot of twenty-first century techno adrenaline. This can be done now, not in two years or somewhere down the road. At the Institute of American Indian Arts in Santa Fe, where Professor Daniel Banks is hard at work reviving the school's moribund theater program, teleconferencing has already made a significant contribution to that effort. Professor Banks has, via the technology of teleconferencing, brought several American Indian theater artists, academics and performers to the campus to give lectures, interviews and other contributions to students in his classes. I taught his class in the spring semester of 2015 on four different occasions from my office in Macgowan Hall on the UCLA campus, and I met and shared discussions with the class members virtually face to face. I'd like to have done this live and in person, but this was a way to do it, and we made it work and we all felt good about being able to participate.

A comprehensive curriculum for the new American Indian theater and performing arts programming can be produced and presented by American Indian theater teachers online and could include some or all of the following courses, seminars and study areas: Introduction to American Indian Theater; American Indian Plays and Drama; American Indian Acting; Writing for the American Indian Theater; Introduction to Directing for American Indian Theater; American Indian Ceremonial Performance; Developing American Indian Theater in Tribal Communities; American Indian Dance, and Research for American Indian Theater and Performance. Syllabi for these courses and seminars are available from various schools and programs where they have been taught, along with teaching guides, reading lists, bibliographies and a substantial body of critical studies writings and research.

Renewed and re-focused creativity

By now we should be mature enough and prepared to consider how American Indian storytelling, or certain aspects of it, can be re-imagined, replaced, renewed. How? The emergence of a new identity for Indian people, of a new self image and the re-taking of ownership of our knowledge, of our histories, our traditions, our stories, our beliefs and values, offers a fantastic range of opportunity and responsibility for an almost endless number of stories, narratives, myths and storytelling. American Indian playwrights are securely positioned to move immediately into this fantastic bounty of ideas, sources and inspiration and form a creative vanguard to produce new works that will fill the theaters with energy, excitement, awe and genuine originality. I think this will be one of the outstanding major creative opportunities for playwrights and storytellers for several generations—and we can tell these new stories and tales exactly and precisely the way we want to tell them.

We need to revisit and respond to some of our long unanswered questions and challenges, ideally in a national gathering of writers, poets, novelists, playwrights, screenwriters, television writers, as well as painters and creative intellectuals with a conference title such as Re-Imagining American Indian Storytelling Traditions. I would urge as topics for debate any or all of these: the inevitability of cultural renewal and how we have had to adapt to modern realities; the directions that American Indian storytelling might take in the future; an updated vocabulary and lexicon of American Indian stereotypes and misperceptions; the pros and cons of writing and creating in English, and exploring how we might, as tribal people, incorporate some other peoples' experiences into our own ways, our own values, our own world views. And we can employ all that technology has to offer to assist in this.

A simple and very effective strategy for establishing that we have taken control and possession of our identity would be a nationwide pan-tribal playwriting competition to select five new works that dramatize and explore aspects of the new Indian-ness that is starting to come to life. This would definitely jump-start a crucial component of the fight for achieving and maintaining cultural sovereignty!

Creating our own methods of sustainability

Leaders of the American Indian theater movement must develop an agenda of proposals for funding and support for a wide range of projects and present these to funders over the next several months. Recent developments, including the discouraging acknowledgement that American Indians have almost zero presence in the Hollywood process, have sparked a remarkably powerful and widespread response from American Indian citizens and thousands of supporters, with calls for Indian artists and performers themselves to step forward and fashion remedies for the current lack of representation and professional opportunities. An agenda of programs and ideas that can help American Indians become better prepared to participate fully in creating movies, television series and entertainments about American Indian life and presenting real American Indian characters and stories would be enthusiastically welcomed and received by Indian people and many others who support and appreciate American Indian arts and culture.

A centerpiece of this work should be laying the groundwork for the creation of a National American Indian Performing Arts Center and Academy, a project that can give the Indian theater movement a powerful boost for years and years to come. Under one roof, in an accessible-to-all location, many crucial and necessary programs and functions can be conducted and administered: an annual national theater conference and play festival; a national network of tele-conferencing to share classes, seminars, lectures and arts conferences with other tribal colleges, tribal communities and American colleges and universities; a talented staff of artists and educators; an educational and training program featuring a full and evolving curriculum for the study of and development of American Indian performing arts; establishment of an Institute for Development of Theater and Performance in Tribal Communities; a research library and archives; resident professional theater and dance companies that will produce, perform and tour nationally and internationally, and a publishing program that could produce texts, anthologies and teaching videos.

This programming could be developed in phases and would almost certainly be attractive to funders and national philanthropic organizations such as the Mellon and Ford Foundations, the MacArthur Foundation as well as numerous corporations and companies in the American entertainment industry. All of this would, of course, require a number of artistic and administrative personnel for full and part-time employment. Several of these projects could easily be managed as for-profit enterprises that would be economically self-supporting and long-range sustainable on a national and even international level.

Creating sustainability, continued . . .

We must renew our efforts to establish two organizations to represent, promote and advocate greater visibility and a stronger presence for American Indian Theater: an American Indian theater and Performing Arts National Alliance and the American Indian Playwrights Guild. Unfortunately, initial work to create these organizations stalled from a lack of volunteers. Funding must be secured to adequately compensate the individuals who will take on this work and its accompanying responsibilities and to support them for several years in these efforts.

Both the National Alliance and the Playwrights Guild should be created as soon as possible. The directors of both organizations should move determinedly to figure out how to provide funding, support, and programs and services. These two organizations could be housed in the national center. A sense of security and confidence will ensue when the artists know they have the support and advocacy that the Alliance and Guild should be providing.

Special efforts must be made to improve and expand our relationships with philanthropic foundations, especially the Mellon Foundation, which funds large-scale and long-term projects such as the Guild and the Alliance. One of the goals of the Alliance could be to establish a national American Indian Theater Production Fund, with the immediate intent of raising $2.5 million to be given out in annual grants for production of new works as well as revivals of older shows and productions. The Playwrights Guild and Performing Arts Alliance leaders should work with the Native Arts and Cultures Foundation to provide at least two grants a year in its budget to support American Indian theater.

We should look for every opportunity to collaborate and cooperate with all theaters of color in America and the rest of the world. We should be willing to cast other people of color in our plays. We should share space when we can and ask for space sharing when we need it. We should lend a hand when asked. We should be spiritually connected. And we should back up, defend and stand united with all artists of color.

American Indian studies departments and programs and other areas of academia are aware of the need for and value of American Indian theater in curricula and programming. Over the past ten years Project HOOP maintained a close working relationship with the UCLA American Indian Studies Center, and in this collaboration a kind of model for American Indian artistic and academic synergy emerged. The collaboration sponsored five national American Indian theater conferences on the campus and nurtured a number of theater development residencies in tribal communities around the country. Project HOOP and the Center have co-sponsored the publication of the Native American Performance and Critical Studies Series in association with the Center's Publications Unit. This series now includes eight titles, comprising five anthologies of American Indian plays, as well as two volumes of critical essays on Native American theater.

Another promising area is developing a relationship between American Indian theater and performing arts groups and five major museums in America with extensive American Indian collections and profiles: the Autry in Los Angeles; the Heard Museum in Phoenix; the National Museum of the American Indian in Washington, DC; the Gilcrease in Tulsa, and the Eiteljorg in Indianapolis. Such an alliance could provide excellent performance and workshop residencies for Indian theater artists and groups at each of these institutions, programming that could be ongoing and the source of creative innovation and expansion for all participants.

A similar relationship should be created between American Indian theater and performing arts and the thirty-three tribal colleges that make up the American Indian Higher Education Consortium (AIHEC). These colleges and universities could become, along with the five major museums discussed above, the initial component of a national touring circuit for Indian companies and productions that would be a major educational and cultural advancement for American Indians.

A concerted effort should be undertaken to revive the relationships with the television networks and major film studios in Hollywood. They helped before, and they can be persuaded to help again. The entertainment industry has not been fully diversified as some wrongfully claim, far from it, and we can join with other diverse communities to work with the entertainment industry to accomplish diversity and develop our work.

Honoring and supporting our artists

American Indian theater and performing arts are being kept alive by a small cadre of creative Indians who are strongly committed to the cause, who have sacrificed, been disappointed, dispirited, disillusioned, down and out for years and years, but who have not given up. When it is possible to do so, formally, respectfully, and responsibly, we must present awards for service, contributions and dedication to such honorable folks as Jane Lind, Jaye Darby, William YellowRobe Jr., Teri Gomez, Marcie Rendon, Jana Rhoades, Julie LittleThunder, Bruce King, Annette Arkeketa, Diane Fraher, Gloria and Muriel Miguel and their late sister, Lisa Mayo, Mark Anthony Rolo, Pat Melody, Diane Yeahquo Reyner, Phyllis Brisson, Keith Conway, and Donna Couteau Brooks and Joe Cross. They each deserve highest honors and respect for all of the good work they have contributed. Aho, aho to all of them.

Renewing the vision

To be sure, one can always tap into a small reservoir of hope and determination when one ponders if there really is a future for American Indian theater. It's become a kind of automatic reflex to make rosy, positive forecasts. During the 2009 videoconference of Project HOOP: Assiniboine playwright and director William Yellow Robe Jr. has strongly declared, "We've never had money. We have always existed in poverty. We won't let it stop us. We can and will survive." And Muriel Miguel, founding director of the Spiderwoman Theater in New York added, "I'm hopeful. It's important to do this work. I refuse to be invisible." We must harness this kind of positivity in order to move forward.

A crucial task that must be tended to constantly is doing all that's possible to make Indian theater important and meaningful to our communities, make it needed, functional and synergistic, fun and happy. There is no question that we have the creative ability, the creative energy required to do this. We must try to move forward sensibly and with confidence. We must make the decisions about what we want and need for our future, including deciding if we really do want to hold on to our culture, our arts, our traditions of creativity, and to maintain a distinct presence in and view of the world. We have a long way to go to fully develop a confident, mature and productive American Indian theater and also an American Indian cinema. What we have now is actually a respectable beginning. If we really do want an American Indian theater, we will continue to work on building it with some of the ideas presented here as well as the continuing flow of creative energy we are given by the Creator.

I think of the time in the early 1970s when I walked all over New York City looking for all the off-off Broadway theaters, all over the city. It was so cool, theaters in some of the most unexpected places, in converted store fronts and parking garages, converted lofts, many of them housing "hits." I especially remember the Mercer Street Playhouse, the WPA Theater on the Bowery, the Negro Ensemble at the corner of St. Marks Place and Second Avenue, the Theater for the New City on Second Avenue, and the 13th Street Theater. I dreamed right then of this being duplicated in Indian Country. Building a chain of playhouses in tribal communities is a fabulous goal, a doable goal, one we should definitely include in the agenda for the next 25 years. The rewards will be beautiful: all kinds of American Indian shows, written, acted and produced by us, on all those stages, all over Indian Country. Aho.

Chapter 15

Culture, ethnicity and the inherent theater of hip-hop

Joseph Schloss

A century ago, America was in crisis. Dark-skinned immigrants were swarming into the United States, filling its cities with raucous music, spicy foods and suspect morality. It was abundantly clear to observers that by the 1950s, whites would be a minority and their culture would be dead. Writing in 1911, the prominent biologist Charles B. Davenport warned that

> it appears certain that, unless conditions change of themselves or are radically changed, the population of the United States will . . . rapidly become darker in pigmentation, smaller in stature, more mercurial, more attached to music and art, [and] more given to crimes of larceny, kidnapping, assault, murder, rape and sex-immorality.[1]

But whiteness managed to survive, and it did so with a brilliantly counterintuitive gambit: Rather than resist these strangers and their frightening cultures, it absorbed them. Italians, Greeks, Jews, Armenians and other racially questionable Europeans became white.[2]

In spite of our everyday perceptions, ethnic and racial categories—like "white"—are neither coherent nor stable. Ethnicity is a social construct, and it is subject to the same pressures and influences as any other aspect of American culture. But possibly the most paradoxical aspect of the social construct of ethnicity is the belief that it is *not* a social construct. We want our sense of ethnic identity to be real, to be permanent, to be dependable, and so we convince ourselves that it is all of these things. But the truth is that ethnicity and culture have always been more like a pair of jazz musicians, each constantly adjusting their playing in response to the other. And this reciprocal, improvisational dynamic is as central to American life today as it was one hundred years ago.

One aim of this anthology is to envision the social and political changes that America's shifting ethnic demographics could bring over the next half century. But in doing so, it is essential to remember that the influence is always mutual. We must acknowledge that our culture is just as likely to change ethnicity over the coming decades as it is to be changed by it. For all we know, the dominant ethnic group of 2050 might be a community that doesn't even exist yet.[3] So if we agree that ethnicity is one of the major factors structuring American society, and we also accept the potential of culture to redefine ethnicity, then I am suggesting that our artists may have far more power than even they realize. Because they are the ones who produce culture.

The most significant contemporary art form to work with the relationship between ethnicity and culture is hip-hop. In this chapter, I will consider how the hip-hop aesthetic—as both a theory and a practice—has already shaped our understanding of ethnicity, and speculate on the implications of its influence for the future.[4] Over the last forty years, the hip-hop community has articulated a coherent set of artistic principles, and proceeded to apply them to performance in a wide range of media, including music, dance, drama and graphic design. These principles were specifically designed to increase marginalized groups' ability to define their own identity. Moreover, in most cases this process was intended to be realized in the context of real-time, public performances. For that reason, I argue that there is little practical difference between the kinds of hip-hop performances that constitute "theater" *per se* and the kinds of hip-hop performances that constitute the other elements of hip-hop. In keeping with the theme of this collection, it is my intention here to focus on aspects of the hip-hop aesthetic that have particular relevance to stage performance. But ultimately I would argue that *all* hip-hop is a kind of theater.[5]

This chapter is itself a product of the New WORLD Theater, albeit an indirect one. In September of 1986, I enrolled as an undergraduate at Hampshire College, a partner in the tightly knit Five College Consortium (along with Amherst College, Mt. Holyoke College, Smith College and the University of Massachusetts). A little over a month later, ten African American students at the University of Massachusetts were assaulted by white students after the Boston Red Sox lost to the New York Mets in the World Series. This event set off an era of soul-searching and activism in the Five Colleges that continued for several years.[6] Among other actions, students at UMass occupied New Africa House for six days, and students at Hampshire College later occupied Dakin House as part of a wave of campus activism that specifically sought to address the politics of ethnicity and culture.[7] This activism built on the foundation of the existing anti-apartheid movement, and was reinforced by the rise of a new brand of highly politicized hip-hop music that was just beginning to emerge from New York. Culture, art and activism were increasing bound together in both our classes and our lives.

New WORLD Theater was one of the main forces serving to define that cultural moment in the Five Colleges. For me, as someone specifically interested in music and politics, New WORLD Theater's "Bright Moments" summer concert series was particularly influential, allowing me the opportunity to experience firsthand the work of musicians who explored these issues in their art, such as Fela Anikulapo Kuti. Having thus been introduced to both music and cultural politics through participant observation, I was already inclined to approach my scholarship from a similar perspective. I began to understand hip-hop as a series of choices being made by individuals in specific social contexts, as well as to explore the political implications of this understanding. As I moved forward,

I began to take this as not only a practical orientation, but also as a methodological and theoretical one as well.

My first book, *Making Beats: The Art of Sample-Based Hip-Hop*,[8] focused on the musical aspects of hip-hop, presenting sampling as the deliberate product of a series of aesthetic and moral choices made by its creators, as opposed to being the inevitable result of larger social or economic forces (which was how it was often presented at the time). This is not to minimize the significance of the social challenges faced by hip-hop's pioneers (including urban de-industrialization, individual and institutional violence, and the government's "benign neglect" of minority communities). Rather, it is to say that the hip-hop performance aesthetic was not so much a *result* of these pressures as it was a *response* to them, with all the intentionality, creativity, and agency that that implies. My second book, *Foundation: B-Boys, B-Girls and Hip-Hop Culture in New York*,[9] took a similar approach to hip-hop dance. Like hip-hop producers, b-boys and b-girls also expressed a clear and consistent philosophy of hip-hop art, one that was specifically designed to guide practitioners toward effective performance in real time.

Most contemporary hip-hop scholarship focuses on hip-hop as a form of popular music. From this point of view, the final work of art that emerges into the marketplace/culture is naturally far more central to the analysis than the process by which that art was originally produced. Even if researchers study the creative process, they do so primarily to develop a deeper understanding of the completed work. But I take virtually the opposite approach. Rather than study the process to understand the result, I study the result to understand the process. And as with any artistic process, the creation of hip-hop art reflects a number of contextual factors, including the artist's sense of personal identity, their sense of how that identity fits into larger social contexts, how they express their understanding of that relationship, and the resources (material, intellectual and social) that they have at their disposal to do so. Moreover, these processes include not only the specific actions of individual artists but also the way those actions are collectively framed by the community, as well as the way those frames are revised and renegotiated over time. Hip-hop artists make each of their choices with a strong consciousness of how their decisions are being perceived by peers. In that sense, again, all hip-hop is theater. And I would suggest that these two acts—hip-hop communities' collective negotiation of performance criteria and their evaluation of specific performances according to these criteria—are among the most politically potent weapons in hip-hop's arsenal. They not only teach practitioners how to take action, but also how to influence the criteria by which their action is to be judged. Mastery of form is the ultimate lesson of all hip-hop arts. As a result, I assert that hip-hop's political strength comes more from its style than from its content.

By taking this position, I am intentionally avoiding the most obvious way that hip-hop and politics have been linked by writers and scholars: that hip-hop serves as a venue for the expression of radical political messages. Though hip-hop certainly has done that in many cases, to make it the sole basis of our interpretation of hip-hop's politics is problematic because it limits analysis to the interpretation of the message itself. By putting the focus on the overt political content of any given work, this approach minimizes the significance of the deeper aesthetic principles through which that content is expressed. That, in turn, not only obscures an important aspect of hip-hop's cultural politics, it may also unintentionally reinforce many of the precise ideological biases that hip-hop was created to fight.

More specifically, the idea that hip-hop lacks a coherent set of aesthetic principles often reflects a logic that assumes that any disparity between hip-hop and mainstream ideologies necessarily can only reflect a deficiency on hip-hop's part. Since much of the hip-hop aesthetic was intentionally designed by marginalized groups to challenge mainstream society's ideologies about cultural production, this critique quickly becomes circular: hip-hop's rejection of mainstream culture can't be taken seriously because it rejects mainstream culture. Marginalized groups should be marginalized because they are marginalized. By its very construction, this logic implicitly rejects the possibility that the hip-hop aesthetic could include a legitimate critique of contemporary social and cultural norms. It leaves only the conclusion that hip-hop is—and is meant to be—a nihilistic violation of those norms. From this point of view, sample-based hip-hop producers can't create an alternative approach to intellectual property; they can only steal other people's music. Graffiti writers can't challenge the use of state power to restrict access to public space; they can only trespass and vandalize. B-boys and b-girls can't create new competitive dance forms based on traditional Afro-Diasporic cultural and spiritual principles; they can only spin on their heads. MCs cannot challenge conventional poetic forms; they can only fail to be poets.

Historically, hip-hop's response to such prejudices has been to ignore them and maintain its aesthetic principles unbowed. By doing so, it makes its outlaw status an artistic issue as much as a moral one, intentionally blurring the line between art and politics. Not only is this true even when the work contains no obvious political message, it is arguably *more* true in such cases. Simply put, the performance doesn't have to be a venue for politics; it is political just by existing. As Clyde Valentin, Executive Director of the Hip-Hop Theater Festival reflects,

> *All* of it is political as far as we're concerned. In terms of [how it's done], who we're bringing together, why we're doing it, who we're looking to reach. All of that is aesthetic as far as we're concerned, in terms of who we are as makers, as people in the mix who have knowledge, have resources, and have the ability to create.[10]

In the pages that follow, I will explore this proposition as it relates to three specific aspects of the hip-hop aesthetic: sampling, battling, and the embodiment of a "character."

Among the most obvious clues to hip-hop's performative approach is the almost universal practice of hip-hop artists mediating their actions through characters that are distinct from their personal identity. In fact, this practice is actually so common that it often goes unnoted by insiders and outsiders alike. Performing in character not only gives the artist a sense of critical distance from their own performance, but also provides the opportunity to make the conscious framing and re-framing of those actions into part of the artistic process itself. As a result, it is extremely rare for hip-hop musicians to perform under their given name. During formal interviews and informal conversations over several decades, hip-hop artists have explicitly and consistently stated to me that their hip-hop names represent characters that they see as being distinct from their everyday personalities. This principle even allows hip-hop artists to perform as multiple characters, a practice that is rare in other art forms.

A good example of the phenomenon is Daniel Dumile, a highly respected emcee who became a major figure in the underground hip-hop scene of the late 1990s and 2000s under the name "MF Doom." But ten years earlier, as "Zev Love X," he was best known as a member of the golden era hip-hop group KMD. Stylistically, Zev Love X and MF Doom are quite different, and are viewed by most fans as essentially unrelated artists despite the fact that they are widely known to be the same person. And the picture became even more complicated in 2009, when Dumile acknowledged in an interview that the masked individual performing concerts as MF Doom was not always him. "I liken it to this," he told an interviewer. "I'm a director as well as a writer. I choose different characters, I choose their direction and where I want to put them. So who I choose to put as the character is up to me. . . . I'm not gonna play the part of that character every time."[11] Though this is a somewhat extreme example, it clearly has its roots within the deeper principles of hip-hop culture.

The importance of character as a conceptual building block of hip-hop is also the reason that names themselves are a central focus of attention in many aspects of hip-hop practice. There is no intrinsic reason, for example, why graffiti writers had to focus their art on writing their names. They could just as easily have painted images or slogans. Yet they chose to devote their energy to the creation and illumination of a name, and by extension, to the articulation of a persona associated with that name. Looking at pictures of old school graffiti writers posing with their work in the 1970s and 1980s, one is often struck by the radical disjuncture between societal stereotypes of graffiti writers (scowling, street-hardened, gang members in their late teens or early twenties), and the actual writer in question (often a fresh-faced, smiling, twelve- or thirteen-year-old). While it would be easy (and to some degree accurate) to ascribe this difference to social prejudice, we must recognize that it was also part of the intention of the writers themselves. To play with—and ultimately exert control over—the way you are stereotyped is both a kind of performance and a kind of power.[12]

Similarly, Clyde Valentin notes that the rapper Jay-Z's ability to become one of the most prominent mainstream businessmen in the United States while simultaneously retaining the aura of an admitted drug dealer from the streets of Brooklyn can itself be read as a complex performance of self-definition. In fact—technically speaking—Jay-Z himself is not even a person at all, but a character, created and performed by the notoriously private artist Shawn Carter.

> The Jay-Z we see is not Shawn Carter, necessarily. And there's an investment that Jay has made . . . to kind of foster this narrative of who he is. That's an incredible amount of work that we discount because it's essentially unseen work. But that's a tremendous amount of work.
>
> I mean, this man and his wife attended the inaugural ceremony and sat *feet away* from the president. And this dude was like the same dude that stabbed up Lance "Un" Rivera in the club for fucking leaking his album. On some godfather shit! Like, *that really happened*. Or it didn't; I don't really know. Maybe it's all part of the mythology![13]

It is probably impossible to say exactly how the adoption and development of a new name and character came to be one of the central aspects of hip-hop culture, but there were clearly several factors involved. Foremost among these was the youth of hip-hop's creators. Using experimentation to develop and situate an adult identity is a central part of adolescence in most contemporary cultures. Filtering this experimentation through a [14] "character" that is similar, but not identical, to the performer is a very effective strategy for achieving this goal. It gives the performer a critical distance that allows them to improve quickly, a kind of plausible deniability in the case of failed attempts, and the option to simply create a new character when the old one no longer suits them. Another influence was the fact that hip-hop evolved from cultural interactions between at least three different Afro-Diasporic cultures (African American, West Indian, and Afro-Latino), and thus tended to emphasize the performative traditions that they shared. One significant aspect of many West African derived traditions is the maintenance of one's reputation within an oral culture. In such cultures, the name itself is often seen as the repository for that reputation; individuals build their reputation by investing in their names. In the case of hip-hop, names remain jealously guarded, and taking the name of another artist or crew is considered a grave sin. To do so is essentially to take credit for their accomplishments.[15]

Given all of this, perhaps the more interesting question is not why name and character are so central to hip-hop culture, but why that fact has been so widely overlooked. Valentin feels that this lapse is indicative of a larger failure to appreciate hip-hop as a coherent aesthetic:

> I think that dismissal comes from ignorance. Because there is no groundedness in the fact that this culture has its own precedents and history, and we've all lived through it. We've all learned the rules the way we've learned them along the way, to [be able to] say, "I am hip-hop." . . . I've learned what those rules are and those tenets are, along the way, and I practice it on the daily. . . . It's too easy for people . . . to just outright dismiss that, because they don't know it.[16]

Scholar and actor Nicole Hodges Persley attributes the oversight to a more general ideology that denies people of color the ability to think critically about their own position:

> No one wants to understand . . . that these men and women are smart enough to create characters that can do the work that they want to do and [also] have a life of their own. . . . What we want to do, I think, with particular artists of color . . . is that we want to [assume] that "your experience is your art." Like, "you are your art." Whereas, I think that with white artists . . . we don't try to link it to autobiography.[17]

In this case, the ideology is not only reflected in the work itself, but also in the relationship between the work and its multiple audiences: blindness to hip-hop's strategic creativity is itself part of the problem that the strategy was intended to combat. Hip-hop's aesthetic principles demonstrate that people of color have the ability to analyze their experiences within a philosophical framework of their own design. This is a political statement in and of itself. Moreover, not only does hip-hop's emphasis on character make this argument on a philosophical level, it also serves as a pedagogical system that trains participants in how to actually negotiate the issue in everyday life. Hip-hop's emphasis on character, the perception of character, and the value of having power over those perceptions, all point to the deeper political significance of the practice: hip-hop is a training ground for meta-cognition on the presentation of identity. Hip-hop not only thinks about identity, but it thinks about how it thinks about it. By making this idea an artistic principle, hip-hop creates a situation whereby any artistic expression that falls under its umbrella *automatically* critiques longstanding ideologies about identity and power just by virtue of the way it is constructed, regardless of the content of the final product.

One important way that hip-hop accomplishes this is through its emphasis on "sampling." In the narrowest sense, sampling is defined as the use of portions of one or more previously recorded works in a new musical composition. The practice became popular in the late 1980s, with the development of digital technology that allowed sound to be manipulated much more extensively and with much less degradation than previously possible. The concept of sampling has subsequently come to be used more generally as a metaphor for similar impulses—borrowing, collage, and juxtaposition of diverse aesthetics—in hip-hop, regardless of whether an actual digital sampler is used, or even whether the object being sampled is sound.

As with the use of characters, sampling reflects a performative approach that simultaneously considers both the performance itself and the way the performance is framed. While the rules and standards of each form of hip-hop are collectively constructed by the community, each individual builds their own character within that framework, often borrowing and juxtaposing elements from diverse cultural contexts to do so. This automatically creates a work of art that accomplishes three goals simultaneously. First, the framework ties the performance to the hip-hop cultural tradition and the African Diaspora generally. Second, the diverse individual elements chosen by any given practitioner tie the work to the original context from which the materials were taken, as well as to the larger social and cultural forces that brought them to into the world of the artist. Finally, the new context reflects the character and intentions of the performer; it represents their ability to conceptualize and control the relationships between the elements. Most importantly, it reflects a consciousness about its audience and how they will interpret the gesture. When sampling is understood as a performance, its relevance to theater becomes clear. "I think that the sampling aesthetic is much larger than just a musical sample," notes Nicole Hodges-Persley. "I mean, we have all types of visual samples. Sound, beyond just music, from the sounds of previous life experiences. References to the past, the present, the future. . . . All these ways that the sample has been used [are] to me one of the defining parts of a hip-hop aesthetic."

In the context of theater, the impulses towards character and sampling have often been combined. It is noteworthy that a significant number of prominent hip-hop theater pieces—including the breakthrough works of Danny Hoch, Sarah Jones and John Leguizamo—have consisted of one-person shows, performed by their authors, in which the artists each portray multiple characters. In fact, this format has arguably become a default structure for hip-hop theater generally. Its very popularity may obscure the fact that it represents an extremely specific set of characteristics to have been chosen coincidentally by so many of the significant voices in the field. But if we do allow ourselves to ask why this format was chosen, we may find that it offers a clue to some of the deeper aesthetic imperatives associated with hip-hop.

In a musical context, the sample-based artist is saying that their artistic vision is best expressed as a relationship between fragments of pre-existing musical recordings; their performance consists of choosing and juxtaposing these fragments. In a theater context, the sample-based artist is saying that their artistic vision is best expressed as a relationship between fragments of pre-existing *personae*. The performance also consists of choosing and juxtaposing these fragments. Taken individually, each character carries the artistic potential discussed earlier. But when these characters are presented collectively, the piece can than make an additional statement through their relationship to each other. Again, the art of sampling is not just the choice of fragments, but also the organization of these fragments into a whole that is greater than the sum of its parts. This requires an ability to see in each fragment the implication of new contexts for which it may be suitable. The initial assessment, the selection of particular elements, and the compilations of these elements into a larger work of sampled art require a series of artistic choices on the part of the creator. And each of these choices is a performance. The process is about presenting the artist's ability to create and control these new relationships and perspectives, as well as the audience's ability to understand and interpret them. In other words, it is about exercising—and performing—social power. And that, again, is political.

Another important interpretive principle in all hip-hop arts is that the performance itself is only the final stage in a long process of preparation, and that audiences are evaluating the preparation as much as the performance itself. In a sense, both are performances, and they comment on each other. In musical sampling, the preparation involves finding and assessing potential sound fragments by searching for rare records. A hip-hop song made by sampling a rare out-of-print vinyl album may be viewed differently from a song that sampled the same music from a downloaded sound file, in spite of the fact that the final products would sound the same. Similarly, the performance of characters becomes a display of research, and is evaluated as such. "People think that there's no research, a lot of times, to the work of hip-hop artists," notes Hodges-Persley:

> So that when they're making a song, or they're making a video, that they just "oh, it just came out like that" or "that's the director." But there's a lot of rich research that goes into making this work. You could spend hours just decoding [it].[18]

At the Nuyorican Poet's Café in New York in early 2011, for example, Sarah Jones presented a series of one-woman performances in which she portrayed a range of characters. Unlike her typical performances, which are largely scripted, the majority of this show consisted of each character responding to questions from the audience. When audience members asked characters about defining experiences in their lives, or opinions that were presumably based on a lifetime of thought from their particular point of view, Jones had to credibly simulate the actual responses that such characters would give. Naturally, this required a seamless integration of preparation and improvisation. More importantly, as a performance it is an all-or-nothing proposition; the character either seems like a real person or it does not. Unlike other forms of theater, there is no possibility of being merely adequate. This approach, in both process and interpretation, reflects another important part of the hip-hop aesthetic: the battle.

Battling is arguably the single most important aspect of hip-hop culture. Even when a performance is not explicitly presented as a battle, the concept is never far below the surface. Almost by definition, there is no such thing as non-competitive hip-hop. This expectation has three major implications for performers. First, it frames each act within the implicit context of performance. A song is understood not only as a work of art unto itself, but also as a challenge to other artists. It is "active," and thus performative in that sense. Second, by being the most adversarial possible performance environment, battling motivates performers to hold themselves to the highest standards, simply to avoid being embarrassed. It is the equivalent of a comedian preparing to perform in front of an audience composed entirely of hecklers. Finally, the performer must contend not only with an audience that will notice any actual failures, but also with an opponent who is actively trying to provoke mistakes. These factors combine to create a kind of Darwinian performance environment. If only the strong survive, then by surviving one learns to become strong. There are many skills that come into play in such an environment, but two of the most important are improvisation and humor.

In this context, improvisation doesn't only provide an opportunity for self-expression (e.g., as in Jazz), but also a way of exercising control over perceptions of one's artistic abilities. It is intimately tied to the artist's (or character's) projection of competence. In this sense, Hodges-Persley suggests, hip-hop style improvisation is directly applicable to theater: "To me, the best hip-hop artists across genres are those who can improvise on the spot and they never let you see them sweat. Period. If I mess up a line in my show, you will *never ever* know. You'll never know." Improvisation protects the integrity of the performance, the character, and the artist.

Humor is another important part of battle strategy, particularly the practice of shifting the frame of reference around a given act (often referred to as "flipping" material). Not only is this an extremely effective tactic in the context of hip-hop battling, but by training themselves in how to deploy it in battle, hip-hop performers also train themselves to deploy it in life. Though it often goes unnoticed by scholars, some form of joke, pun, or satire appears in virtually every work of hip-hop art, including the most deadly serious ones. By reframing material, humor serves to create critical distance. Its integration into a larger hip-hop performance aesthetic reinforces the centrality of the power of framing as an important part of hip-hop performance practice.

Again, I am arguing here for a definition of hip-hop performance that is based on the conscious application of a set of aesthetic principles—the form—rather than upon the specific content of any given work. Having reviewed three elements of the hip-hop performance aesthetic (character, sampling, and battling) and some of the strategies associated with each (naming, collage, improvisation and humor) we can now begin to see how they work together. Collectively, the principles of hip-hop performance guide practitioners to create characters who are similar to, but not identical with, themselves. Using sampling, they develop resources for this character to use, and they test the efficacy of these resources (individually and in various combinations) in literal or figurative battle. Battles also simultaneously test various meta-strategies, particularly the ability to reframe conflicts into more manageable forms through humor. With these performance strategies in mind, then, it is clear that "hip-hop theater" is not so much a matter of making hip-hop theatrical as it is of adapting hip-hop's existing theatricality to a new setting.

A good example of this can be found in the "cypher." Common to many forms of hip-hop performance, the cypher is, on the most basic level, simply a group of people standing in a circle. But as a performance space, it embodies many fundamental qualities of hip-hop. Perhaps the most significant of these is a lack of distinction between performer and audience. Not only is there no raised stage, but there is not even a "front" towards which people are expected to direct their attention. Every participant can see every other participant at all times, and all an audience member has to do to become a performer is to start performing. When combined with the battle aesthetic, this means that every audience member is not only a potential performer, but also a potential *challenger* to each of the others. Even when unacknowledged, this underlying attitude is a fundamental building block of the hip-hop aesthetic, and it is reinforced by the space. On a deeper level, then, the cypher serves to frame the performances not only physically, but also socially and philosophically.[19]

It should be no surprise, then, that hip-hop performers feel an obligation to bring the cypher to the stage, in spite of its profound impracticality in that setting (the most obvious problem being that it would block the audience's view of the performers). Almost all staged performances of hip-hop dance—along with many performances of other hip-hop arts—use a "half-cypher" configuration in which inactive performers form a semi-circle behind the featured dancer or dancers, leaving the audience to symbolically form the other half of the circle. As b-girl and choreographer MiRi Park notes, however, this solution is far from ideal:

> Trying to present a cypher in a concert dance setting . . . is really problematic because the cypher in and of itself is unending, by concept and in practice. And it's also about a sort of equality. Each man stands for himself; each woman stands for herself inside the cypher. And there's a definite and palpable energy exchange. And then everyone is literally on the same level.
>
> So when you put the cypher on a proscenium and you have this presentational setting at this point, and then you're opening up half of the cypher to an audience, where there's an audience that's literally just sitting there and absorbing, but not really necessarily [contributing] to the energy. It essentially changes the cypher. It's no longer a cypher. It's meant to open up and present it, but really it's sort of draining it from its life force.[20]

The expectations of a theater audience are often directly contradictory to those of a cypher participant. Not only is a cypher participant expected to be prepared to enter the circle and challenge the others at any moment, but that potential—even if unrealized—is an important part of the context in which the performance occurs. By contrast, such behavior (jumping on stage and challenging the performers) would be an obvious violation of the expectations for a theater audience. More to the point, it is so contrary to the norms of theatrical etiquette that it would not even be part of the audience's mentality, and thus not part of the way they interpret the performance.

So why would performers even bother to try to bring the cypher into a theatrical setting? Clearly they feel that in spite of the practical difficulties it represents something important. And it is equally clear that what it represents is not content, but the hip-hop frame itself: the hip-hop way of doing things and the hip-hop way of seeing what is done. It represents a form of interpretive power.

For Clyde Valentin, the cypher represents a more general conceptual model for creating spaces in which performances can be evaluated:

> I'm more for a democratic approach to that work. Where . . . it's like if you show up to the cypher and rock it? . . . You can jump in at your own risk, then you get put on because you shine. . . . But there [has to be] a cypher to begin with, you know what I'm saying?
>
> So what does that look like in the context of the stuff that *we* do? The [Hip-Hop Theater] Festival increasingly is becoming that sort of space for us. Where it doesn't really matter where you are [in the development of the work]. It doesn't matter if it's a little rough. It doesn't matter if it's just an idea. It's a space that you can jump into. Where people can watch—and *we* can watch—to see what you're bringing to the table.[21]

Returning to my earlier point, just the very idea that the hip-hop community is capable of developing and using such power carries deep political implications, regardless of how that power is deployed. As part of a historically marginalized Afro-Diasporic community, hip-hop's founders were struggling to become cultural subjects rather than objects, and this was a powerful weapon in that struggle.

As Stuart Hall has written:

> The ways in which black people, black experiences, were positioned and subjected in the dominant regimes of representation were the effects of a critical exercise of cultural power and normalization. Not only, in Said's "Orientalist" sense, were we constructed as different and other within the categories of knowledge of the West by those regimes. They had the power to make us see and experience *ourselves* as "Other." Every regime of representation is a regime of power formed, as Foucault reminds us, by the fatal couplet "power/knowledge." But this kind of knowledge is internal not external. It is one thing to position a subject or set of peoples as the Other of a dominant discourse. It is quite another thing to subject them to that "knowledge," not only as a matter of imposed will and domination, by the power of inner compulsion and subjective conformation to the norm.[22]

Not only are we all expected to see the world through the eyes of the powerful, but we are encouraged to take the fact that we are doing so as a given. A severely limited perspective becomes normalized. But hip-hop rejects this idea to its very bones. The foundational principles of hip-hop give marginalized communities the power to reframe performances so that they can represent their own points of view.[23] In so doing, they also make the process itself visible. Both of these actions can have significant public policy implications.

As an indication of the way the hip-hop aesthetic could potentially help to reframe the discourse around race, we may take as an example a 2011 study, which reports:

> The median wealth of white households is 20 times that of black households and 18 times that of Hispanic households, according to a Pew Research Center analysis of newly available government data from 2009 . . . These lopsided wealth ratios are the largest since the government began publishing such data a quarter century ago and roughly twice the size of the ratios that had prevailed between these three groups for the two decades prior to the Great Recession that ended in 2009.[24]

If one views the average white net worth as the norm, then indeed the net worths of the other communities are clearly low by comparison. For someone who saw the issue from this perspective—as most Americans would, regardless of race—the search for solutions to such a problem would begin with an investigation into the reasons for the low net worth of African Americans and Latinos, and continue with the advocacy of remedies for whatever those deficiencies are found to be. Without even thinking about it, most of us would naturally tend to confine our inquiries to causes and remedies that were specific to the African American and Latino communities.

But what if we considered African American or Latino net worth to be normative? Then the picture begins to look very different. From this perspective, we see Americans in general as having a net worth that is comparable to the rest of the world, with the striking exception of *white* Americans, who are much richer. This may lead us to ask very different questions. How has the history of the white community provided it with a dramatically higher net worth than other communities? How has this advantage affected the experiences of other American communities? How could such a concrete economic disparity map onto such an abstract cultural construct as "whiteness" in the first place? Such questions would naturally lead us to look for causes and remedies that are related to the history of social and economic relationships *between* communities in the United States, more so than the supposed deficiencies of the disadvantaged communities themselves. Just to be clear: I am not saying that one of these perspectives is right and the other is wrong; they are simply two different ways to interpret the same data. But what is the benefit of rejecting a possible interpretation without even considering it? We often think of ethnocentricity as a moral failing, but it is equally an intellectual failing. Though a more comprehensive understanding of the diversity of available points of view won't automatically lead to better policy positions, it does offer a more accurate picture of reality, which is an important first step towards action.[25]

Hip-hop performance gives its practitioners theoretical and practical tools to not only reframe discourse to better reflect their own point of view, but also to present these alternative perspectives in a coherent, understandable and engaging way. It does this for both individuals and communities, and particularly for communities of color. Having the intellectual and practical ability to question normativity is a form of power. And it is a form of power that specifically speaks to the nature of ethnicity in the US, because the place of any given community in the hierarchy is an important part of the cultural apparatus of ethnicity itself. The marginalization of recent immigrants at the beginning of the twentieth century was deeply connected to their identity as non-whites. As they became more "white," they became more central to American culture. But at the same time, as they became more central to American culture, they also *became more white*.

The hip-hop performance aesthetic—along with other similar forms of cultural expression that will certainly develop in the coming decades—thus holds far more potential power than may be apparent at first glance. By opening up new possibilities for the relationship between culture and ethnicity, it creates new opportunities to define our identities as individuals and communities, and thus to take an active role in shaping our society in general. Is it grandiose to attribute such power to something as seemingly mundane as hip-hop? Perhaps. But hip-hop counts on being underestimated, just as it knows that even the smallest of cultural shifts, properly deployed, can tip the balance towards a more inclusive society.

Notes

1 Charles B. Davenport, *Heredity in Relation to Eugenics* (New York: Henry Holt, 1911), 219. http://www.archive.org/stream/heredityinrelati00dave/heredityinrelati00dave_djvu.txt, accessed January 5, 2013.
2 For detailed analyses of these transitions, see Noel Ignatiev, *How the Irish Became White* (New York: Routledge Classics, 2008); Matthew Frye Jacobsen, *Whiteness of a Different Color* (Cambridge, MA: Harvard University Press, 1998); and George Lipsitz, *The Possessive Investment in Whiteness* (Philadelphia, PA: Temple University Press, 1998).
3 It may be a mixture of two or more ethnic groups of our era, a subcategory of a single current group, or an identity that is entirely new.
4 I understand that using a term like "theory" to describe a hip-hop mentality may seem startling if one's primary exposure to hip-hop has been to the form of popular music associated with that term (which is of course most people's experience). But popular music is only one of many areas to which the hip-hop aesthetic has been applied, and as I will argue, it is in many ways atypical.
5 Though I am suggesting that the concept of "hip-hop theater" is difficult to distinguish from other forms of hip-hop, it is actually easier to distinguish from other forms of theater. This is because (in my opinion) hip-hop theater is best defined by its aesthetic rather than its content. In other words, I would argue that it is possible to make hip-hop theater about subjects that have little relationship to hip-hop as it is conventionally understood, so long as the aesthetic principles of the work itself emerge from the hip-hop tradition. Conversely, I argue that theater that addresses hip-hop-related topics (however that might be defined) does not *ipso facto* constitute "hip-hop theater."
6 Anthony Kwame Harrison, *Hip-Hop Underground: The Integrity and Ethics of Racial Identification* (Philadelphia, PA: Temple University Press, 2009), 177 n.5.
7 Valeria M. Russ, "Sit-in Continues At UMass: Black Students Allege Racism On Campus," http://articles.philly.com/1988-02-17/news/26240010_1_white-students-black-students-minority-students; Timothy Shary, ed., *A History of Student Activities and Achievements at Hampshire College, 1969–1991,* 1991, http://www.hampshire.edu/library/3848.htm.
8 Middletown, CT: Wesleyan University Press, 2004.
9 New York: Oxford University Press, 2009.
10 Interview with the author, 2013.
11 Andrew Noz,"DOOM: Shadows On The Sun," 2009, http://www.hiphopdx.com/index/interviews/id.1331/title.doom-shadows-on-the-sun.
12 One example of this was an early convention in graffiti in which writers presented their names in the form of film or TV credits: "_______ as _______." In other words, designating themselves as characters was itself the performance.
13 Interview with the author, 2013. See also Mark Anthony's Neal's excellent *Looking for Leroy* (New York: New York University Press, 2013) for additional discussion of "Jay-Z" as a constructed identity.
14 For a nuanced array of analyses of how this process, operates through popular culture, see the anthology *Generations of Youth: Youth Cultures and History in Twentieth-Century America*, ed. Joe Austin and Michael Nevin Willard (New York: New York University Press, 1998).
15 In fact, for much of hip-hop's history—and to some degree, still—if two performers even unintentionally took the same name, it was common to battle for it. An alternative way of addressing such problems, most common among graffiti writers, was a numbering system whereby the original performer would keep the name, but the newcomer could still use it so long as they appended a "2," indicating that they were the second person to use the name, not to be confused with the original. In any case, the number of different strategies that were developed to address name-related conflicts is evidence of the significance of the name within the culture.

16 Interview with the author, 2013.
17 Interview with the author, 2012.
18 Interview with the author, 2012.
19 For a comprehensive and nuanced discussion of the cypher and its social implications see Imani Kai Johnson, "Dark Matter in B-Boying Cyphers: Race and Global Connection in Hip-Hop" (PhD Dissertation, University of Southern California, 2009, http://digitallibrary.usc.edu/cdm/ref/collection/p15799coll127/id/265317).
20 Interview with the author, 2012.
21 Interview with the author, 2013.
22 Stuart Hall, "Cultural Identity and Diaspora," in *Social Theory: Power and Identity in the Global Era*, ed. Roberta Garner (Toronto: University of Toronto Press, 1990), 631–632.
23 Of course, at this point, this is not just a question of ethnicity; it can equally apply to any cultural default (gender, religion, sexuality, etc.). But it was clearly developed in the context of the struggles of people of the African Diaspora.
24 Rakesh Kochhar, Richard Fry, and Paul Taylor, *Twenty-to-One: Wealth Gaps Rise to Record Highs Between Whites, Blacks and Hispanics*, Pew Research Center, July 26, 2011.
25 Haki Madhubuti writes of such a shift in perspective with regard to Malcolm X's philosophical evolution: "I say that Malcolm X was normalized rather than radicalized because he was introduced to ideas that challenged and liberated his mind, ideas that put his people close to the center of civilization . . . From that point on, Malcolm X prepared himself to go on the offensive, to be proactive and combative in a self-reliant and self-protective manner. *Any person, from any culture, functioning sanely would have acted the same way*." Haki R. Madhubuti, *Yellow Black: The First Twenty-One Years of a Poet's Life* (Chicago: Third World Press, 2006), 238, emphasis added.

Chapter 16

We are not alone

A community of common values

Mark Valdez

Until the emergence of the Network of Ensemble Theaters (NET), ensembles spread across the United States had no collective identity. This was the mid-1990s, a time when the general field of theater considered the ensemble form to be a somewhat aberrant organizational structure, admired in theory and practiced in modern-day Europe, perhaps, but of no significant artistic value to theater-making in the US. At best, we were seen as an odd assortment of successes, spread out here and there, but certainly no one had connected the dots to reveal a movement taking shape.

Today, NET has over 350 members representing thirty-six states, the District of Columbia, as well as three international members. Most come to NET to access its various benefits—professional development, knowledge sharing, advocacy, festivals, convenings, grants, to join a national conversation, and so forth—but many have told us that they stay because of the community they find. Our membership is diverse in budget size ($2,000 to $5 million), longevity (2–54 years old), geography (rural, urban, international) and genre (applied theater, community-based, classics, contemporary performance, dance theater, devised work, hip-hop, ice skating, improv, music, puppets, site-specific, youth theater . . . the list goes on).

As for the larger ensemble field, with the exception of two companies (Steppenwolf Theater and Lookingglass Theater, both in Chicago), the largest ensembles are operating with budgets of about $1.5 to $2 million, with the vast majority under $200,000. In fact, of NET's membership, about 60 percent have budgets of $100,000 or less. And although small in scale and diverse in practice, these ensembles are having a positive impact across the arts field and other sectors, such as community development, environment, prison reform, education, and others.

How can this be? In a 2006 article, Margaret Wheatley and Deborah Frieze summarized the Berkana Institute's investigations into how change occurs in nature, and how those lessons might apply to social change. They wrote,

> The world doesn't change one person at a time. It changes as networks and relationships form among people who discover they share a common cause and a vision of what's possible. . . . When separate, local efforts connect with each other as networks, then strengthen as communities of practice, suddenly and surprisingly a new system emerges at a greater level of scale.[1]

Creating a Network of Ensemble Theaters

> A network is a way to build a movement because you've got a way to do something where it can be projected. It can go further than yourself.
>
> — Jan Cohen-Cruz, editor of *Public*

In 1996, eight ensembles gathered for a preliminary planning process at Towson University, funded by the Theater Communications Group, to explore models of collaboration. By 1998, the same eight ensembles (A Traveling Jewish Theater, Bloomsburg Theater Ensemble, Cornerstone Theater Company, Dell'Arte International, Independent Eye, Irondale Ensemble Project, The Road Company, and Touchstone Theater) partnered in a two-year exchange project called the Network of Ensemble Theaters, funded by the National Endowment for the Arts. This not only gave us our name, it seeded an ethos from which a widespread coalition would emerge: one based on exchange, peer learning, relationships, and place.

The NEA grant allowed these companies to tour productions to each other's theaters, establishing a practice that placed art at the center of the exchange, from which discourse could emanate; a practice that, to this day, remains core to our organization. It also afforded them opportunities to spend time together, building and deepening relationships. Many were working in isolation, a result of geography, in rural communities, or simply from the fact that they were the only ensemble in their city. These exchanges fomented a deep desire for a community of ensembles; a space where we could be an "us" and not a "them," where we could talk about our practices, challenges and successes without having to explain or justify why we were working in this manner: it would be understood and known.[2]

The timing was right: each of these organizations had been operating for ten or more years and they were each secure in their own practice and identity. They were ready to go outside themselves, to learn about their own work by learning about somebody else's. Gerard Stropnicky, from Bloomsburg Theater Ensemble, recalls,

> There was a growing sense that we could speed up the individual growth of our companies if we could build trust and learning between us. We were all thinking, 'This could help my company!' and so we worked out these exchanges . . . and there were many, and it worked. We got to hang out together for at least a week, and got to talk about our work and our challenges.[3]

As Wheatley and Frieze explain, networks "are based on self- interest—people usually network together for their own benefit and to develop their own work."[4]

Laurie McCants, also from Bloomsburg Theater Ensemble, adds, "Our movement grew and we had gatherings. We made a manifesto (some of us were kids of the sixties, remember). We had more gatherings. . . . We have great gatherings."[5] These in-person events and convenings were crucial to the formation of the network. They provided opportunities to coalesce a collective identity and culture. Stropnicky adds, "We could have kept chatting forever, but we needed to do something. We recognized that NET had to be more than a place to talk to each other, it would be a place for action—to see work, make work, share work, and collaborate with each other."[6] The NET gatherings brought people together to express their needs and interests for participation and to envision how this organization could meet those needs.

The ensembles also had to build trust—get to know one another so that they could work together—all of which takes time and patience. "Ensemble work isn't easy," says Carlton Turner, co-founder and co-artistic director of the ensemble M.U.G.A.B.E.E:

> It's not a situation where we have more people and so the work is going to be easier. No. You have to respect the diversity of the thought that comes to the table, which means the work is actually a little bit harder [than non-ensemble work]. But at the end of the day, everybody has bought in because their voice was central to the planning.[7]

The project continued to gain momentum after its initial two years, and participation evolved beyond the founding members. Ostensibly, the early incarnation of NET was a group of organizations that were all creating a particular type of work; they were connecting around a shared genre, a form. The emphasis was very much on the external attributes: they produced new works, utilized devising processes, developed productions over long periods of time, artists ran the organizations, etc. In 2004, with support from the Ford Foundation, NET undertook a national strategic planning process, which revealed, among other things, that beyond shared practices (the external attributes), this was a network connected by shared values.

As articulated by the membership, these values include:[8]

- Collaboration: NET promotes and celebrates an infinite range of collaborative relationships among ensembles, artists, presenters, audiences, communities, and more.
- Inclusion: NET is committed to inclusion with regard to place, race, ethnicity, sexual orientation, gender, gender identity, physical/mental/sensory (dis)ability, aesthetic orientation, age of individuals and ensembles, class, and cultural heritage.
- Transparency: NET values making creative and organizational processes transparent to and between its members and the interested public, taking advantage of public dialogue, communication media, and open artistic practices.
- Mutual Respect: NET accepts the responsibility for and promotes a mindfulness of the challenges in working respectfully and effectively within a culturally diverse membership and society.
- Knowledge Building: NET understands that all ensemble projects and strategies, past and present, combine to constitute a body of knowledge. NET is committed to developing this body of knowledge and transmitting the legacy of ensemble practice and culture to current and future generations of artists.

By focusing on values—on the "why" of why we work this way—the ensembles were able to go beyond differences in styles and aesthetics. To be clear, aesthetics is a subject we delve into regularly; it wasn't just an item that the founding ensembles wanted to organize around. Concurrent with the articulation of values, our members ratified a manifesto to give action to our values. It states:

> By joining together in a Network of Ensemble Theaters we strive to give strength to each other; to share our resources; to create a forum for controversy and debate; to document and articulate the heritage and body of work of ensemble practice; and to maximize our ability to bring about change in the world beyond ourselves through the transformative power of collaborative theater.[9]

A community of practice

> Rather than worry about critical mass, our work is to foster critical connections. We don't need to convince large numbers of people to change; instead, we need to connect with kindred spirits.
>
> —Margaret Wheatley and Deborah Frieze, *Using Emergence*

In 2012, NET undertook an initiative called MicroFest USA: Revitalize, Reconnect, Renew to take a fresh look at the role of art and artists in creating healthy, vibrant communities. Focusing on the spectrum of cultural production traditionally regarded as "creative placemaking strategies," we wanted to expand the conversation by looking at this work through a social-justice prism. Our intent was twofold: to acknowledge and advance the pioneering and current work of ensemble theaters committed to community-based practice and positive social change, and to foster mutual learning with a wider spectrum of artists, culture workers, and community partners also contributing to community well-being and social change.

This inquiry grew out of field observations, which started with the question: How does art impact place and place impact art? When we looked across the country we noticed that:

1. Ensembles are place-based entities. Unlike the pick-up company that comes together for a one-time collaboration on a production, ensemble artists are permanent members of the communities they are serving. The artists creating the work are facing the same community challenges as the audiences who see the work. This allows for a different type of conversation to transpire, from one production to the next, unfolding over time. Hence, the relationship between artists and audience is not so much that of producer/consumer, but of friends and neighbors.
2. Much of the work we were seeing was taking place site-specifically in community venues, cultural centers, lakesides, skid row, store fronts, church halls, warehouses, bars, etc. There is a complex relationship to buildings, as their very function is to protect what is inside by keeping the outside world at bay. For a long time in theater history, this included keeping certain audience

members away. This is further complicated by a history of redlining, of class divisions, elitism, and so forth. Now there appears to have been a shift: the work is moving into accessible, communal spaces that are already occupied by intended audiences.

3 Perhaps because many of these productions exist outside the confines of traditional theater spaces, the relationship to audiences was noticeably different. Oftentimes, the work invited audience participation and dialogue (both in its creation and execution); it acknowledged the presence of the audience, of the community. Through this dialogue, the work seemed to be activating civic participation, not only activating neighborhood spaces, but also re-presenting the community to itself, with community agency.

As a result of these conditions, alongside the values driving the work, ensembles are poised to catalyze and lead efforts towards community transformation. Their work can frame and mediate the difficult conversations. Quoting Jo Carson, Gerard Stropnicky reminds us, "A play (or any work of art) will not itself 'solve the problem.' But art can provide a view through the fog."[10]

As a national organization, it's important to NET that we have a real, regular, and meaningful presence around the country. Particularly in the communities of Detroit, Appalachia (Harlan County, Kentucky, and Knoxville, Tennessee), New Orleans, and Honolulu—places challenged in the extreme by economic, social, and environmental issues, but also places where rich and distinctive cultural forms have thrived—we saw innovative strategies emerging for renewal and revitalizing through cross-sector, interdisciplinary collaborations. Too often, though, these communities remain overlooked, or else we merely accept the public narrative that has been created: "They're back-woods hillbillies," or "Detroit is bombed out and dangerous," and so forth. Since much of the work transpiring in our host communities is done under-scale or is focused on specific neighborhoods, it remains invisible to many across the nation. We wanted to pay attention, to learn, to share, to support, to bear witness; and what we found has transformed our organization.

Whether urban or rural, or in neighborhoods, wards, or "hollers," the most successful and creative strategies for making a vibrant place that we saw included cross-sector/cross-disciplinary collaborations, which involve community participation alongside arts and non-arts professionals. The merging of multiple perspectives and expertise (i.e., ensemble practice) enables fresh and holistic solutions to some of the community's most pressing needs and challenges.

Below are some examples of the work we highlighted at the MicroFests.

In Detroit: Earth & Sky Repose

Resourced and facilitated by the Community + Public Art: Detroit (CPAD) program of the College for Creative Studies, local artists worked with community residents to activate a vacant lot in Detroit's North End. The actual site was chosen and the artwork came to fruition through substantial neighborhood participation. When asked what was needed from this public art opportunity, community members answered: "Food, jobs, and a safe place for our kids." Together, artists and community members created a stone pathway, lined with benches and sculptures, which also function as a water collection system for the on-site community garden and greenhouse.

This project brought together an array of partners: the Christian Community Development Organization, which owned the property; the Vanguard CDC, a youth service organization; the Greater Woodward CDC, a service organization for the homeless which buys food from the garden with a grant from Whole Foods; the Central Detroit Christian organization; and Home Depot, which donated supplies. Gardening labor was supplied by individuals working off community service hours as well as by young people who have taken "real ownership" of the garden.[11]

In Appalachia: Higher Ground

Based at Southeast Community and Technical College, Higher Ground has developed a cycle of plays based on a multi-decade story-gathering process that speaks to the challenges families and communities are facing in their area, such as land ownership and land use, outmigration, drug abuse, the changing coalmining industry, and so forth. With cast sizes of seventy or more community members, the Higher Ground plays create an open forum for discussing the important issues facing Harlan County residents while also creating opportunities for participants to form ties that extend beyond the project.

In describing the project, Mark Kidd writes,

> The Higher Ground project has used its creative forms—story gathering, play creation, and performance—to enact what Imaging America's Curriculum Project Report describes as community cultural development: "self-directed development strategies, where members of a community define their own aims and determine their own paths to reach them."[12]

Their latest production will be staged in unoccupied buildings throughout the county, bringing residents together to imagine a new future for real estate that has been inaccessible for public uses.

In New Orleans: Cry You One

A collaboration between two ensembles, Mondo Bizarro and Art Spot Productions, working with the support and cooperation of a variety of local environmental activist groups, Cry You One is an outdoor performance and online storytelling platform that journeys into the heart of Louisiana's disappearing wetlands.[13] Described as "a funeral for the land," the performance borrowed from the "second lines" in New Orleans jazz funerals, where mourners parade down the streets following a brass band. In this instance, instead of following a jazz band down a city street, the audience followed actors and musicians alongside the levees and wetlands of St. Bernard Parish, mourning the disappearance of the land, culture, and people that will be lost, the result of weak and reckless environmental policies.

At the end of the five-hour performance, the audience was invited to share a meal, prepared by local food-justice groups and chefs, and to learn more about the environmental damage to the Gulf Coast. Environmental groups such as the Gulf Coast Restoration Network, government departments such as the Louisiana Department of Natural Resources, and individuals such as Lloyd "Wimpy" Serigne, who grew up on Delacroix Island—land which is now under water—were on hand to lead and take part in the conversations.

In Hawaii: Urban 808

A collective of cultural workers, artists, and organizers, Urban 808 develops youth leadership and provides mentorship for "at-risk" youth through urban arts (graffiti and mural painting). Among their programs is the Junior Board Initiative, a "comprehensive mentorship program focusing on a movement to unite our youth, while inspiring Hawaii's next leaders to mobilize and govern action toward improving the quality of life within their own communities."[14]

At the MicroFest, these young leaders guided participants in a tour of the Kaka'ako neighborhood, where Urban 808 is located. The youth expertly guided participants through streets and alleys, parks and warehouse, showing attendees several of the 50 or more murals they have created. The mural projects reflect local history and culture, embodying indigenous stories and values, such as *aloha aina* (love of the land). The program brings together youth from various high schools, including private schools. According to founder John "Prime" Hina, at first "the 'snobby, rich kids' and the 'ghetto kids' didn't want to work with each other, but after a year, they were like family." Marcus Renner, one of the attendees, recounted, "One of the youth explained how working on the mural has helped her develop leadership and public speaking skills."[15]

In their neighborhood, one of the fastest gentrifying areas of Oahu, artists and longtime residents are at risk of displacement. The youth, working with the Urban 808 Founders, are organizing community dialogues with the various local stakeholders, including residents, business owners, and developers to envision a collective future for their neighborhood.

Toward systems of influence

> The third stage in emergence can never be predicted. It is the sudden appearance of a system that has real power and influence. Pioneering efforts that hovered at the periphery suddenly become the norm. The practices developed by courageous communities become the accepted standard.
>
> (Margaret Wheatley and Deborah Frieze, *Using Emergence*)

NET defines an ensemble as "a group of individuals dedicated to collaborative creation, committed to working together consistently over years to develop a distinctive body of work and practices."[16] Stropnicky observes,

> Workers in all disciplines—musicians, sculptors, muralists, community gardeners, environmental activists, organizers—including many who may not self-define as artists, come comfortably within that definition and have joined this national conversation. NET's stated core values of collaboration, inclusion, transparency, excellence, and respect aren't exclusive to Theater artists.[17]

Following are some examples of the companies included in NET and at the MicroFests.

In Detroit: Young Nation

Young Nation is a youth-development program whose mission is to "promote holistic development of youth in urban settings through building relationships, community education, and passion-driven projects."[18] According to youth leader Nyasia Valdez (no relation to the author), "Young Nation started out in 2008, from a group called Expression. There was a need to build relationships between youth and adults, graffiti artists and lower riders. We wanted to connect young people with their passions."[19] Projects include the Alley Project, a youth program that encourages homeowners in Southwest Detroit to invite graffiti artists to paint garage doors, transforming "dangerous" alleys into public galleries; and Inside Southwest Detroit, an online platform to share the stories, issues, history of the neighborhood through pictures, articles, blogs, tweets, instagrams and videos.

Young Nation's approach to youth development

> attempts to affect change not by power, assumption, or coercion but instead inspiring young minds through example and engagement. Implicit in this approach is that youth are involved in participatory processes, that principles of positive youth development are promoted, and that there are cultural and developmental competencies that work together toward the processes and ends of the initiative.[20]

When I asked Valdez why she remains involved in Young Nation, she cited the effectiveness of this strategy and the opportunities for deep involvement and visioning. "They want it to be youth led and they want your input. That's what keeps me here."

The role of youth leadership mirrors how NET views ensembles, where the artists are empowered in the direction and visioning of the organization. Both draw on lateral, collaborative structures, value mutual respect and embrace transparency in decision making.

In Appalachia: On The Creek

Robert "BobbyB" Martin, co-founder of On The Creek, describes the group as "an ensemble that is open to collaborators from the Eastern Kentucky region; people of different backgrounds (artist or not) who want to share in commemorating, investigating, and visioning our (the people and the land of this area) stories (past, present, and future)."[21]

Martin came to NET as a Fellow for the MicroFest initiative, one of eight individuals representing the four partner communities (two Fellows were selected from each community). Through his involvement, he brought along his collaborators, understanding the benefits to the group of coming into contact with like-minded artists. Recalling the formation of On The Creek, he explained that they came together to organize the Clear Creek Festival, a multidisciplinary healing arts festival. Company members include storytellers, musicians, carpenters, blacksmiths, social workers, researchers, and others. In fact, only one person self-identifies as a theater practitioner. Through their participation and attendance at the MicroFests, they began to understand and see their work as ensemble. Martin explains,

> In our area there are few examples of an ensemble practicing culture together. We were in a practice where we were identifying as people working in culture (musicians, singer/songwriters, craftsmen—metal and wood workers, etc.). Our members were not experienced with others doing ensemble practices. As we came into contact with others at the MicroFests, we said, "Yeah, we're that." It gave us a community we were lacking. Seeing work, sharing work, affirming the work . . . we were gravitating towards [ensemble practice] but didn't know the impact of [it].

In New Orleans: Art Spot Productions

Already a longtime NET member, Art Spot Productions is representative of a growing number of ensembles that are expressing ensemble values and practices through a variety of interconnected programs. Three core programs have remained constant throughout the five-member ensemble's twenty-year history. First is the creation of original, devised performance. Next is IROC (Individuals Relating and Overcoming Conflict), an education program for local high school students that draws on the company's devising practices for student dialogue around the themes of identity, gender, sex and sexuality, conflict resolution, and cultural organizing. Last is the Drama Club, a theater program with and for the inmates of the Louisiana Correctional Institute for Women. Founded in 1996, this program has served hundreds of women with opportunities for creative expression and personal examination, using theater. Most recently, a new group has formed, called the Graduates, composed of formerly incarcerated participants in the Drama Club, allowing these women to continue their work.

"All of the layers of the work begin to feed each other," says Kathy Randels, founder and Artistic Director of Art Spot. "There are physical exercises, games we share with each [other]. The principle of bringing in research and personal material to create performance is shared across." However beyond methodological crossover, Randels explains that the company's value of honoring individual voices and experiences also runs through each program:

> Everyone is asked to contribute. It allows us a way to bring everyone's voice into the material. With the Graduates, for instance, we facilitate exercises to get to what it is they want to say and meld it with the other stories getting told. We help them hone these stories on the page and in rehearsals. They have the authority of what they say about themselves. . . . Especially with the incarcerated women and formerly incarcerated women, it gets me questioning theater a lot. . . . What are we doing when we are creating the stories? What stories do we have a right to tell? . . . Who can tell them?[22]

In Honolulu: PA'I Foundation

Founded in 2001 to preserve and perpetuate Hawaiian cultural traditions for the next generation, the PA'I Foundation is the non-profit organization of Pua Ali'i 'Ilima, a *hālau hula*, or school of Hawaiian dance, founded by *kumu hula* (master teacher) Vicky Holt Takamine. While the organization is centered around and supported by *hālau* members, the purpose of the PA'I Foundation is not centered around servicing the needs of the *hālau*, but addressing and serving the needs of native Hawaiians and those who make Hawaii their home.[23]

As a primary partner for NET's Honolulu MicroFest, Takamine states,

> Our collaboration made sense. Hula is our performing art; it is our *mo'olelo* (story), our indigenous form of theater. I think of my *hālau* as an ensemble—maybe not a theater—but an ensemble. When you make a commitment to join a *hālau,* there is a real feeling of trust, responsibility and belonging to a family. When we build an ensemble, we are building a community. It's about being inclusive; about connecting with each other, an audience, support . . . finding help and support for the work and for the community.[24]

With the spectrum of cultural production represented within the ensemble field, folk and traditional arts are forms of community empowerment, expressions of deep cultural knowledge and durability, creativity, and community values. Forms like hula provide a critical connection to the past, fostering intergenerational connection and understanding and linking history to contemporary issues toward deeper understanding. They name and interpret their experience, and affirm cultural continuity in the face of social concerns. Cultural workers, activists, and others intentionally draw upon folk and traditional arts and culture to unite people in celebration of place, as well as mobilize people on political or social issues. To this point Takamine adds,

> We did not have a written language. The tradition of *oli* [chanting] and hula were handed down from generation to generation. Our activism revolves around perpetuating these forms. There were efforts to ban our language and hula, but they have survived *Ku'e* [resistance] by perpetuating culture.

Today in NET, we find ourselves at a moment with a broad and diverse constituency. More complicated than ironing out differences between types of theaters, our challenge right now is to find common ground between ensembles working in different sectors (muralists, gardeners, architects, hula, coalminers, and so forth). This is significant for an organization that has defined itself as a network of ensemble *theaters*. Our values of inclusion, collaboration, mutual respect, and so forth, drive us to preserve these relationships; to make this a home for all ensembles. As before, the connecting thread is ensemble, the values and spirit that underpin ensemble practice, which transcend discipline and sectors. We are at the moment of formalizing this expansion. The conversations are complicated and the challenges known. Some members are concerned that they will lose something, some are worried that the organization will be diluted, some are skeptical that we can meet all the needs from multiple sectors when we struggle enough to meet those of the theater field, and more.

These concerns are real and ones that we will confront. But we will also look at the benefits. What the MicroFests taught us is that we are not alone, that the impact of our work is far-reaching, that our practice is vital to community transformation, and that the work matters. Again, as in the early days of NET, we learned about our work by learning about somebody else's. We are a community affiliated by values—a community of practice, building a system of influence, and as our mission demands of us, "propelling ensemble practice to the forefront of American culture and society."

Notes

1 Margaret Wheatley and Deborah Frieze, "Using Emergence to Take Social Innovation to Scale," *Berkana Institute*, 2006, www.berkana.org/lifecycle.htm, www.margaretwheatley.com/articles/emergence.html, accessed February 2014.
2 Though I was affiliated with one of the founding ensembles at this time, and took part in the exchange activities funded by the NEA grant, I was not personally involved in the conversations or active in the founding of NET. I am writing in the first person voice to represent what this meant to the ensemble field.
3 Telephone Interview with Gerard Stropnicky, February 5, 2014.
4 Wheatley and Frieze, "Using Emergence."
5 "The Ensemble Theater Movement," speech delivered at the Theater Communications Group annual conference in Dallas, June 2013.
6 Telephone interview, February 5, 2014.
7 NET promo video, http://vimeo.com/85632926.
8 www.ensembletheaters.net/about/values.
9 www.ensembletheaters.net/about/manifesto.

10 "A Community of Practice: NET Learning in Place," *Animating Democracy*, 2013, http://animatingdemocracy.org/resource/community-practice-net-learning-place.
11 Pam Korza, "MicroFest USA: A Synthesis of Learning About Art, Culture, and Place," 2013, www.ensembletheaters.net.
12 Mark Kidd, "MicroFest: Democratic Arts in Appalachia's Coal Country," 2013, www.ensembletheaters.net.
13 http://www.cryyouone.com/.
14 http://808urban.org/.
15 Quoted in Sonny Ganaden, "MicroFest: Honolulu Theater and Society in the Center of the Sea," 2013, www.ensembletheaters.net.
16 www.ensembletheaters.net.
17 Gerard Stropnicky, "Three Lenses on MicroFest USA: Intentions, Values and Prepositions," 2013, http://www.ensembletheaters.net/sites/default/files/files/StropnickyNOLAPaper_Final.pdf.
18 http://youngnation.us/mission.html.
19 Telephone interview, January 22, 2014.
20 http://youngnation.us/approach.html.
21 Telephone interview, January 15, 2014.
22 Interview, January 19, 2015.
23 http://www.paifoundation.org/about-2/.
24 Telephone interview, January 20, 2014.

Chapter 17

Tear the pages out

lê thi diem thúy

In 1996, with the help of New WORLD Theater, and under the direction of Roberta Uno, I developed a solo performance exploring the psychic trauma of Vietnamese refugees. Drawn in part from my own experience as one among the millions of Vietnamese boat people who fled Vietnam in the aftermath of the American/Vietnam war, *the bodies between us* was not about catharsis or release. Its aim was to enter into the deeply disorienting experience of those who are in a state of abeyance, having departed the old world but not yet arrived in the new one. Or, having arrived, are constantly drawn back toward the world that they left behind, and the memory of the people and places that remain there.

What if, in answer to the question, "where are you from?" the audience saw the ways in which the loss of a homeland and a mother tongue give way to an unfixed and undefined (i.e. seemingly eternal) state of floating? The question posed cannot be answered definitively, but only considered for the barbed riddle that it is.

If the characters could bring the sea itself—and all that it held—ashore with them.

If they themselves were proof of bodies (of land, water, memory) spilling over.

Then we might be able to trouble the framework of what is seen and remembered about the war and its aftermath. Then we might be able to show that nothing in the experience is linear, not the journey, not the memory, not the telling.

During a particularly difficult rehearsal, when I was running in circles around the stage, trying to channel a sense of lightness and flight, but only feeling weighed down by the darkness of the piece's ending, where the two main characters speak about running into the sea, I balked. Standing still, my breath arriving in gasps, I heard myself say, "I can't." To which Roberta replied, "Someone lives to tell the story." The sentence was bracing in its clarity. It pulled me from the sea and coaxed me back.

I make work—poems, stories, performances—about things I cannot bear. Something in my mind and my body requires that I find a way to approach the very things I know but cannot accept. Art is what we make when the facts are not sufficient to contain the heartbreak.

* * *

What is the difference between distance and death? This is a question the child in *the bodies between us* considers in regard to her mother, from whom she and her father are separated. If the mother has not died, then what keeps her from joining them? If that world has not vanished, then where is it? Her consciousness will have to grow to allow for the reality of much that is not visible, entire realms of experience that go largely unvoiced, a here and a there that are separate yet simultaneous.

There are so many countries, so many borders, so many crossings. Grief is one. Terror is another. Rage is another. Love is another. The dream of freedom is yet another.

My mother died in March of 2001, after a brief and vicious fight with cancer. My youngest brother was her favorite child, her golden child, the boy born in America. They were tight. She had gone back to her childhood home in Vietnam to live out her last days, and he was in San Diego. When I wrote to tell him that she had died he wrote back and described a dream he'd had. I wrote it down in my notebook:

> in the dream, it was like a replay of the last time he saw her—that night they caught him and brought him by the house before taking him down to the station—she was lying in the bed and he was sitting beside her—she told him to be good, to stay out of trouble, and he said he would try—when it was time for him to leave, he leaned down to hug her—her body shook as he held her and he knew—he woke and said, my mother died—and the boy who was his cellmate replied, no—don't talk like that—homes.

If I told you that my brother had been in and out of corrections facilities since he was 11 years old; that when he was 17 he was tried and convicted as an adult for a home invasion, which he served a seven year sentence for; that less than three months after being released he was arrested and charged with assault; that there was a trial and he was convicted; that because this conviction was his second felony strike, his six year sentence was doubled to twelve years; that while he was serving that sentence he was involved in yet another case, of trying to smuggle a small amount of drugs—ecstasy and marijuana—into the prison where he was an inmate; that if convicted of this case, which would be his third felony strike, he would be facing 25-to-life; that his public defender and the prosecutor worked out a plea that spared my brother 25-to-life; that he instead got a seven year sentence which, if you add it to his twelve-year sentence, means he will get out in nineteen years; that he'll then be 47, which is older than I am now, though only four years younger than my mother was when she died; would you feel you knew everything there was to know about him? Would you see him as the career criminal the state of California insists he is? Would you tell me that nineteen years is a long time, but it is not life? Would you remind me that there is a stark difference between distance and death—that one can be crossed and the other cannot—and that I should, therefore, be grateful?

I won't make excuses for my brother, who has made some supremely poor choices in life. And I will not argue the merits of any of his cases here, but if mistakes and transgressions are a mark of youth, why do so many young people of color have to pay with what amounts to their life for what others get to apologize for yet still walk away from, future largely intact—and bright?

I had thought the challenge for my family was getting to America, finding our footing, and being well here. I thought ours was a story of becoming Americans while not letting go of Vietnam, the place from which a war had violently propelled us, but also the place where our deepest roots lay.

In my brother's story I see how tenuous citizenship and belonging are. Once my brother had been deemed a criminal, it became increasingly difficult to keep him from becoming a statistic: a young man without a name, without a face; a young man who was counted merely as a body, a number; a young man at once captive and unmoored.

In a sense you could say that trying not to lose sight of my brother, I found myself, once more, out in deep waters.

* * *

I returned to San Diego in 1998 to attend the trial of my brother and three of his friends on assault charges. It was almost a year to the day from when I had last been in San Diego, to celebrate my brother's release from prison after serving a seven-year sentence for a robbery conviction from when he was a teenager.

My brother, who was then 25, had been in and out of corrections facilities since he was 11. Which is to say, he grew up on the inside, and being out was like landing on another planet and being hurled backwards and then forwards in time. He returned to the old neighborhood, where the streets looked the same, but nothing else in his life was. Our mother had died. Our father had moved back to Vietnam. He found it hard to breathe.

Despite this, at the time of his arrest, he had been set on turning his life around. He had completed his mandatory anger management courses, was going on job interviews, and was exploring the possibility of taking some courses at a local community college. He was dating a young woman who had a good job and her own apartment, and nothing to do with the gang life. He wanted to record an album of songs he'd written in prison and new ones since his release. We had tentative plans that he would come visit me in Massachusetts in the spring or summer, once the weather was kinder. We were hopeful and determined, but also foolish and unfocused, we thought the hard part was behind us.

A third of all parolees in this country return to prison within two years, my brother would be no different: another name, another number, after being out for less than five months, he'd caught another case. Now, due to California's 'three-strikes' and gang enhancement laws, if convicted, he was looking at a serious round of time.

* * *

I wrote a letter to the judge who would sentence my brother. I admitted that it was a strange letter, filled with argument about the case, as much as with love for my brother. But what could I do?

I sketched the trajectory of my brother's life beside my own, how our paths diverged, how I went on to college and he stayed behind and was schooled primarily by the culture of gang life and of the various corrections facilities he was admitted to. I wanted to convey how very little separated my brother and me, how if I had been born a boy I might have made some of the same decisions. Who could say? After all, I, too, had begun leaving home at a young age in order to escape what felt like the insurmountable pressures of our family life. If it weren't for the teachers who took me in and guided me, who saw my talents and encouraged me, I don't know where I would be now.

I tried to write back the time and to write back the tide. I tried to explain things that could not really be explained, my parents' failed efforts to find a footing in this country, my father's addictions and rage, my mother's illness and early death, how very many years my family had spent apart from one another, separated by war, reeducation camps, entire continents, oceans.

I asked for mercy for my brother and for the three young men who would be sentenced with him. Mercy, as if they were facing a death sentence. One of the young men would be released on probation; one would receive four years; another would receive six; my brother was sentenced to twelve years, four for assault, three for the gang enhancement, five more because this was his second 'strike' felony. Twelve years, for being present at the scene of a fight, where no one, not the alleged victim nor the lone witness, had seen him throw a punch. My brother did try to run that night; he leapt a fence and ran across a few suburban lawns and turned a corner and was caught. He was running for his life; he mistakenly believed that he already had two strikes and that if he was caught, charged, and convicted, this would be his third strike, game over, out, for life.

* * *

When my brother was about 14 I dreamed that he had died in a youth detention facility where he was being kept. The authorities called my parents and my parents woke me. Somehow my mother was able to tell me the terrible news, just with her eyes. In the dream I was disconsolate and wild with grief. I kept shouting, "How do you know? Who told you? How do you know?" I insisted that we wait to see his body. We need proof, I said. But my parents said we would not be allowed to, my brother had already been buried. I couldn't absorb what they were telling me and I felt the walls of the dream closing in on me until I woke up, sobbing.

Time, of which we say it is 'hard' when it promises pain, which 'flies' when filled with pleasure, which is 'fleeting' when it holds something we want to savor, which is 'on our side' when we are optimistic, 'against us' when we are not, 'immemorial' when it reaches back beyond the grasp of memory, which will 'tell' what we don't yet know, the fabric of which seems 'torn' when we are confronted with something we can't accept, which 'darkens' in order to illuminate; a sentence is a prisoner's ultimate measure of time. If all goes well, he will be released at the end date, if not, the end date keeps getting rewritten, it becomes a once open door slowly closing, a lock impervious to all keys.

In the span of a sentence's hold, sits a man or a woman on the inside, invisibly linked to a chain of people going about life on the outside. So am I linked to my brother, as he serves his sentence and awaits his appeal, so is he linked to the mother and grandmother of the young man who sat beside him during visiting hour, so are we all linked to the guards who stood watch over our visit, and to the woman who counted out many hundred dollar bills in bail money to the clerk downstairs, who is linked to the young Somali woman coming through the visiting room doors, who is linked to the memory of my mother and father, Vietnamese refugees newly arrived in San Diego, trailing myself and my baby sister, the four of us wandering a dim stretch of downtown searching for a movie theater to disappear into, not yet Americans, but wanting to do what Americans did.

The darkness of that theater is linked to the brightness of November 4, 2008, when, opening the door of the apartment I was renting in downtown San Diego, I heard people cheering in the streets, and saw on the television Jesse Jackson Sr. weeping with abandon in Chicago's Hyde Park, his tearful gaze seeming to take in an immense river of time.

* * *

Denial may be neither a matter of telling the truth nor intentionally telling a lie. There seem to be states of mind, or even whole cultures, in which we know and don't know at the same time.[1] To be bound to someone who is doing time is to acknowledge, through experience, the reality of a largely invisible world, one that depends on the dehumanization of masses of people, many of whom are young, and the majority of whom are of color. My brother's trial, conviction, and return into the mass incarceration system coincided with the triumphant days of Barack Obama's election and inauguration. For me, this brought into high relief some of the deep contradictions of our time.

While he often eschewed directly addressing the topic of race during his presidential campaign (unless he had to, as with the speech he gave in response to the Reverend Jeremiah Wright scandal), Barack Obama often alluded to the struggles and hopes of the civil rights era as a time when Americans across all walks of life united around a common purpose. By doing so, it seemed he was tying that time to ours. We were reminded that because a group of people sought to cross a bridge in Selma even as they were badly beaten back; because thousands marched, and many were killed; because men and women faced the sting of fire hoses and police dogs in Birmingham; because a girl in Little Rock set out for school, and a preacher in Atlanta raised his eyes and his voice to the mountain top, we know that we can, that we must, that we shall.

The struggles of the Civil Rights era remain deeply relevant, though perhaps not in the ways we would like to think. Law professor Michelle Alexander eloquently, and persuasively, argues in her book *The New Jim Crow*, that we have become a nation of people that abides the disappearance of millions of our fellow citizens into a new caste system, one in which a felony conviction often results in the loss of hard earned civil rights, including the right to vote, the right to serve on a jury, the right to live in public housing or receive public assistance. To lose such rights creates a second class of people in our society, people for whom living in a democracy is not marked by a place at the table, but rather, by rigid and relentless refusal.

The United States locks up a greater percentage of its population than any other nation on earth. This is due, in part, to the "war on drugs," mandatory minimum sentencing laws, tough-on-crime measures like California's three strikes law, and the privatization of the corrections industry. Sentences have ballooned out of proportion to the crimes committed, defying logic and common sense, let alone justice. A turn away from reform and rehabilitation toward containment means more and more people are warehoused, biding time, with little hope and little change in sight.

According to a 2012 report by the Sentencing Project there are currently 6.98 million people in our nation's mass incarceration system. This same report states that 6 million Americans are unable to vote due to felon disenfranchisement laws. While the election and re-election of Barack Obama to the highest seat in the nation is testament to the fact that some deeply entrenched barriers have indeed fallen—the rate of disenfranchisement among voting age black Americans, at 8 percent, is also the nation's highest, a bitter distinction indeed.

What does the promise of America mean to my brother? Or to the many men and women who could not cast a vote for anyone, let alone for the man who would become our nation's first black president? Surely for them, caught inside the machine of our nation's mass incarceration system, doing time in prison, in jail, on probation, or on parole, this day is much like the last and will be much like the next, it has not yet transformed into the longed for day, the one whose arrival might break the hard chain of days.

One day my brother, and the many inmates like him, will walk out of their prison cells and come home. The men and women they'll be, and the homes they'll find will depend not only on their individual actions, but also on our collective will.

If my brother had made it to Massachusetts to join me, as we'd hoped, New WORLD Theater's youth initiative, Project 2050, would have been a revelation to him. More than just drawing attention to the shifting demographics of our country—2050 is the year in which it is projected that people of color will become the majority in the US—Project 2050 asked what that might mean for our democracy.

Here were young people of color forming a community, through art, to engage with the most pressing questions of their times, including that of incarceration, one of the main themes in New WORLD Theater's Project 2050 Summer Camp in

2002. Working in collaboration with artists and scholars, erasing the line between activism and art, empowering themselves and their communities through education and self-expression, these were young people fiercely and whole-heartedly prepared to face the future. What would have been so revelatory to my brother? A central premise of the initiative: that the future is brighter with these young people in it, active participants in the play of democracy.

While the scale of our mass incarceration problem is staggering—when we consider the number of people caught within the draconian loop of it, the amount of federal and state dollars wasted on it, the recidivism rate, the level of disenfranchisement, the families broken, the futures effectively erased—what's more alarming still is what becomes of us, as a nation, if we don't face it.

If our nation's rate of incarceration continues at its current clip, it is quite likely that the year 2050 will signal not only when people of color represent the majority in the US but also when being in the majority mattered so little. If communities of color remain those most impacted by mass incarceration—through higher levels of disenfranchisement and the employment, housing, and education discrimination that a criminal record often incurs—this will have a profound effect on the health of our democracy. Stripped of the civil rights that earlier generations fought and died for, holding on by whatever means possible, shut out of the American Dream, communities of color may be systematically relegated, for generations, to running in place or slipping further behind. Precisely because the problem is systemic, activists, scholars, policy makers, engaged citizens, must all play a part in the movement to dismantle mass incarceration in our country.

The legacy of New WORLD Theater reminds us that art has a unique role to play in such a movement. Art is a means of giving voice and making visible. Looked at in light of our nation's mass incarceration problem, art can be a means of individual and collective resistance. To show the human toll of mass incarceration, it isn't enough to get the facts out. As in portraits of war, numbers and statistics—whether they are casualty counts or incarceration rates—can be difficult to absorb unless we are able to put a name and a face and a feeling to the facts. And as in all true portraits, it is necessary to show or suggest that there was, in fact, a before, and there may, one hopes, be a time after, one that is able to salvage from the bomb blast or the long sentence a life worth living.

I believe that art alone allows us to get closer, not only to what we know and care about, but more importantly, what we don't know or perhaps don't wish to know. We are offered a glimpse into other lives, a glimpse from the inside out, a telling detail that makes the humanity of another person more difficult to deny.

My brother understands something about art's essential urgency. No one needs to tell him that it can save your life, make time stop, break down walls, make visible an invisible man.

When my book, *The Gangster We Are All Looking For* was first published, I sent a copy to my brother who was then an inmate at Folsom State Prison. A prison guard informed him that the book had arrived, but he could not receive it.

Inmates are not allowed to receive hardcover books because drugs and weapons might be concealed in them. My brother said, "You can take the whole thing apart. Tear the covers off. I don't care. Tear the pages out. Just give the words to me."

* * *

Art is a song of freedom. Freedom is the dream of a new reality. Reality is the thing that must be faced. Facing it will free you.

Note

1 Stanley Cohen, *States of Denial: Knowing about Atrocities and Suffering* (Cambridge: Polity Press, 2001).

Chapter 18

"Not a prophecy, but description"

Rethinking multiculturalism in the "post-racial" moment

Jeff Chang

Back in 2006, when Barack Obama was still just a freshman senator, I was pitching my book editor on a followup to *Can't Stop Won't Stop*: hip-hop, I told her, had followed a number of historical cultural uprisings, but perhaps the least understood of them—and perhaps the most important to understanding the moment we were living through—was the multiculturalism movement. I admitted to her that I had become obsessed with it and how it had moved from a radical avant-garde to a state and corporate "ideology from above."

I gave it my best shot: beginning in the mid-1970s, a ragtag group of U.S. artists of color mounted a challenge to mainstream whiteness. They protested racist representations in media and the arts and the educational system, and fought to advance their own counter-representations. In doing so, they sparked a broad backlash. By the late 1980s and early 1990s, the pitched debates over multiculturalism marked the outbreak of the North American culture wars.

But then something happened. Just a decade later, at the turn of the millennium, the era of Clarence Thomas, Condoleeza Rice, and Richard Parsons opened. One scholar and assimilationist declared, "We are all multiculturalists now." What had once appeared as an insurgency against invisibility now felt like a mere correction. What had happened to the revolution? *That* was what I wanted to write about.

Monique laughed gently, and in the sweetest way possible, said, "Multiculturalism. Oh, I don't know. Who cares about that now?"

She was right. Outside her Flatiron office, on city billboards, Diddy was selling aspirational consumer goods with a smirk. On TV, *The Boondocks* and *South Park* mocked earnest multiculturalists as cartoon punchlines—passive, platitudinous white teachers, high on diversity the way hippies had been on Flower Power.

What was I thinking? I had recently curated a panel at the Ford Foundation on hip-hop aesthetics, featuring Greg Tate, Mark Anthony Neal, Vijay Prashad, and Brian Cross. In my own earnest way, I had asked them to think about framing hip-hop aesthetics within the context of the victories of the multiculturalism movement that had preceded it. I was surprised to hear Mark and Vijay issue strong critiques.

Mark said that when he had been a college student activist, multiculturalism simply meant that he could get a budget to put on Black History month events and recruit faculty of color. But it quickly became a trap, a way for bureaucracies to essentialize identities and contain radicalism.

Vijay added,

> Multiculturalism was an ideology from above. It was about the institutional management of diversity, and it decided not to engage with the principal feature of the antisubordination movements, the antiracist movements which fought white supremacy and power. Multiculturalism became about celebration; it was about dealing with your history and your past. But white power and white supremacy was off the table and out of the room.[1]

Good grief. I had pitched Monique a book no one wanted to read, not even my own friends.

For his part, Greg pushed back, noting the germinal 1970s Bay Area literary journal, *The Yardbird Reader*, started by the writers Ishmael Reed and Al Young and featuring a multiracial core of young poets and novelists. What they and other like-minded artists had started *was* an insurgency against invisibility.

The waning of the Civil Rights era and the end of formal legal desegregation had left a nation bereft of a vision for a new America. Artists were best positioned to articulate the end of the invisibility of people of color and the recognition of identity, not just in a legal sense, but a cultural sense as well. With recognition could come a new understanding not merely of "diversity," but of national culture itself. The Yardbird collective argued that American culture had never been only white and Western, a singular, unitary, exceptionalist model. America had *always* been multicultural. Their argument seems so obvious now, yet it was radical back then. And the transformation they called for remains only partially realized.

But as a book topic in 2006, all this seemed a non-starter, as relevant as last month's tweets, worth only embarrassment or indifference.

Then suddenly Barack Obama was running for president, a biracial man from Hawai'i whose own passage into consciousness occurred just as the culture wars were being fought on the campuses. It seemed natural that he should invoke a personal and national narrative of reconciliation, and he offered his own biracial selfhood as a hope that the culture wars would end. Many pundits were ready to believe him, inventing a new word "post-racial" to describe the new republic Obama was supposedly leading us towards—one in which all of the US's inconvenient racial history, the kind that conjured only embarrassment or indifference—simply melted into air.

But Obama's campaign of hope unleashed old hatreds and desires. If Ronald Reagan had turned the 1980s toward a restaging of the national cultural divisions of the Vietnam war era, where the forces of restored order would tame the incoming demographic tides of youth and color, it now seemed as if conservatives wanted to turn Obama's candidacy and then presidency into a way to refight the culture wars of the Reagan-Bush era.

Like all wars, the culture wars were not inevitable. But in the last epoch of the twentieth century these wars erupted because demographic change and multiculturalism had prompted new discussions about democracy, particularly around contested values of expression, recognition, inclusion, and empathy. Back then Pat Buchanan—who had declared the culture wars in 1992—and his ilk argued that if multiculturalists were allowed to triumph, American democracy would crumble. From the start the culture wars had been framed as a struggle for the soul of America, a clash of competing narratives: the story of the great America we are in danger of losing forever versus the story of a hopeful emerging America. The nation's colorization might lead to the end of American civilization or the beginning of a great national transformation.

The specter of an Obama presidency seemed to require nothing less than a last stand against the end of the great white America. In Buchanan's Obama-era polemic, *Suicide Of A Superpower: Will America Survive to 2025?* he wrote: "What happened to the America we all grew up in?" Both questions—the first inseparable from the second—pointed to an aching imperial nostalgia, an ideal of a homogenous Christian nation, and a quaking fear of a future conditioned by cultural and racial change.

So as the country began to tear itself asunder over race, identity, and culture once again, I decided—with characteristically poor judgment and no irony at all—to take Monique's dismissal as a challenge.

What was it about multiculturalism that had been important? Why did even those of us who had been among its adherents feel so ambivalent and critical of it now? What did it mean to the unfinished projects of desegregation, cultural equity and racial justice in the US?

The return of the culture wars made recovering a narrative about multiculturalism something worth doing.

* * *

A common narrative of the American desegregation struggle begins with the outbreak of civil protest in Montgomery, Alabama, in 1954, and peaks in the year between the summers of 1963 and 1964, bookended by the March on Washington for Jobs and Freedom and the passage of the Civil Rights Act. From there, the post-Civil Rights era—which might be said to have begun in the summer of 1965, after the assassination of Malcolm X, the passage of the Voting Rights Act, and the days of rage and nights of fire in Watts—looks like a long, tragic dissipation.

If the history of race in America is taken solely as one of traditional political and social movements, framed as a narrative of the actions of the state, then that tragedy certainly continues almost a half-century of summers later through to the trial of George Zimmerman and *Shelby County v. Holder*. But true integration required much more than simply changing the formal dictates of the law. It required a shift in consciousness, too.

After legal segregation was wiped away, the question of cultural desegregation became paramount. Another way to understand the civil rights era is to begin from a different point of view: cultural change made political change possible. Change had not just happened through sit-ins and occupations and marches. Spaces like pop radio, the Southern Black church, and the major league baseball park helped move the national imagination to make *Brown v. Board of Education* and the Civil Rights Act of 1964 conceivable.

The end of *de jure* segregation set the field for the culture wars of the 1980s. After formal political change, cultural workers shouldered the way forward out of segregation. In this sense, the multiculturalism movement was an insurgency against invisibility. The backlash that it spawned was about quelling claims around the terms of real integration and equality. Both sides were moved by the urgency of demographic change—and as one side fought for cultural transformation, the other took a stand for white racial restoration.

The aims of what would become the multiculturalism movement were clarified at the very beginning of Ralph Ellison's 1952 novel, *The Invisible Man*. "I am invisible, understand, simply because people refuse to see me," his fictional protagonist famously remarked. "When they approach me they see only my surroundings, themselves, or figments of their imagination—indeed, everything and anything but me."

Race began as a visual problem between appearance and the perception of difference. In Ellison's telling, whites could not see the people of color in their lived truth. For people of color, invisibility meant lack of representation and misrepresentation. The result was cultural segregation, a condition of racial inequality that denied both the segregator and the segregated the possibility of connection or empathy, much less transformation.

With Kenneth and Mamie Clark's experiments in Black children's self-image in mind, Martin Luther King, Jr. often told his audiences: "You see, equality is not only a matter of mathematics and geometry, but it's a matter of psychology . . . It's not only a quantitative something, but it is a qualitative something. And it is possible to have a quantitative equality and qualitative *in*equality."[2]

Here was where the legal and legislative breakthroughs of the Civil Rights Movement could no longer point the way forward. Civil Rights activists had attacked differential treatment under the law, the engine of racial segregation and inequity. But the law could only set the basic terms on how we were to interact. What would guide the creation of a new nation? That was the space of values and visions. It was cultural work.

Differing notions of "integration" illustrated this problem. Integration meant one thing in education, public accommodations, and housing. In culture, it meant another. The central question to Brown v. Board had been, "(D)oes segregation of children in public schools solely on the basis of race, even though the physical facilities and other 'tangible' factors may be equal, deprive the children of the minority group of equal educational opportunities?" In arguing that it did, the Warren Court argued that segregation always implied "the inferiority of the negro group." In this context formal integration had been delivered under the shadow of the white man's burden.

To the multiculturalists, "integration" implied cultural inferiority as much as structural inequality, unequal distribution of ability as much as unequal access to opportunity. From the majority's point of view, the new freedom afforded by *Brown v. Board* left a person of color with a single option: assimilation. Instead, the multiculturalists would begin at the point where the law ended and the culture began. They set out to eliminate the gap between formal integration and cultural equity, between the kind of integration that changed just the minority and the kind that changed everyone.

Understood this way, integration was not just about reaching mere numerical diversity. It was about fostering a radical diversity, the wild protean ecological sort. It was about what might flower when people could really have a mutual exchange across the lines that still existed after the legal restraints had fallen. Real integration would not be a one-way process. It would vector in all directions, opening everyone to new stories, new worldviews, and the possibility that these exchanges could leave everyone changed for the better.

Just as Ellison's nameless narrator in *The Invisible Man* had concluded, "Our fate is to become one, yet remain many—This is not prophecy, but description."

* * *

Multiculturalism's antecedents could be traced to west-coast Third Worldist spaces, which often grew directly out of the Black Arts Movement, and Chicano, American Indian, Asian American and feminist of color identity movements. During the early 1970s, places like the Inner City Cultural Center in Los Angeles or the Kearny Street Workshop in San Francisco became hubs of interracial arts production. Feminists of color played a central role in defining ideas of a united struggle. One of the earliest multiculturalist documents is the anthology *Third World Women*, edited in 1972 by Janice Mirikitani and produced by a collective that emerged in part out of the San Francisco State University Third World Strike in 1968.

If it is possible to fix the birth of the multiculturalism movement, one date might be December 12, 1975, when Ishmael Reed declared its arrival in *The Berkeley Barb*, saying,

> The multi-cultural movement is the movement of the Seventies. In the Sixties you had the Black Arts group, which was very narrow and Black; and the counterculture movement, which was very narrow and white. Now you have the multi-cultural movement, which is mixed up. This is the wave of the future for the whole country.

The word "multi-cultural" was hyphenated in the article, as if to highlight the paradox inherent in a conception of culture that was not unitary.

Reed had moved to Northern California in 1969 to teach at U.C. Berkeley. He soon fell in with a crowd of Third World writers—including Al Young, Lawson Inada, Frank Chin, Ntozake Shange, Thulani Davis, Toni Cade Bambara, Victor

Cruz, and Jessica Hagedorn. By 1976, he had transformed *The Yardbird Reader*, which began as a Black literary journal, into the first multicultural literary journal. Members of the collective went on to form the Before Columbus Foundation, whose mission was to popularize the notion that, "'Multiculturalism' is not a description of a category of American writing—it is a definition of all American writing."[3]

This argument would undergird the twinned efforts to increase the representation of people of color, in both the aesthetic and institutional senses of the word. Multiculturalism meant rethinking canons of whiteness, redefining notions of identity and nation, and broadening the range of narratives and interpretations available. In another sense, it meant structural reform challenging institutional racism and cultural inequity.

By the mid-1980s, activists had been increasingly and loudly demonstrating against minority underrepresentation and mainstream misrepresentations in Hollywood films like *Fort Apache: The Bronx* and *Charlie Chan*, and the Broadway play, *Miss Saigon*. At the same time, a vibrant infrastructure of community arts organizations—emerging from the convergence of protest movements, cultural uprisings, and government funding and often community-based philanthropy—had created spaces to incubate and platforms to promote new voices. The founding of New World Theater in 1979 marked an important moment in this era of expansion.

The coming decade was one of real breakthroughs. In 1983, Alice Walker's *The Color Purple* won the Pulitzer and the National Book Award. Soon the list of writers of color who won a Pulitzer or a National Book Award grew to include Toni Morrison, August Wilson, Gloria Naylor, and Maxine Hong Kingston. Blockbuster exhibitions such as the massive "Chicano Art: Resistance and Affirmation" exhibition found large audiences in ten cities. Books such as Lucy Lippard's *Mixed Blessings: New Art In A Multicultural America* and the anthologies, *Race, Writing, and Difference* and *Out There: Marginalization and Contemporary Cultures* helped to transform theoretical approaches in the academy.

On a national level, the Association of American Cultures began meeting in the mid-1980s to convene art activists and local arts agency administrators from around the country to explore how to better foster pluralism through policy and support for cultural organizations and arts projects. The Caribbean Cultural Center in New York City began organizing Cultural Diversity Based On Cultural Grounding conferences, where artists, scholars, policymakers, and educators, from Appalachians to Afrocentrists, began redefining the idea of cultural equity. Their agenda would include a pluralistic rethinking of criteria of aesthetic excellence, a commitment to developing "the cultural empowerment of our communities," and parity in representation in everything from exhibitions to decision-making positions.[4]

Such initiatives were often supported by the National Endowment for the Arts' Expansion Arts program, established in 1971 to especially reach emerging organizations "deeply rooted in and reflective of culturally diverse, inner-city, rural, or tribal communities."[5] In turn, the Expansion Arts program reflected a growth in state and municipal arts funding for culturally underrepresented groups, particularly the San Francisco Arts Commission's innovative Cultural Equity grants program. In 1992, the NEA published a broad national survey on 543 cultural centers of color, marking a moment of official recognition of the contributions that multiculturalists had made to the "unique cultural and artistic pluralism of the United States."[6]

By this time, multiculturalism could be described as a broad, decentered movement that had defined a new pole in debates over aesthetics, philosophy, politics, and ethics. Indeed it could claim a large number of victories, that is, if it was aware of itself as a united concern. But the movement had become so vast it had spawned its own internecine battles, as artists fought over issues of authenticity and commodification. And the same massive demographic and cultural shifts that had made multiculturalism viable had also begun to spark a backlash.

* * *

In the early 1990s, the movement seemed to reach its apex. New census data revealed a nation transformed by people of color. The spaces that came under most scrutiny and pressure were college campuses, where the implications of the new diversity could be felt most viscerally. As a result, reactionary culture warriors focused first on containing multiculturalism on the campuses.

In 1988, not long after the faculty of Stanford University voted to replace a Western Civilizations graduation requirement with a more pluralistic one called Cultures, Ideas, and Values, the conservative National Association of Scholars formed, vowing to confront affirmative action, diversity trainings, "tenured radicals" and their "oppression studies." So began the sustained attack of the multiculturalism movement.

The backlash brought together colorblind neoconservatives, Moral Majoritarians, and Anglo-American restorationists. Over the next five years, these culture warriors would ravage public funding for the arts, unleash a wave of state censorship of public art, begin a rollback of affirmative action and other policies designed to desegregate public institutions, and silence a generation of artists of color who had just begun to crack the bamboo ceilings.

One of the great battles in this period of the culture wars came in the 1993 Biennial at the Whitney Museum of American Art. Curators hoped to stage the spirit of democratization and emergence of the period. Only 36 percent of the more than eighty artists selected for the show were white males. The lineup included future superstars Glenn Ligon, Coco Fusco, Lorna Simpson, Gary Simmons, Jimmie Durham, Fred Wilson, and Trinh Minh-ha, alongside Cindy Sherman, Nancy Spero, Matthew Barney and Chris Burden. It was the most diverse exhibition ever held in a major American museum.

Thelma Golden laid out the mission and in her essay, "What's White . . . ?":

> Artists in the nineties have begun to fully deconstruct the marginality-centrality paradigm. Marginality, in effect, becomes the norm while the

> center is increasingly undefinable and perhaps irrelevant. Although many may call this Biennial the "multicultural" or "politically correct" Biennial, it should be read as a larger project which insists that decentralization and the embracing of the margins have become dominant.[7]

But critics instead mounted what might be described as a revolt of the elites. They called it "a showcase for political correctness" and "one extended exhibitionistic frenzy of victimization and self-pity."[8] It was about "multicultural anger . . . at the European-American White Male" and had the "cordite aroma of cultural reparations."[9] One pundit declared the show to be "a cultural war to destabilize and break the mainstream."[10]

In the wake of the Biennial, formalism was fully restored as the dominant language of aesthetic judgment. The word "identity" itself became verboten, not just in the visual arts but across many other genres. If one practiced "identity art," one was certainly not practicing what any serious critic would consider "good art."

In theater, a similar debate broke out, resulting in the spectacle of an actual showdown onstage. In 1997, playwright August Wilson and the critic Robert Brustein faced off at the Town Hall in Manhattan to argue multiculturalism in the theater. Over the course of the evening, the two tangled on issues of race, culture, and the role of art in social change.

Wilson pointed out that only one of the sixty-six regional theaters was a black one. Brustein decried Wilson as separatist. Why, Wilson asked, should the white experience be considered as universal, while the black experience be seen as specific, as if it were somehow less than fully American?

Brustein argued that theater should not aspire to be "ideological art," that an artist should "speak truth to power," not seek power. When an audience member asked Brustein how one could speak "truth to power" without invoking the power and politics, Brustein stated, "Art does not change social consciousness."

Wilson countered brusquely, "Art changes individuals, and individuals change society."[11]

* * *

But things had already begun to change quickly. By the turn of the millennium, multiculturalism had lost its edge. The Bush cabinet was multicultural. Disneyland and Coca-Cola were multicultural. As the author Paul Beatty put it in his classic hip-hop novel *The White-Boy Shuffle*, everything was multicultural and nothing was multicultural.

And this was where we had found ourselves—still—in 2006 as we discussed the rise of hip-hop after multiculturalism. Still debating whether or not what multiculturalism and hip-hop had accomplished was true integration. Still dealing with the shadow of invisibility—the lack of representation and presence of misrepresentation.

Multiculturalism is remembered now less as a movement than as an idea, less as an aesthetic idea than a social and philosophical idea, and less as a transformative idea than a failed one. And yet there had always been a difference between the multiculturalism movement launched by artists and cultural critics of color, and the multiculturalism expressed by capital and the state. Especially after 9/11, it became clear that a kind of state multiculturalism could be mobilized against the new Other—Arab-, Muslim-, and South Asian-Americans—and that this could fit comfortably in with a corporate "keep calm and continue shopping" multiculturalism.

It is no wonder many felt the need to distance themselves from this kind of multiculturalism of excess and essentialism. It had become something no one could recognize or defend.

As early as 1991, Henry Louis Gates had criticized what he called multiculturalism's confusion of "political representation" with "textual representation"—a defense of (still elusive) aesthetic standards that used almost exactly the kind of argument white formalists had deployed for decades to exclude artists of color:

> What could confer "equity" on "culture"? The phrase assumes that works of culture can be measured on some scalar metric—and decreed, from some Archimedean vantage point, to be equal. The question is why anyone should care about "culture" of this sort, let alone fight for a claim upon its title.[12]

Not even white liberal defenders of multiculturalism had been so transparent in their disdain. But by the millennium, formalism and its cranky cult of "quality" was once again ascendant.

Oddly enough, what made bad theory created new openings for art. A subversively hopeful critique marked the post-multicultural art of the new millennium. In 1999, Thelma Golden famously—if half-jokingly—declared, "Post-black was the new black." She was on to something. The post-1993 Biennial art world had bound artists of color not to talk race explicitly. But they had been freed conceptually to express race in myriad new ways, and did so usually in brainy, ironic, and exuberant kinds of ways.

Post-multiculturalism was about hijacking the language of formalism to both demonstrate competency and quietly undermine its exclusionist tendencies. Golden's notion of post-blackness was as much a strategic retreat before an art-world ready to lock its gates as it was a door-jamming for new artists of color to enter the mainstream. It said "Don't judge me as a Black artist, judge me as an artist. But I will reserve the right to express my Blackness any way I want to."

But if post-multiculturalism fought formalism to a draw and opened up space to play in cultural politics, it lost language to address the politics of culture. In part this is because multiculturalism had triumphed in an important sense. By the turn of the millennium, with hip-hop at the spearhead, popular culture had been more visually desegregated than ever before. Opponents of multiculturalism could turn its very success against itself.

In striking down the heart of the Voting Rights Act in *Shelby County v. Holder*, Chief Justice John Roberts wrote, "Our country has changed, and while any racial discrimination in voting is too much, Congress must ensure that the legislation it passes to remedy that problem speaks to current conditions." He was referring to the progress that had been made in "minority representation." Well, yes, Your Honor. But also, no. As Justice Ruth Bader Ginsburg dissented, the Court had terminated "the very remedy that proved to be best suited to block that discrimination."

There lingers a paradox at the heart of the post-racial moment—while our images show a mostly optimistic nation moving toward cultural desegregation and racial equality, our modes of living together reflect distancing and blindness, rancor and silence, our politics bespeak deep pessimism and a desire for disengagement, and our social indexes reveal increasing social resegregation and racial inequality.

A prematurely celebratory air has pervaded the post-multiculturalism era. There are more artists of color represented than ever. But there still seems precious language to discuss how the new systems maintained modes of invisibility for artists of color. Questions of access, distribution, cultural criticism, and privatization—all issues that had driven the multiculturalists to seek cultural equity and that are now being reconfigured into, appropriating Justice Ginsburg's felicitous phrase, "second-generation barriers"—seem to have melted into air.

For these reasons, not all artists see post-multiculturalism's contortions as the way to move forward. Hip-hop celebrates the irrepressible energy and optimism of bricolage-creativity. At its best it reveals youth identity-making informed by radically invididual and local idiosyncrasy with a global ambition. New World Theater's Project 2050, forefronting demographic and cultural change in its name, meant to catalyze the promethean powers of youth to create new forms and content that might suggest approaches toward a more thoroughly colorized American future.

After the millennium many mainstream cultural organizations find themselves unable to quickly enough devise new modes of engagement to stem a crisis of declining audiences. But in Project 2050, the same youth at the spearhead of demographic change—working in communities that were 85 percent white but also undergoing their own process of change—were invited to dialogue and imagine how to respond and lead cultural change through the arts. Their projects organically led to hip-hop, and an interdisciplinary hybrid of spoken word, movement, and theater that spoke to crucial issues such as immigration, incarceration, and identity.

Demographic change and cultural change will of course continue. Demographer William Frey has devised a simple metric to encapsulate the implications of these twin changes. He calls it "the cultural generation gap." Frey measures the cultural generation gap by simply subtracting the proportion of white children in a state from the proportion of white seniors. In Arizona, the state with the widest gap, 83 percent of seniors were white and only 43 percent of children were. The next five gap states were Nevada (34% gap), California (33%), Texas (32%), New Mexico (31%), and Florida (29%).[13]

Non-white births in the US now exceed white births. Yet the most politically influential American demographic, the post-World War II generation known as the Baby Boom, remained four-fifths white. Political scientist Ron Brownstein writes,

> Over time, the major focus in this struggle is likely to be the tension between an aging white population that appears increasingly resistant to taxes and dubious of public spending, and a minority population that overwhelmingly views government education, health, and social-welfare programs as the best ladder of opportunity for its children.[14]

What is clear now is that the multiculturalism movement really grasped the implications of these shifts. The anti-multiculturalist backlash was also conditioned by a dawning realization that demographic change and cultural change were inextricably linked. And our efforts to truly end these wars are hindered by a huge (color) blind spot, the same blind spot that has perhaps prevented us from fully understanding the promise and also the tragedy of the rise and fall of the movement.

When massive cultural change can be reduced to a cartoonish parade of styles, to affections of language or clothing, of course it can prove worthy only of embarrassment or indifference. It's important to recover multiculturalism because it's important to remember the stakes the movement was fighting for.

What the ongoing culture wars—in all of their rage and rancor—mask over is the continuing need for not just for racial justice, but cultural equity, the call for a transformation in the very way we see all the colors that make up America, the call sounded in the civil rights movement, but pressed forward by the multiculturalism movement.

In the same way we need cultural work now that honestly addresses difference, culture, and privilege, while providing modes that advance cultural equity. Such projects begin not from a morally bankrupt, culturally oppressive nostalgia, but from the hope for a more empathetic and egalitarian future, toward finishing the projects of desegregation, cultural equity, and racial justice. We need work that will ask us to imagine what can happen in—not *to*—the America and the world we are *all* growing up in, the one we are all making together.

Notes

1 Vijay Prashad in "Got Next: A Roundtable on Identity and Aesthetics after Multiculturalism" in *Total Chaos: The Art and Aesthetics of Hip-Hop*, ed. Jeff Chang (New York: Basic Civitas, 2006), 37.
2 Martin Luther King Jr., "Desegregation and the Future," address delivered at the annual luncheon of the National Committee for Rural Schools, New York, NY, December 15, 1956, in *The Papers Of Martin Luther King, Jr.: Birth of a New Age, December 1955–December 1956* (The Martin Luther King, Jr. Papers Project, University of California Press, 1997), 475, http://mlk-kpp01.stanford.edu/primarydocuments/Vol3/15-Dec-1956_DesegregationAndTheFuture.pdf.

3 Ishmael Reed, Kathryn Trueblood, and Shawn Wong, eds., *The Before Columbus Foundation Fiction Anthology* (New York: Norton, 1992), xi.
4 Marta Moreno Vega and Cheryll Y. Greene, eds., *Voices from the Battlefront: Achieving Cultural Equity* (Trenton, NJ: Africa World Press, 1993), 177–78.
5 Elinor Bowles, *Cultural Centers of Color: Report on a National Survey* (Washington, DC: National Endowment for the Arts, 1992), 7.
6 Ibid., 21.
7 Thelma Golden, "What's White?" in *1993 Biennial Exhibition* (New York: Whitney Museum of American Art, 1993), 35.
8 Deborah Solomon, "A Showcase for Political Correctness," *Wall Street Journal*, March 5, 1993; John Taylor, "Mope Art: Deconstructing the Biennial," *New York,* March 22, 1993.
9 Fredric Koeppel, "Art Tirades at Biennial Simply Get Tiresome," *Memphis Commercial Appeal*, March 28, 1993; Peter Plagens, "Fade From White," *Newsweek*, March 14, 1993.
10 John Leo, "Cultural War at the Whitney," *U.S. News & World Report*, March 22, 1993.
11 Quoted in William Grimes, "Face-to-Face Encounter on Race in the Theater," *New York Times*, January 29, 1997, http://www.nytimes.com/1997/01/29/theater/face-to-face-encounter-on-race-in-the-theater.html?pagewanted=print&src=pm.
12 Henry Louis Gates Jr., "Good-Bye, Columbus? Notes on the Culture of Criticism," in *Multiculturalism: A Critical Reader*, ed. David Theo Goldberg (Malden: Blackwell, 1994), 206–207.
13 William Frey, *Diversity Explosion: How New Racial Demographics Are Remaking America* (Washington, DC: Brookings Institute Press, 2014).
14 Ronald Brownstein, "The Gray and the Brown: The Generational Mismatch," *National Journal*, July 24, 2010, http://www.nationaljournal.com/magazine/the-gray-and-the-brown-the-generational-mismatch-20100724.

Afterword

Bill Rauch

Reading this collection of chapters in their entirety is for me, in part, the experience of being overwhelmed with gratitude for the influence of Roberta Uno and the New WORLD Theater. I am just one member of the larger American theater community groping forward in an effort to help build a field that is more equitable, one that realizes the prophetic vision of Project 2050. And yet in my single case, the connections are too numerous to mention here so I will cite just three examples.

As the founding artistic director of the community-based Cornerstone Theater Company, I vividly remember New WORLD Theater inviting us to send representatives to a conference in Amherst—I was thrilled—but making it clear that the invitation extended only to our company members of color. It was a defining moment for me in understanding the limitations of my white and male privileges, an indelible lesson in the fact that sometimes room has to be made at the table by someone actually getting up and stepping aside. As I read the insightful reflections of current Cornerstone artistic director Michael John Garcés in this volume, I come face to face with how the theater company that I co-founded has evolved, irrevocably influenced by the work of New WORLD Theater.

Many years ago, too many to count, I was part of a memorable meal-time break-out session at a Theater Communications Group conference with a handful of members of sister ensembles from across the country. We were giddy in our connection-making; we couldn't drink in one another's insights fast enough, and these conversations eventually led to the formation of the Network of Ensemble Theaters. Mark Valdez's chapter chronicling the growth and vitality of that network reminds me of the example set by New WORLD Theater: traditional, often hierarchal models, are not only not the only but often not the most effective way to create world-transforming art.

In my current capacity as artistic director of the Oregon Shakespeare Festival, we have hosted what we originally called Hip-Hop Boot Camp, later renamed Mixing Texts. A deep immersion into the intersection of classical texts and what Roberta brilliantly termed "Future Aesthetics," this work has brought our company and audiences into contact with many of the artists whose hip-hop aesthetic was nurtured by New WORLD Theater. In fact, UNIVERSES, an ensemble that honed its innovative aesthetic in Amherst, has become the ensemble in residence at OSF, and two of its founders—Steve Sapp and Mildred Ruiz—now reside in Ashland, Oregon.

I could go on listing the connections throughout this book to my own life's work, but I know that most of my colleagues could embark on the same exercise with ease. In its thirty-year existence, New WORLD Theater planted seeds that continue to bear fruit throughout the world. How fortunate that all of us are nourished by that fruit. How beautiful to see the towering mature trees, the surprising grafts and the courageous seedlings that form our collective work.

As I write these words, late in 2015, I have my good days and my bad days in terms of being able to celebrate the progress of our field and of the theater company that is my artistic home. As my colleagues and I try to transform the large-budget, historically white-majority institution that is the Oregon Shakespeare Festival (talk about barriers to inclusion: we have Oregon and Shakespeare in our name, for goodness' sake!) into a progressive center of equity for our field, I am especially grateful for this book. For its frankly anti-racist, youth-empowering, pro-community, pro-human global agenda.

As I hungrily absorb its pages looking for common themes and lessons in how to strengthen our efforts to model the United States of 2050, here is what strikes me in that beautiful simple way that the deepest truths often do.

Against all odds, in an unlikely place, with imagination and chutzpah and moral clarity and perhaps even some moral outrage, a group of people was willing to envision the future and to transform the present to get us there. Unhelpful distinctions between amateur and professional; artificial dichotomies between excellence and community; false hierarchies of exclusion and power were all ignored, rejected, dismantled. In their place, the foundation of every endeavor of New WORLD Theater (and its powerful descendants) was a simple but powerful twinning of respect and love. What better example could be set for us today in this particularly polarizing, fear-fraught environment in which we find ourselves, than to remember that respect and love must be the coin of our realm?

If you have chosen to sample these chapters or better yet to read this book cover to cover, you are part of an unstoppable force for good that was begun in 1979 but has not stopped and will not stop.

Index